Drum nadrochi m

R. NESSIE R

DOUBTERS

STERS' DOUBT

g the Loch Ness Monster swimming in the s
e second "public appearance" within a we

r William Adie (27), Borlum
Mr Robert Macdonald (62),
rumnadrochit, said the famous
he centre of th loch between
c. and
was moving sort of
—from my right to shores.
m, said: "I
nd Mr Adie

ere as fast as I could."

reau operations chief ily seer
Simon. He said yester-hree h
ming up very abruptly apar
a great lick. He lookedf the
en when he got out and the
is creature."   o has
r t

until yesterday before In
of the bureau's sighting er
ped the creature's texture lie
h and its colour as brown.
olours the water may have
oression. It is so thick that
wn 50ft. in the water visi

was sp
when I turned to
loch and saw these th
in the middle of the
were circling around

GLASGOW HERALD

SCHOOL MA
SEES LOCH
MONSTER

The first sighting tl
of the Loch Ness
was reported yesterday
W. V. Turl, an English
master.

Mr Turl, of Warley, W
tershire, was travelling
his family along the lo
near Drumnadrochit,
they saw three hu

MONSTER HUNT

MONSTER

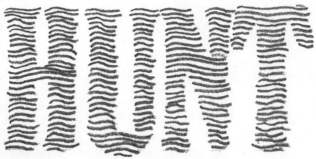

HUNT

By

Tim Dinsdale

A.R.Ae.S.
Director of Photography Loch Ness Investigation Bureau

FOREWORD BY
ROBERT H. RINES
President of the Academy
of Applied Science

PUBLISHED BY **ACROPOLIS BOOKS LTD.** ● WASHINGTON, D.C. 20009

Originally published under the title
"The Leviathans" by Routledge & Kegan Paul Ltd., London in 1966.

First printing of this completely updated
and expanded volume in the United States of America
April 1972
© Copyright 1966, 1972 by Tim Dinsdale

Published in cooperation with Routledge & Kegan Paul Ltd. by
ACROPOLIS BOOKS LTD.
Colortone Building, 2400 17th St., N.W.
Washington, D.C. 20009
All inquiries should be directed to Acropolis Books Ltd., at above address.

Printed in the United States of America by
COLORTONE PRESS Creative Graphics Inc., *Washington, D.C. 20009*

Type set in Baskerville
by Colortone Typographic Division, Inc.

Design by Design and Art Studio 2400

Library of Congress Catalog Number 71-184717
Standard Book No. 87491-325-X

To a friend
TORQUIL MACLEOD
Adventurer
Free Spirit

CONTENTS

FOREWORD

As live television made us witnesses to man's excursions upon the moon, an eighty-four year old grandmother shook her head and remarked that this was all a fake—a gigantic television studio fraud, perpetrated to cover up the millions that our politicians had been secreting away, under the guise of a space program.

At an earlier stage, when America had not yet caught up to the Soviets in space-probing, a very able physicist friend had similar comments of disbelief when Russia produced photographs from the rear face of the self-same lunar satellite.

The world abounds with disbelievers—educated and uneducated—of all kinds of issues. Even in our everyday technological world, the cynicism of the 'knowledgeable' towards new ideas, the resistance to novel concept and change, the straightjacket (or is it the smothering cape?) of 'not-invented-here,' holds back the progress of man and almost extinguishes the seemingly divine flicker of incentive. Indeed, the word 'invention' itself connotes what was not obvious to all the other trained minds.

And so it was that several well-trained and noted scientists and technologists from the Academy of Applied Science approached the explorers at Loch Ness, Scotland, who insisted that there were monstrous creatures in that long, deep, and mysterious loch, which just kept resisting posing for that unequivocally clear picture; and whose discovery might well shake man's imagination and add suddenly and immeasurably to his knowledge, as did the feats of our moon voyagers.

The intrepid work of the British Loch Ness Investigation Bureau, in spite of the budgetary problems of all noncommercial ventures, and the actual ridicule of the press and the so-called scientific community, intrigued our Academy. The fact that the *author of this book, Tim Dinsdale, could find no true scientific sponsor or sponsorship—even after producing an amazing motion-picture record of a large, clearly animate object in Loch Ness—made our blood boil.*

But why should we be agitated? They ridiculed Pasteur and Lester; they pooh-poohed the Wright brothers and their heavier-than-air machine; they initially turned a deaf ear to Goddard and rocketry and an even deafer ear to Whittle and the jet engine. Why shouldn't the new breed of 'know-it-alls' reject the existence of large unknown creatures in Loch Ness—or anywhere else?

And why shouldn't they, in their infinite wisdom and self-granted monopoly on knowledge, reject all photographic proof produced by investigators and all accounts of visual observations—be they from former trained naval and air officers, forestry officials, police officers, priests, lawyers, doctors, businessmen or ordinary folk—obviously all possessing no skill or intellect to distinguish artifact from reality, and perpetually being under the influence of Scotch whiskey or the local chamber of tourism?

The gauntlet was down.

In the fall of 1970 and in the summer and fall of 1971, our Academy team, including noted sonar manufacturer and underwater explorer Martin Klein (President of Klein Associates, Salem, New Hampshire) and Isaac S. Blonder (Chairman of the Board of Blonder-Tongue Laboratories, Oldbridge, New Jersey), aided by complementary equipment, supplies, and consulting services from a "Who's Who" of American organizations, supplied (and are still supplying) a strong right hand to Tim Dinsdale, Bob Love, and others of the Loch Ness Investigation Bureau, to supplement, among other projects, the earlier sonar searches of the University of Birmingham Electrical Engineering Department group and of the Worldbook Encyclopedia program headed by Love.

We were provided with the Klein high-definition side-scan sonar; with special hydrophone listening and recording equip-

ment from Blonder-Tongue Laboratories and H. H. Scott, Inc.; with underwater strobe light equipment from United States Scientific Instruments, Inc., of Watertown, Massachusetts; with hormone and other synthesized lures, developed and contributed by International Flavors and Fragrances of New Jersey (which both the American and British press heralded as "sex" lures for attracting Nessie); with "Sea-Klear" compounds for increasing underwater photographic range, provided by Food and Chemical Research Laboratories of Seattle, Washington; with further hormone, excreta, and other scents of a wide variety of underwater creatures, prepared from solutions supplied by the Miami Seaquarium of Florida and freeze-dried to enable portability and reconstituting at lochside with the aid of scientists from the United States Army Natick Laboratories and the Harvard Medical School; salmon oil, blood, and other parts from the northwestern United States and Canada; recorded sounds of a wide variety of types of underwater creatures from the University of Rhode Island and the Woods Hole Oceanographic Institute; and more recently, ingenious elapsed-time underwater strobe and camera equipment from MIT's reknowned Professor Harold E. Edgerton ("Papa Flash" of Jacques Cousteau's adventures); and more mundane equipment from others who also have become intrigued with this adventure.

Tim Dinsdale describes some of the exciting sonar contacts we made with large, moving underwater objects, in the latter part of this book. Until recently, my own faith abounded in these contacts, in photographs that I deemed reliable from my personal investigation and study, and in accounts from persons I have adjudged to be competent, truthful, and reliable reporters.

And then it happened, on June 23, 1971, at dusk, on a calm, barely still-lit evening, in the company of our Academy historian Carol Williamson Hurley and former RAF Wing Commander Basil Cary and his wife, Winifred, who has had several sightings of large 'beasties' over the years! There arose in Urquhart Bay a large hump, somewhat triangular in shape and void of any detectable fin. We measured its dimensions by telescopic comparison between this phenomenon, two-thirds of a mile away, and a nearby anchored 53-foot fishing vessel. Nessie, 20 feet long and about 4 to 6 feet out of the water at her apex, slowly moved toward us into the bay, turned, and then submerged.

And so I can tell you, not just intellectually from sonar studies or mere research of the reports of others, that I have seen an amazingly large animate object in Loch Ness, a mere part of its body measuring over 20 feet long. It was not artifact; I was not drinking; and I observed it with others. Having derived considerable skill as a water observer from wartime experience, sonar experience, and long years of fishing and boating experiences, I can tell you it was a real creature.

But what intrigues us most—since we know that soon we will have those clear and definitive movies—is to observe the red faces of the scientific community when the Loch Ness Investigation Bureau and its associates present the final evidence and identification.

We even know what will be the response: 'Oh, we thought there was something there—just not enough earlier proof.'

If the scientific community thinks there's 'something there,' this is probably their last chance to come aboard as true scientists and help provide the final proof. Come with open minds, finances, equipment, and brains!

Robert H. Rines
Academy of Applied Science
Belmont, Massachusetts

I

THE QUESTING INSTINCT

ON a sparkling April morning in 1960 I found myself gazing incredulously through binoculars at the back of a great animal, far below and away across the inky waters of Loch Ness. For a while it lay motionless, and then moved off in a ponderous manner creating a surge of ripples.

Following its zigzag course I turned to my ciné-camera – and reached out towards it briefly through a telephoto lens . . .

In the months and years since that time I have followed its wake, gaining slowly in knowledge and experience, and although for the most part the animal has remained hidden in the depths – remote – mysterious – immovable – enveloped by the dark waters of prejudice surrounding it, there have been moments of excitement, and progress too.

Occasionally it has broken surface, adding something to the existing store of evidence, but more important, exposing itself to the penetrating light of inquiry which is now beginning to illuminate parts of the great area of surface water contained by the shores of the loch. Independent inquiry, vitalized by the questing instinct of private groups, and individuals – who pit their resources and initiative against the apparently overwhelming odds – and it is with the 'human element' this chapter is concerned, because herein lies the key to a remarkable discovery.

But before dealing with it, and to gain a sense of perspective, it is necessary to turn the clock back a little further to the time when unknown aquatic animals were first reported with consistency in Loch Ness. This was in 1933, with the construction of a motor-road along the northern shore. The continuous rock-blasting, the presence of many people, the felling of trees exposing a view of surface water all combined to dramatically focus world attention to the 'Monster' as it came to be known.

With the passage of time there were photographs, films, books and a multitude of eyewitness reports outlining its features – a small head, long serpentine neck, enormous length of body with hump-like proturberances along the back capable of changing shape; two pairs of limbs developed for swimming, and a long tail thought to be used in propelling it through the water.

Sometimes it was reported travelling at speed, throwing up an almost ship-like wash, and at others lolling on the surface. Sometimes more than one monster was seen – and on a very few occasions people claimed they had seen it out of water! But despite all these statements, words and photographs, and a legendary history going back to the sixth century, no one succeeded in proving the beast to a coldly aloof, and distantly inactive scientific establishment – who appeared to rule it out on the grounds of technical absurdity.

This was the situation which existed when after a year of probing, and piecing together of parts, I went to Loch Ness and obtained the film which is (at the time of writing) still the most significant piece of evidence of its kind. The proof of some huge animate object, swimming in a lake where there should be nothing larger than a salmon – its humped back and wake in distinct contrast to a motor-boat, filmed afterwards for comparison.

But, if this sequence failed, like all the previous evidence, to cause a change in the official attitude towards the Monster, when shown to the public on television it had the opposite effect.

Before long I was answering letters from people who expressed a desire to enter the arena, and do battle with the odds. Sensible letters, full of encouragement; and I realized the best way to foster this crusading spirit would be to write a book – a form of 'monster-hunters' manual – analysing the subject as it stood, and describing how the individual might equip himself, and join the hunt. Two expeditions had shown me that field-work involved long hours of concentrated watching, and that without long-range camera equipment it was a waste of time and money.

In May of 1961 the book *Loch Ness Monster*[1] appeared in Britain, and the year following in America.

It contained, if nothing else, an interesting collection of photographs of the 'phenomenon', and some practical advice.

Reviewed by some forty newspapers and journals, and on television, it was evident that whatever my shortcomings as a writer, interest in the *subject* remained as great as ever; and quite as controversial; but in the spring of 1961 there was every reason to suppose that close-up ciné-film would at last be obtained. There was no lack of activity. Two major expeditions were in the planning stage, and I was about to make a third attempt with much improved equipment.

Back in the field towards the end of March with a battery of lenses, I spent a great many hours watching from different places along the sixty miles of shoreline – sleeping when and where I could. It was a cold hunt, in more senses than one, and I found for all its solitude and etherial beauty at dawn, when the vast area of water would sometimes stretch like a mirror of coloured glass to the horizon, a lack of weatherproof clothing could demoralize the watcher to a point where these scenic effects were lost, and vigilance reduced to a state of numbed indifference.

But, I learned something from it – that too much equipment was as much a handicap as too little. I had with me a giant 36-inch telephoto lens and gun-mount tripod; a 20-inch adaptor; still and ciné-cameras; 130- and 300-mm. lenses with separate tripods. Altogether a pile of gadgetry which I juggled about

[1] Routledge and Kegan Paul Ltd, London. 1961. Chilton Books, Philadelphia. 1962. Now in paperback, refer Routledge, 68 Carter Lane, London, EC4V 5EL.

when I should have been scanning through binoculars . . .
better to operate a single high-quality camera and lens, because
in the emergency there would be room for only one finger on
the button, and one eye at the viewing aperture.

Another thing – to set up this equipment blatantly on the
shoreline, without camouflage, was equally mistaken, because I
had watched the animal cruising just beneath the surface along
the fringe of the loch (where local fishermen troll for salmon),
and I knew this type of encounter to be a possibility.

Returning home empty-handed, I experienced the crushing
influence of defeat, but during the long journey had time to re-
view the problem. With the coming of summer and the small
army of volunteers I felt sure our luck would change – and there
was the chance I could get back for another attempt, later on in
the season.

The difficulties, hazards and technical problems fascinated
me, as they had so many other people in the years preceding –
and this overrode any tremulous feelings of doubt I had about a
repeated sighting. Surely, if I stuck it out, and refused to ack-
nowledge defeat, and drilled myself in the art and discipline of
effective monster-hunting, I might overcome the odds? But,
this would mean continuing to work on a solitary basis, for
reasons of economy. The cost of three expeditions with most of
the equipment on loan had been heavy; and the hire of professional gear in the future would increase this by half as much
again. But if I was going to work alone there would be the ad-
vantage of a type of discipline I could not expect to impose on
others: and this would result – must result, in efficiency.

Despite these hopes and resolutions, however, and a fourth
expedition in June, the year 1961 passed without any startling
success – both major expeditions having been postponed until
1962. But, it was an important year because opinion had begun
to resolve into opposite camps – the 'For' and 'Against'ers' who
quickly took up defensive positions, and viewed each other
fiercely across a common no-man's-land of doubt, both sides
quite determined not to yield an inch.

4

Before long a heavy verbal crossfire opened up, and I had
difficulty in avoiding it – but as the real battlefront was far removed, around the shores of Loch Ness, I was fortunate at this
time to meet a man who was to play a dynamic part in the setting up of expeditions, and a Bureau for examining the evidence.

David James, M.B.E., D.S.C., Member of Parliament and
Antarctic traveller, was one of the few British naval officers to
have escaped from a German prison camp, and get clean away
with it – in short a man with the natural gift of initiative, who
enjoyed, amongst other things, a sense of humour. It was not
long before he collected about him a bustling team of enthusiasts, and had become a member of the select and quietly
determined Board of Directors of the Loch Ness Phenomena
Investigation Bureau Ltd. – a non-profit-making company.

Invited to join as 'Chief-field-investigator', I attended a
number of meetings, but in view of the research to which I was
already committed asked for this to be changed to 'Field
Associate', and as time and opportunity allowed, continued
with the task of trying to promote interest, by giving talks, and
showing the film.

Prior to the formation of the Bureau, this was the only means
by which one could hope to gain a hearing – but it was uphill
work, and Zoologists showed such an obvious tendency to shy
away from the facts, it forced one to the conclusion they did not
want to become involved, as much for political reasons as any
other. Science had put them in a very difficult position. For years
it had bluntly refused to take part in an official expedition,
and poo-hoo'd the mounting pile of evidence, and it seemed that
with one or two odd exceptions, individuals were *afraid* to make
a stand on it – and if this was the case it was pointless to pursue
the matter with them.

It would be wiser to concentrate on getting evidence which
no one could refute, and to avoid the whirlpool currents of
emotion which surrounded the Monster; engulfing those who
were drawn into them.

My decision was influenced to some extent by the death of a

man for whom I had a great friendship and respect; who spent the last two years of his life at Loch Ness, researching into its depths, in company with his Australian wife and helper.

His story was a strange and moving one, and I first came to hear of it through a rumour, suggesting that in early 1960 a man had watched the Monster lying partly out of water on the shore – and later on, through the good offices of Mrs. Constance Whyte, of *More Than a Legend*[2] fame, arranged to contact him during my second expedition in July of that year.

We met on the southern shore at a place known locally as the 'Wall', where the line of General Wade's original garrison supply route rounds an outcrop near the water. Torquil and Elizabeth MacLeod arrived in rumbling war-surplus vehicle, a 5-ton radio truck in which they lived before making a home in a remote croft-house high up in the mountains.

He was a small man, and yet there radiated from him some special quality of personality, which the drawn lines of his face could not hide – the marks of the rare disease which was killing him.

Moving freely in the caravan-like body of the vehicle, we brewed up a cup of tea, then I sat transfixed and listened. Torquil had seen the Monster on two occasions, and although bound by anonymity, the condition on which his full-time research depended, he was later to let me publish both accounts.

In due course these appeared on pages 137 and 143 of *Loch Ness Monster* together with sketches of the beast he had measured out of water through graticulated lenses – a saurian-like animal, the visible parts of which he estimated at 45–55 feet in length: but with his name excluded, these reports were of course inadmissible as evidence.

We parted friends, and during the March hunt in 1961 I was able to visit the MacLeods at their croft, and get to know them better. Sleeping outside in the army vehicle I rose at dawn, in the bitter cold, to find a swath of falling snow trailing across the landscape, like an off-white tablecloth – and began to appreci-

[2] Published in 1957 by Hamish Hamilton, London.

ate why the area was known to some as 'Little Siberia'; but for all that there was peace to found in its haunting loneliness, and I knew that both Tor and Lis were happy there.

During the course of the morning we watched from the northern shore, with telephoto cameras peering through the narrow windows of the truck, and I learned something more of Torquil's extraordinary life, and the unique line of research he was following. He was artist, adventurer, and brilliant innovator all rolled into one, and salt water coursed through his veins.

From sailing at an early age in square-rigged ships to fishing for sharks off the Australian Barrier Reef, to navigating his own graceful wooden ketch the *Airy Mouse* in home waters, he had tried his hand – and chanced his arm – at many things, and when in 1950 he was found to be suffering from Hodgkin's disease,[3] an incurable complaint, instead of giving up he laid the plans for this last daring undertaking, which he followed through to his death, without concession; and although his work remained unfinished, if success should be measured in terms of courage then *he did achieve it*, in full measure – because of his indomitable spirit.

Just before his death he journeyed to London, a return trip of over twelve-hundred miles or so, to give evidence before a private panel of experts. It was the last time we met, and I could see how very ill he was – but he spoke with convincing clarity of his second encounter in August of 1960, when he and Lis had watched the beast from the northern shore ploughing up the surface water close to a motorized yacht.

As luck would have it, her skipper and company director, Mr. R. H. Lowrie, came forward with his family to give evidence, which, with supporting 'wake' photographs taken from the deck, and a further simultaneous report from the southern shore presented a case for the Monster which was irrefutable – and yet, incredibly, without any positive result.

[3] Which is not, incidentally, a contributory cause to hallucination. The disease attacks the lymph glands of the body.

It was this verdict which convinced me of the *futility* of argument – and determined me with fixed resolve to continue with the hunt. But as Torquil's anonymous reports were, I believe, of such accuracy it is important to corroborate one of them by publishing the Log from the yacht *Finola* kindly submitted by her owner, who notes:

'On this Sunday morning we went to the ancient Priory,[4] as our custom is, where the Order of Benedictine Monks are settled, and about eleven o'clock – a dull, heavy, wet day, we departed under motor intending to cover the twenty-five miles to the other end of Loch Ness.' The log reads:

2.20 p.m. Smooth as glass. (Having washing palaver.)

3.05 p.m. Strone Point Castle abeam. 5 knots. 13 miles.

4.15 p.m. Brian on watch. Family below for Sunday lunch. Brian inquired 'What is this monster supposed to look like? There is something coming up astern.' All hands on deck witness a curious form coming up astern between 6 and 10 knots looking like a couple of ducks, occasionally submerging, and a neck-like protrusion breaking surface. The Monster – nothing less. As it came abeam we were fascinated, so much so that it had passed to starboard before anyone remembered that we had an old camera aboard.

After about ten minutes it swung away to starboard towards Aldourie Point, and some photographs were then taken. It swam quickly causing considerable disturbance and showing a large area of green and brown, and proceeded on a collision reciprocal course to our own.

A hurried family conference unanimously decided something sinister was approaching, and that we should alter course to avoid close contact.

4.48 p.m. Arrived Loch Dochfour eighteen minutes after seeing Nessie, eighteen minutes overdue.

[4] St. Benedicts, at Fort Augustus, south-west end of loch.

1   Each arm of the long 'V' wake created by a 30 ft. fishing boat travelling down the centre of Loch Ness . . .

2   . . . reaches shore some 20 minutes later as an extremely localised bar pattern of ripples, when viewed from *above*. When viewed from the *side* at a shallow angle, wake arms appear as a line on the surface.

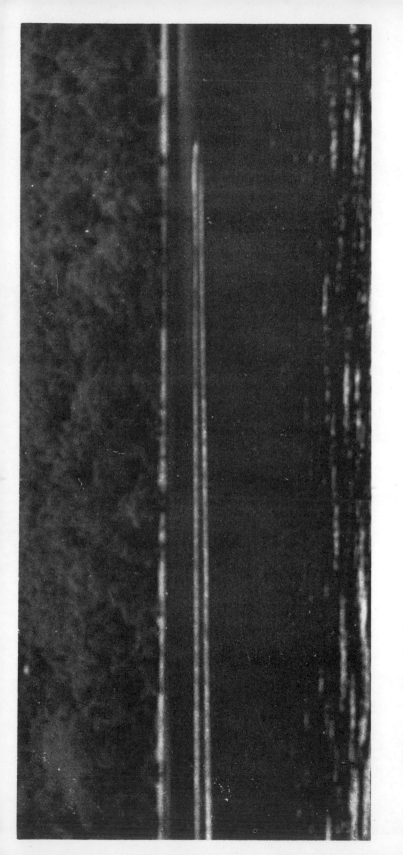

3 The Lowrie 'V' wake photograph taken with an old camera from the deck of the yacht *Finola*; Summer 1960, Loch Ness. The Monster swam past almost totally submerged, but "causing considerable disturbance and showing a large area of green and brown". The Log continues ". . . a hurried family conference unanimously decided something sinister was approaching, and that we should alter course to avoid close contact".

5.00 p.m. Mr. MacLeod, a naturalist arrived and reported he
had himself observed Nessie following *Finola* as also
had his wife. . . . Kindly warned us of Press interest,
which seemed to us good advice – agreed we would
say nothing and take care of photographs when developed.

NOTES: Made bow wave similar to *Finola*'s and appeared
frightened by noise of all hands on deck.
Certainly appeared to follow *Finola* for a time.

To which I should add that when questioned about the size
of the beast Mr. Lowrie had said it was difficult to estimate, but
that the parts visible below water suggested it was as big as the
boat – which measured 40 feet in length.

The photographs were not of good quality, appearing to be
slightly out of focus. The best is reproduced on Plate 3, and
shows the long wake created by the animal swimming just submerged. Having watched and filmed this myself I know it is
typical, and although no part of the body is discernible, Mr.
Lowrie enclosed in his letter 'scribbles' made shortly after the encounter showing three humps, with spray and wash. (Refer to
Sketch 2.)

On Plate 6 the only photograph I have of Torquil MacLeod
appears. Standing in characteristic pose there can be seen behind him the simple beehive-like monument erected by the
people of Glen Urquhart to 'a very gallant Gentleman'. It commemorates John Cobb's fatal attempt on the world water-speed
record in his jet-boat *Crusader*, marking the spot where it struck an
area of disturbed water, on the morning of September 29th, 1952.

With regard to this event I would like to digress for a moment
and deal with some odd information given to me by Torquil,
that frosty morning when we stood gazing out over the water. I
can even remember his words . . .

'Do you know,' he said, 'there is a rumour that people watching the record-breaking run from high up on this shore saw

9

Nessie's wake developing, and that when *Crusader* came charging by, it ran into it.... It's possible, isn't it?'

Turning the matter over in my mind later I had to admit that it was, because if one of these animals had been lying near the surface the scream of jet-engine noise could have frightened it, causing it to swim rapidly and create a foot-high wave, and several hundred yards of trailing wash[5] – and with the boat travelling at over 200 miles an hour, in a few moments it would overrun a great area of water. At such a speed too, ripples only a few inches high would prove disastrous.

Recalling the news film, which had shown the apparently instantaneous break-up, I decided to try and obtain a copy, and study it, and also get in touch with the cameraman who had followed the run of the boat.

The film posed no great difficulty, and within a month I had both a positive and negative copy – but it was two years before I met up with Jock Gemmel, retired veteran camerman for Pathé News. In forty-seven years of experience he had filmed many record-breaking attempts, and was in consequence the best type of witness.

Filming from the mountainside from the southern shore opposite, with a 35-mm. camera and 17-inch lens he was told the early morning attempt had been cancelled, due to ruffled water. It was one of a series of postponements, keeping him at his post for more than a week, waiting for a jelly-like calm.

Later in the morning conditions improved, and from a distance of over a mile he filmed *Crusader* on her last fateful run.

From where he stood the water appeared to be completely calm – but when viewed through the film, due partly to the foreshortening effect of the big telephoto lens, it is anything but calm; and if each frame is studied individually through an enlarger the boat is seen to approach and enter this troubled area of water.

[5] It is surprising how long a wake can 'live' in calm water. I once timed a 30-foot motorised fishing boat steering down the middle of Loch Ness. The wake reached shore over twenty minutes later, with waves 6–8 inches high. (Refer to Plates 1 and 2.)

At first it pitches rapidly and irregularly, and then performs three distinct pitching movements, which in engineering terms demonstrate a classic 'undamped oscillation' which, becoming more pronounced, finally results in the prow digging in, tilted slightly to one side.

The boat disintegrates in the space of one frame, which at the huge speed is to be expected.

From the normal projection of this film, there is no noticeable indication of a wake, but when examined frame by frame at the point of disintegration there is a reflection on the water in the foreground which could possibly indicate a line-wake, similar to that shown in the Lowrie photograph. (Pictures appear on Plates 4 and 5.)

Delving into the British Museum archives at Colindale, I turned up three newspaper headline stories of the 30th September, 1952, the day following the accident.

The *Daily Mail* commented on the fact that John Cobb momentarily closed his throttle about 150 yards from the post (end of measured mile), before the boat disintegrated after bouncing up and down two or three times. The *Daily Telegraph* quoted Mr. Angus Barr, a Wakefield Oil representative who said that *Crusader* hit three waves, the first two of which she rode. It also noted that Cobb saw these waves, because observers on the hillside saw him throttle down.

A *Daily Express* staff reporter wrote: 'John Cobb fastest man on land, became the fastest man on water today and was then killed – by three ripples, it is thought.

'As his £15,000 speedboat *Crusader* slackened to 205 m.p.h. a ripple of the sunlit waters of Loch Ness caught the boat's underside. Then another.

'A third V-shaped ripple struck – and John Cobb was thrown as *Crusader* disintegrated in a plume of spray. All this I saw from the bow of the yacht *Maureen*, 400 yards away.'

With this report, several clear stills from a film punctuate the last few yards of *Crusader's* run. It was obviously shot from above, on the northern shore, and the pitching action of the boat has been captured. The water appears to be jelly-like, but with a distinct bar pattern of ripples through which the boat is running.

Considering this information, and these photographs, and the fact that a V wake created by any large object travelling through the water appears as a line-wake from the *side;* and a series of regularly spaced ripples oblique to the object's line of travel from *above* – it is conceivable that the reflection in the Pathé News picture is one arm of a V wake, and that *Crusader* ran through the local pattern of ripples created by the other.

We shall never know whether the Monster, or, to be more specific, one of the colony of large animals inhabiting Loch Ness caused this accident, but the possibility exists: and for this reason I believe the lake should be barred to any further record-breaking attempts.

It is of course unlikely this view will be endorsed until their existence is accepted as a fact – and until it is, we must continue with the hunt.

In 1962 there was a great deal of activity, and some useful results obtained. The Monster was seen and filmed, though not conclusively – and this continuing failure to close with it, whetted the appetite of some and destroyed the faith of others – faith in themselves and their ability to overcome the odds imposed by the very nature of the task. The great size of the lake, the wind, the weather, the tantalizing rare appearances, the lack of support and funds and the sneers of criticism all combined to demoralize, and in some cases defeat the watcher. But as in every challenging situation losses were more than made up by the reserves of energy and enthusiasm, which are a part of human nature; and most important of all, the infusion of new blood from volunteers.

Commencing in early June, Lt.-Colonel H. G. Hasler,[6] D.S.O., O.B.E. organized a continuous day and night patrol from his yacht *Jester*, and during the next two months he and some fifty-six volunteers watched and listened in shifts – waiting to record underwater sounds from hydrophones, or photograph the beast at the surface, and during this time his unusual junk-sailed craft became a familiar object, sailing or drifting under bare poles.

The search was carried out to a pattern, and every morning a rendezvous made with a base on shore. Here a relief crew would be taken aboard to work in shifts during the next twenty-four hours.

In early July a Cambridge undergraduates' expedition took up station, under the leadership of two Scientific Graduates, Mark Westwood and Peter Baker, who piloted a similar venture in 1960. Equipped with long-range photographic gear mounted at intervals high up on the shoreline, and echo-sounding apparatus in boats the lake was probed and peered at as never before, and yet both these expeditions retired exhausted, with results which barely compensated for the huge expenditure of energy.

Once again, it seemed, the Monster had given the slip to its pursuers, showing just enough of itself to prove to them it was no figment of the imagination.

Excellent reports on both these undertakings appeared in the *Observer* Sunday newspaper; Hasler contributing on 3rd June and 19th August, and Baker and Westwood combining to analyse their work on 26th August. Hydrophone noises, hump, back and possible momentary neck sightings, and three strong echo traces made up the bag of unexplained phenomena – a meagre return in total; but none the less intriguing.

In the spring and autumn of the year I put in two more expeditions, without success, but on each my equipment

---

[6] Founder of the transatlantic singlehanded yachtsman's race. Colonel Hasler led the famous canoe raid against German shipping during the war, which became the subject of the book and film 'Cockleshell Heroes'.

improved and I graduated from amateur to professional powered cameras, with variable focus lenses and transistorized sound. This resulted in a loss of mobility, but as my objective had changed it no longer mattered; and more important still with six hundred hours of solitary watching behind me I was becoming immune to failure, and the wretched effect it could have on morale.

In mid October David James and twenty-six of his merry men joined in with a pair of searchlights, hoping to attract the beast and film it at night, down the beam. A day watch was also maintained, and from this expedition some really valuable evidence emerged, including a short length of 35-mm. film showing a dark underwater body moving contrary to wind and ripple, before which salmon had been seen to leap, by a number of witnesses, in broad daylight. Some 10 feet in visible length, about 3 feet of it emerged from the water, momentarily.

Results from this venture were submitted to a panel of four scientists and naturalists, specializing in marine biology, wildlife photography and otter behaviour. The chairman was impartial, and in no way connected with the issue – but when, in due course, a report appeared its conclusions stated flatly that: 'We find there is some unidentified animate object in Loch Ness, which, if it be a mammal, amphibian, reptile, fish or mollusc of any known order, is of such a size as to be worthy of careful scientific examination and identification . . .'

The effect this conclusion, and subsequent TV programme, had on the Official Attitude can be measured by events, because in 1963 activity was again voluntary – though supported by a growing body of corporate opinion. ATV put up money and equipment, and in June of that year a two-week expedition manned by the David James brigade watched and waited, and exposed several lengths of film.

Shot at extreme range, or through an advection fog, or 'Har', as it is known locally, the Monster was caught on the surface, and on the fringe of a distant shore, but again without sufficient clarity. Nor were private expeditions more successful with photography: but a most unusual interview was tape-recorded by a Mr. F. W. Holiday who had seen the beast himself the year before, at Foyer's Bay.

Having met Ted Holiday, known for his articles in fishing magazines, I do not hesitate to include excerpts from his 'Report on Loch Ness Phenomena' submitted to the bureau as evidence, with names of witnesses, (who would otherwise prefer to remain anonymous). . . .

'Item 3' reads – 'The McI . . . – C . . . Sighting'.

The sighting occurred on an evening in July 1963. It is the nearest sighting of an adult head and neck of which I have record.

Mr. McI. had already evaded several newspaper reporters. However, I met him at his place of work and he gave me a frank account. . . . On the evening in question he and his friend C. were in a boat some 200 yards from Tor Point (north-east end of loch near village of Dores), where they were fishing for sea-trout. Sometime after ten o'clock, Mr. C. commented on the fact that something was rocking the boat. There were no ships about to account for the turbulence.

A little later both men saw a ripple of broken water not far from the boat. Both thought it was caused by the back of a large salmon.

Quite suddenly the head and neck of the Monster reared out of the water to a height of about 4 – 5 feet. It was between 20 – 30 yards away from the boat.

As the anglers looked at the animal it disappeared by sinking straight downwards (i.e. not by diving head first). There was a good deal of froth and water disturbance. The neck then came out a little farther away. It disappeared once more before showing a third and last time at a greater distance.

When the Monster had gone, the anglers continued fishing but enjoyed no further sport. They went ashore fairly soon. McI. had seen the Monster's humps on an earlier occasion near Drumnadrochit. However, this was Mr. C's first sighting. . . . I received the impression that McI. had given a true and objective of a most extraordinary experience. Details and comments by this witness are as follows:

Appearance : The Monster's neck came out of the water quickly. It was powerful and of considerable thickness – a column of at least 1 foot in diameter.

The head was held at a slight angle to the neck. Mr. MacI. said the head reminded him of a bulldog. i.e. Flat on top with a powerful lower face. He saw no eyes or tentacles. Colour of head and neck was blackish brown. The head was wide and extremely ugly. Part of a hump was also visible.

The witness described the beast as 'hairy'. Asked to amplify, he said that the neck was fringed by what looked like coarse black hair. It reminded him of the mane seen on Highland cattle.

Mr. MacI's impressions : MacI. said he had no idea what the animal could be. He thought it was without doubt hunting for fish. At that period the numbers of grilse and sea-trout around the Tor Point area had much improved.

I asked if he wasn't afraid of boating on water containing such large creatures. He remarked that there was no record or tradition of the Monster harming men in a boat. In fact he planned a fishing trip on the day following our meeting.

Mr. MacI. said to me, 'There is certainly a weird beastie in the loch.' He added that he didn't expect anyone to believe in the Monster till they had seen it with their own eyes.

By asking this witness a great many questions about his reactions, etc. I tried to decide on a single adjective that could fairly describe the Loch Ness beast. The best I could arrive at was 'bizarre'. . . .

In his covering letter to me Ted Holliday wrote:

'Had a curious impression when questioning. . . . I couldn't put it in my report. When people are confronted by this fantastic animal at close quarters they seem to be stunned. There is something strange about Nessie that has nothing to do with size or appearance. . . . Odd, isn't it?'

16

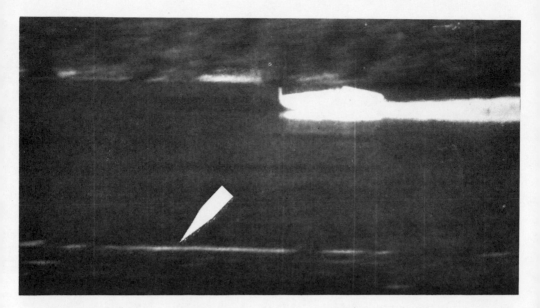

4 ABOVE *Crusader* at the moment of destruction. Stills from the
film shot by Jock Gemmel for Pathé News, in September 1952,
show what could be one arm of a 'V' wake in the foreground.

5 BELOW John Cobb's record breaking attempt ended in disaster
when his jet-boat ran into a local pattern of ripples, the cause of
which has never been established. Speed was over 200 m.p.h.
and the break-up almost instantaneous.

6   Torquil MacLeod standing in characteristic pose, searching the dark mysterious waters of Loch Ness; shortly before his death in 1962. Behind him can be seen the John Cobb memorial. Erected by the people of Glenurquhart, this simple cairn of stones marks the place, and passing, of "a very gallant gentleman".

7   Ruined Castle Urquhart stands amid the ghostly mists of dawn —a guard upon the centuries.

Yes it is odd – so odd in fact that I'm grateful to Ted for mentioning it, because I have noticed the same thing when interviewing witnesses. Perhaps the explanation lies in the sense of unreality – dreaming almost, which affects one when looking at the beast. It is as though one is looking at a *Unicorn*. Something impossible – absurd – incredible, the blatant flesh-and-blood existence of which has quite a bemusing effect.

But whatever MacI's reaction to it, the details of his description oblige one to reconsider the problem of identity – which has, over the years, been the cause of so much heated argument.

Disregarding the more fatuous explanations, there are no less than four serious schools of thought, each of which has its devoted adherents, and something to commend it regarding the Monster; which in turn is considered a mammal, a reptile, an amphibian and a mollusc!

A great deal has already been written on the subject, but summarizing briefly one could say that the first theory has been dealt with by Ivan Sanderson, F.Z.S., as an introduction to *Loch Ness Monster* (American edition), and the second in the book itself, as an adjunct to the careful study made by Mrs. Constance Whyte in *More Than a Legend*, in 1957.

The Amphibian theory was supported by R. T. Gould and Dr. Malcolm Burr, D.Sc., in books and articles[7] in 1934, and by Lt.-Colonel W. H. Lane, who published a curious little pamphlet on it at about the same time, which is now so rare it has become a collector's item.[8]

The mollusc, or giant invertebrate theory (the most recent and technically stimulating) is discussed by F. W. Holiday with much good sense in an article for the *Field* magazine, 1st November, 1962.

[7] *The Loch Ness Monster and Others*, by R. T. Gould. The article 'Sea Serpents and Monsters', February edition of the *Nineteenth Century* magazine, by Dr. Burr.

[8] Pamphlet of eighteen pages, 'The Home of the Loch Ness Monster'. Publishers: Grant & Murray Ltd., 126 Princes St., Edinburgh.

The types of animals considered are, respectively, an un-known species of gigantic long-necked seal, a surviving evolved form of long-necked Plesiosaur, an unknown gigantic species of newt, and lastly a sea-slug!

In relation to these four theories, I would like to comment on two of the details in the McI. sighting, which positively identify (*a*) Hairiness about the neck, and (*b*) The ability to sink straight downwards: both these characteristics having been reported on many previous occasions, but not at so close a range.

My comments are these. Coarse hair may be suggestive of a mammal, but it should be borne in mind that the male hairy frog, which is an amphibian, has developed a great number of *skin* filaments which look like hair, and these, it is thought serve as an aid to respiration by increasing skin area.

Indeed, Gerald Durell in his piece 'Hunt for the Hairy Frogs'[9] states that 'All frogs breathe, to a certain extent, through their skins; that is to say the skin absorbs oxygen from the moisture of the creature's body. In this way a frog has, so to speak, two breathing apparatuses – the skin and the lungs. Thus by breathing through the skin the frog can stay submerged in water for quite considerable periods . . .'

Secondly, the ability of the Monster to sink straight down-wards has been attributed to its ability to alter displacement like a submarine, by 'blowing its tanks' – or adjusting the in-flatable organ along its back, which gives rise to the change in shape of its curious humps – and this may prove to be the case; but when reading a very old and absorbing book *Geology and Mineralogy* by Professor William Buckland,[10] published in 1837 I came across some information which, if correct, could provide a better explanation.

In Chapter fourteen *Proofs of Design in the Structure of Fossil Vertebrate Animals*, Buckland analyses various extinct animal forms, and among them *P. dolichodeirus*, a type of Plesiosaurus, the first specimen of which was found in the lias of Lyme Regis,

[9] Page 90 of *The Barfut Beagles*. Publishers: Rupert Hart-Davis, 1954.
[10] See Appendix, Note A.

England, about 1823: regarding which he says: 'The head exhibits a combination of characters of the Ichthyosaurus, the crocodile and the lizard, but most nearly approaches the latter. It agrees with the Ichthyosaurus in the smallness of its nostrils, and also their position near the *anterior angle of the eye* . . .' (my italics).

'Ribs: The ribs are composed of two parts, one vertebral and one ventral; the ventral portions of one side uniting with those on the opposite side by an intermediate transverse bone, so that each pair of ribs encircled the body with a complete belt, made up of five parts. Cuvier[11] observes that the similarity of this structure to that of the ribs of chameleons and two species of Iguana, seems to show that the lungs of the Plesiosaurus Dolichodeirus, (as in these three sub-genera of living Sauarians,) were very large; and *possibly* that the colour of its skin also was changeable by the varied intensity of its inspirations. This hypothesis of Cuvier is but conjectural respecting the power of the Plesiosaurus to change the colour of its skin; and to the unexperienced in comparative anatomy, it may seem equally conjectural, to deduce any other conclusions respecting such perishable organs as the lungs, from the discovery of peculiar contrivances, and unusual apparatus in the ribs; yet we argue on similar grounds, when from the form and capabilities of these fossil ribs, we infer that they were connected with vast and unusual powers of expansion and contraction of the lungs. . . . The compound character of ribs, probably also gave to the Plesiosaurus the same power of compressing air with its lungs, and in that state taking it to the bottom, which we have considered as resulting from the structure of the steno-costal apparatus of the Ichthyosauri.'

The fact these observations were made more than a hundred years ago does not necessarily invalidate them, because some really brilliant work was done at about this time in the new science of palaeontology – and considering the Monster's ability to sink straight downwards without any audible exhalation, and

[11] Baron Georges Cuvier, the great French paleontologist, 1769–1832.

equally, the variation of colour and blotching attributed to it in reports[12], they are of unusual interest.

However, I have not included them because of my preference for the Plesiosaur theory, but because of the belief that we should be on the alert for information which could possibly be relevant – and in this respect some recent work done in the U.S. on how alligators hold their breath, adds something more for consideration.

In the 13th August, 1963, edition of the magazine *Animals*[13] (edited by Armand Denis) reference is made to two physiologists, H. T. Anderson and P. F. Scholander, who have found out how it is that alligators can stay under water for two hours or more at a stretch – which is a very long time for an air-breathing animal.

The answer lies in their ability to greatly reduce the flow of blood, and heart beat to two or three beats per minute. . . . 'Thus, although half the oxygen stored up before the creature goes under gets used during the first twenty minutes of a two-hour dive, what is left is sufficient to keep it just conscious for the remaining 100.'

Here again nature demonstrates her supreme adaptability – which means that we cannot afford to be too sure about the limits of temperature, or endurance, or the way in which environment affects the colony of unknown animals inhabiting Loch Ness – or (it would appear) other freshwater lakes around the world, and the oceans too, with which these lakes were once connected. . . .

[12] See Appendix Note B.

[13] Page 224, under News and Views – 'How the Alligator holds its breath'.

8 Torquil's artistry. This lovely drawing shows a square-rigged ship (probably the *Winterhude*) in which he sailed before the War, on one of his many adventurous journeys.

9 'Ogopogo' surfaces. This obviously genuine photograph by
Owen Templeton published in 1960 by the Penticton Herald,
British Columbia, outlines the Okanagan Lake Monster in every
detail. Head, neck, humps and tail are clearly in evidence. Note
also refinement in feeding posture . . . .

2

EXPANDING RIPPLES

FRESHWATER-MONSTER reports form the backbone to this chapter, collected from various sources, and arranged on a country of origin basis:

1. North American Reports.
2. Russian Reports.
3. Swedish Reports.
4. Irish Reports.
5. Scottish Highland Reports.

Wherever possible I have made contact with informants, either through the mails, or in person, but in the case of newspaper stories it is not always possible to verify facts, due to time-lapse or the movement of witnesses.

CANADIAN REPORTS

During the course of time a quantity of information has come in on Canadian lake-monsters. In the previous book a section appears on the most famous, in Lake Okanagan, British Columbia; similar in most respects to the L.N.M., but rejoicing in the nickname 'Ogopogo' – but it now seems that counterparts exist in other Canadian lakes, and that two of these have acquired titles in deference to the original – Manipogo, and Igopogo.

But, despite a slightly tongue-in-cheek attitude of the Press most reports appear to be factual, and I am indebted to Mr.

Michael Painter[1] for a balanced assessment and his trouble in providing details of environment at Okanagan, which is probably the only lake open to an effective search, due to its relative narrowness.[2]

Actual sightings of Ogopogo are infrequent, but the 80 miles of water is deep, and there is a noisy surface activity, which Mr. Painter describes in one of his letters:

'When I was small there were few boats on the lake, and those that did go out contained dedicated fishermen. Almost no one had a motor and I remember the scorn we felt for one particularly noisy model. . . . You could look out on the lake and recognize practically any boat by sight. Now in summer it is one mass of water skiers, speedboats, sail boats, even planes, and there is more or less a continuous roar of engines. . . . The rest of us mostly stay ashore to avoid the uproar. You will detect a native's scorn for these happenings, and perhaps I exaggerate the noise. However, while the number of people likely to see Ogopogo has increased vastly, I would think that, seriously, there is sufficient disturbance on any nice summer day to keep him out of sight . . .'

Having lived in Canada I know this description is true of many lakes accessible to the big cities – and in areas visited by people on holiday. They are alive with activity on a scale hard to imagine in Britain. By contrast, during the time spent watching the waters of the Ness, there have been days on end when I have only seen an occasional rowing boat – skulling peacefully along; the only sound a creak of rowlocks and the gentle lap of water on the hull.

But despite the interference there is no doubt that Ogopogo makes regular summer appearances as shown by the record of sightings produced by the *Kelowna Courier* in the form of a book-

[1] Michael Painter, P. Eng., B.C.R.F., M.E.I.C., M.C.I.F., is an engineer and forester, resident at Okanagan Mission, B.C. He has never seen Ogopogo.
[2] In Appendix Note C some facts appear which may prove of interest to the student, regarding depths, fish populations, topography, etc.

let in 1952, *Ogopogo – His Story* by R. P. McLean, in which a dozen or so clear accounts are analysed with impartial good sense. Unfortunately, the copy I have is one of the very few remaining – from which the following brief extracts are taken:

'If the Ogopogo is only a legend, a topic of conversation, it is a pretty lively and enduring one. The story goes back long before the days of the white man and the Indians certainly believed there was something in the lake. So sure were they that they made sacrifices when they ventured into certain sections of the lake. And there are tales from early settlers too. Hearsay, perhaps, but frequent enough and all with a similarity to give substance to the Indian Legends. And there is a growing body of present-day, practical people who are now quite convinced that Ogopogo, whatever it may be, is real. . . . Descriptions vary . . . but broadly follow the same general pattern. The length is placed from thirty to seventy feet. . . . The infrequent descriptions of the head agree that it has the general appearance of a horse or a sheep. Some claim there were whiskers or a beard. Almost all observers report that the body was coiled or humped, the tops of the humps showing plainly above the lake's surface. All agree too that he can move very rapidly. . . . Let's take a look at the evidence. There is a great deal, so let's select a few specimens from the files of the Okanagan newspapers. . . . On 10th July of this year, 1952, The *Courier* reported that on the previous Sunday Mrs. E. A. Fred Campbell was sitting on the lawn of her home 2420 Abbot St., between three and four in the afternoon. With her was Mrs. E. W. Campbell of Vancouver, and Mrs. Evelyn Little from Scotland, hardly two enthusiastic Regatta promoters.

'They suddenly saw Ogopogo a few hundred feet away. The Vancouver woman told the *Courier:* "I am a stranger here. I did not even know such a thing existed. But I saw it so plainly. A head like a cow or a horse that reared right up out of the water. It was a wonderful sight. The coils glistened like two huge wheels. . . . There were ragged edges like a saw. It was so beautiful with the sun shining on it. It was all so very clear, so extraordinary. It came up three times, then submerged and disappeared."'

'The *Pentiction Herald* reported that on Saturday 12th August, 1950, Rev. W. S. Beams, rector of St. Saviours Anglican Church Pentiction, saw an amazing spectacle in the lake in front of his Naramanta cottage. It was about 4.30 and the day was sunny and bright while the lake was calm. Suddenly there was a terrific disturbance in the lake and several humps appeared in view. "It was like a huge hose threshing about in the water," declared Rev. Beames. This went on for three or four minutes, then the "animal" appeared to dive under and the humps disappeared, leaving a terrific wake behind. Then the lake was perfectly calm again.'

'Sqdn. Leader Bruce Millar, and Mrs. Millar were driving along the Naramanta Road one Sunday evening when they saw Ogopogo in the lake below them. They stopped their car and watched him for quite some time, stopping other passing cars. They described him as a "lithe, sinewy monster, 75 feet in length with a coiled back and dignified demeanour. Periodically his progress would be halted as he lay quietly on the water, head well raised, as he surveyed the lake with calm dignity . . . then his tail would rise, there would be a splash and he would weigh anchor."'

Of the many other reports selected, three stand out. One describes a 50 foot specimen with between ten and twelve 'loops' of body showing, another when two separate specimens were apparently seen at approximately the same time, one near the shore and the other in the middle of the lake, and thirdly the report of Captain Jack McLeod: 'I'm a sceptical sea captain and I've travelled the waters of Okanagan Lake for twenty-seven years without seeing any signs of a Monster. However, at last I've seen Ogopogo, and this is no second-hand story as I saw it with my own eyes.'

The *Kelowna Courier* has reported several recent sightings: for example on 17th July, 1963, 'Seventy-two-year-old Sy Jenkins was fishing in the bay at Naramanta when he noticed a commotion in an overgrown section of the lake. A 20 foot long black object, showing three humps about five feet apart, travelled past the boat and moved into deep water. Mr. Jenkins said the serpent was visible for more than a minute. A Naramanta resident for a number of years he has never before seen the Ogopogo, though he has fished in the lake a great deal.'

Summer, 1964. 'A Mr. and Mrs. Leslie Kerry, 2188 Abbott St. saw something about 300 yards off shore, creating a large wave. It moved about a mile down the lake, watched carefully through binoculars. Mr. Kerry said: "I could distinctly see a head and part of a shoulder. It looked very much like a seal head, although I thought I could make out two horns. It was travelling very fast, and making quite a commotion . . ."'

September 3rd. 1964. 'Kenny Unser, aged 15, throwing sticks into the water for his dog, near the Kelowna old Ferry wharf noticed high waves, and then about three feet of dark green tail came out of the water, and hit the wharf with a crash . . . "It was about 75 yards away. It was about a foot thick, with big scales, and rounded off at the end like a chopped-off dog's tail . . . it hit hard, and water splashed up onto the wharf."

'Frightened, Kenny got his dog out of the water and went home. His family treated his story as a joke until they learned two other people had reported seeing something large moving in the water a few hours previously, near the Ogopogo statue; close to the old Ferry wharf. Mrs. Dorothy Parrish, and Mrs. Betty Nordvie noticed something about 100 yards out and wondered if it could be a submarine, but realized it was too shallow. "They could see the water moving over what appeared to be three humps . . ." There were no boats in the area at the time.'

It is encouraging to read of such recent evidence, because unless I am mistaken, the Ogopogo will in due time become a

focal point of interest, and Okanagan lake subject to the most
intense scientific probing : but he will not lack for competition. . .

Oakville Journal Record, 27th July, 1963, Keswick, Ontario. 'A
Presbyterian minister, a funeral director and their families are
the latest to claim to have seen "Igopogo", the Lake Simcoe sea-
serpent. The Rev. L. B. Williams of Mount Albert, and Neil
Lathangue of Bradford, their wives and children were boating
in the lake Monday when something came towards them, Mr.
Lathangue said it was charcoal coloured, 30–70 feet long and
had dorsal fins. Igopogo was first reported eleven years ago by
an Indian trapper, and has since been described as a "dog faced
animal with a neck the diameter of a stove-pipe".'

Ken Anderson of Oakville, Ontario, who sent this clipping
rightly points out that the lake is frozen over during the winter
– and I know from experience that in summer it is a play-
ground; barely forty miles from the vast city of Toronto. However, it covers a good area, being 15–20 miles in diameter and
is fed by several rivers. Fish population may be dwindling due to
the intense activity of sportsmen who trail their glittering lures
everywhere – and on the strength of this one report it would
probably be wise to reserve judgement on 'Igopogo' – whereas
the information on 'Manipogo', to the westward is far more extensive. . . .

Winnipeg Free Press 5th August, 1961. 'THAT MONSTER
AGAIN – Hunt on for Manipogo – A University of Manitoba
professor, if he can get equipment and skilled helpers will return
to Lake Winnipegosis this summer as the only Canadian scientist to be officially interested in the existence of Manitoba's sea
monster. Dr. James A. McLeod, the University's head zoologist
hopes to search the lake this summer for either Manipogo himself or his remains . . .'

Winnipeg Free Press 21st August, 1961. 'MANIPOGO'S ON
THE GO – Manipogo has made his 1961 début. The Lake
Manitoba-Winnipegosis-Dauphin Lake Monster put in his first

reported appearance of the year Saturday evening at sunset. A group of seven were watching the sunset at Twin Beaches on Lake Manitoba between 8.30 and 9 p.m. when Mrs. Blanche Konecki sighted an object a few hundred feet off shore. Blanche saw it and said, "Isn't that a boat sinking?" and someone said, "No, it's the Monster," Patrick Rakowski, of 488 Giroux Street, St. Boniface, told the *Free Press*.

'The group on the shore watched the "thing" for four or five minutes. Patrick said: "It was over 40 feet long, with one large hump – about 35 feet long – and a short hump at each end. It was yellowy-brown, and looked slimy."

'The group decided it was travelling from five to seven miles an hour . . .'

Another article from the file of newspaper clippings I have on this subject outlines Manipogo's history. Written by Erik Watt, it describes events leading up to the publication of a photograph in the *Free Press*, 15th August, 1962, purporting to show the monster at a range of 50–75 yards – and can be summarized as follows:

1909. In September Valentine McKay, a Hudson's Bay Company fur trader (who lives in Grand Rapids today) was travelling by canoe on Cedar Lake. Rounding Graves Point he saw 'on the glossy surface of the water 400 yards from shore . . . a huge creature travelling at about 2 m.p.h. It had a dark upper surface which glistened, and part of its body projected about four feet in the air, vertically. The water was considerably disturbed.' It disappeared behind an island.

1918. April. Fullers Bay, Lake Winnipegosis. Oscar Frederickson was shooting duck on ice a foot or so in thickness, when suddenly 'something heaved the ice upwards in two or three feet of water . . . slivers of ice a foot long fell on the south side, and a piece of loose ice six to eight feet wide began to rotate slowly'. He didn't see the cause, but suspected the lake Monster of which he had heard.

1935. Dirty Water Lake, near north end of Winnipegosis. C. F.

Ross, Manitoba timber inspector, and Tom Spence of Pine Falls, see a strange beast with 'a single horn protruding from the back of its head like a periscope'. The animal's head is small and flat; it has a body like a dinosaur, with slate grey hide 'like an elephant'.

1948. Lake Manitoba, near St. Rose du Lac. C. P. Alarie of St. Boniface describes hearing an unearthly cry, and then at a range of 400 yards in a marsh, sees a 'brownish-black thing about six feet long' which rears up and then disappears.

1955. Graves Point. August. Albert Gott of Pelican Rapids, fishing with Joe Parker and his two sons describe an object 'about four feet out of the water, and 2½ feet thick' which disappeared when they rowed to within 400 yards of it.

Lake Winnipegosis. September. Near the Overflowing River, Charlie Burrell fishing with three Americans, sees four to six feet of an animal's back break water, and then disappear.

1957. Lake Manitoba. Louis Betecher and Eddie Nipanik working on the shore see a strange creature serpent-like in appearance.

1960. July. A. R. Adams of St. Rose reports seeing a creature resembling a large snake. The head is diamond shaped, about 8 inches wide and a wake develops about 8 feet behind the head setting up waves some 15 inches high. Speed estimated at 15 m.p.h. Later, some fourteen miles to the eastward three occupants of a boat report a reptile-like beast surfacing within thirty feet. Its description fits the Adam's account. Chris Stopel of Crane Bay, remains in the boat while his wife and sister leave it in fear, wading ashore through a marsh.

August 12th. Manipogo beach. Seventeen witnesses report seeing three Monsters – two appear to be fully grown and the third much smaller. Three weeks earlier twenty persons reported seeing a single huge 'reptile' from almost the same spot. Numbered amongst these witnesses are Tom Locke, a government land inspector and his wife.

1961. 19th August. Twin Beaches. Seven people describe seeing an animal 40 feet long, with three humps. Yellowy-brown in colour, it travels at five to seven m.p.h.

1962. 15th August. *The Winnipeg Free Press* publishes a photo-graph from an 'original untouched negative' showing some long dark object, with a curious bump in the middle, travelling on the surface of Lake Manitoba. Two fishermen, Dick Vincent of Pembina and John Konefall of Dauphin state it was taken at a range of 50–75 yards, and as the gun'wale of the boat appears in the picture this estimate appears acceptable ... 'We first spotted the object to the left of our boat about 300 yards away,' said Mr. Vincent, 'after swinging into the direction it was heading, we saw what we believed to be a large black snake or eel ... which was swimming with a ripple action ... it was about a foot in girth, and about 12 feet of the Monster was above water. No head was visible.' Despite the power of a ten-horse motor, attempts to catch up with the beast failed.

I have on file a forty page typescript on the subject of lake-monsters by Ivan T. Sanderson, in which he classifies the many Canadian sightings under the broad heading 'Northern Lake Monsters' – or N.L.M.'s for short. In it he refers to the August 1961 *MacCleans Magazine* article 'Scientific Search for Pre-historic Monster', drawing attention to Prof. James McLeod's interest in the Winnipegosis Monster, and the wooden replica of a huge vertebra recovered from the lake by a Mr. Oscar Fredrick-son, a local resident, back in the 1930's.

A picture of this (the original bone seems to have been des-troyed by fire) appears in the 5th August edition of the *Winnipeg Free Press*; and the caption states 'It could have come from a huge reptile'. A point of view qualified by Prof. McLeod who is reported as saying the model was either made by someone who knew his palaeontology – or was the copy of a bone from a crea-ture believed extinct for millions of years.

But quite apart from the recent crop of Canadian sightings one cannot read the Sanderson typescript without coming to the conclusion that there are a number of other lakes in South America, the U.S. and Canada from which similar phenomena have been reported – which is interesting because in August

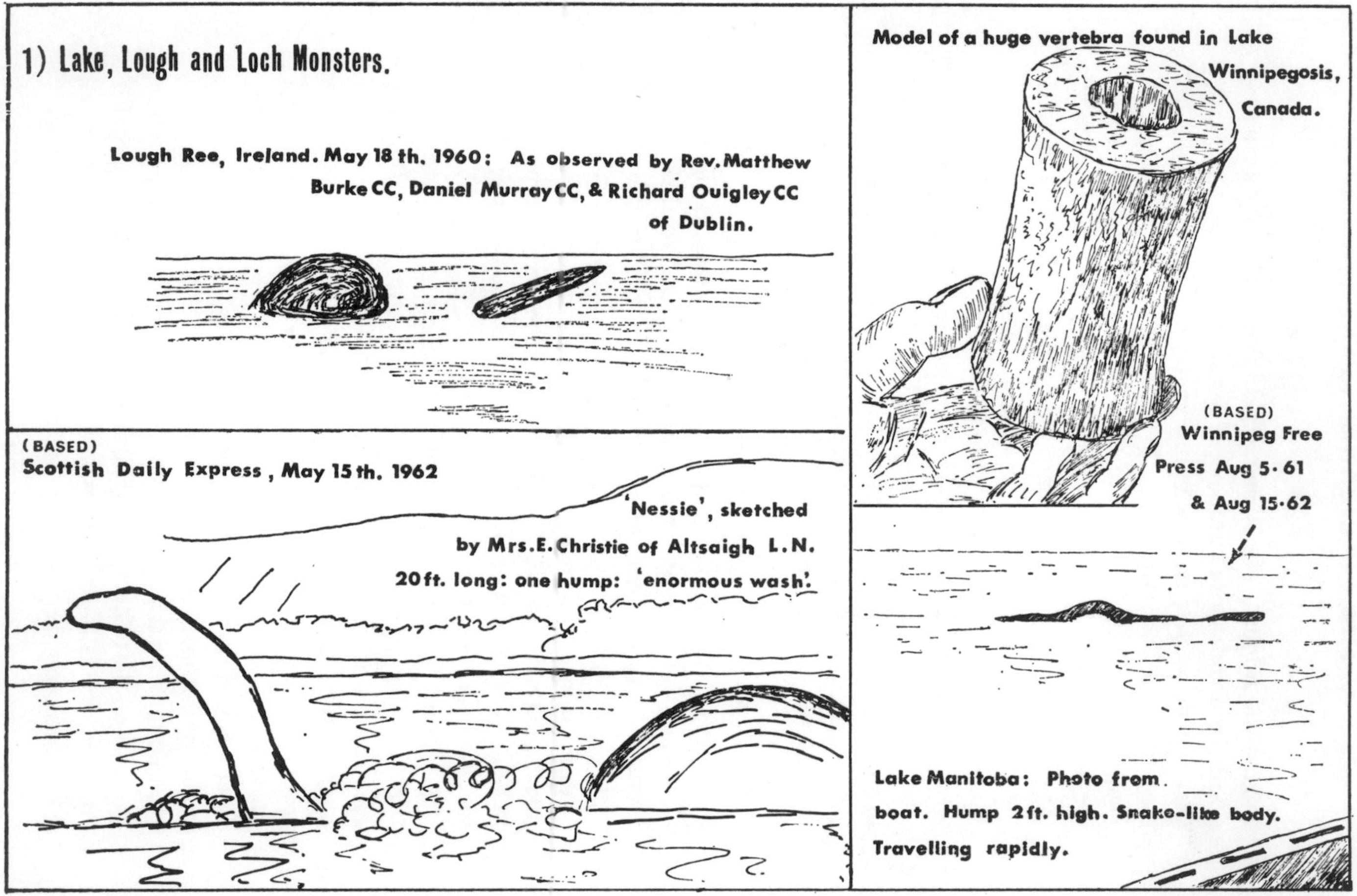

1) Lake, Lough and Loch Monsters.

Lough Ree, Ireland. May 18 th. 1960: As observed by Rev. Matthew Burke CC, Daniel Murray CC, & Richard Ouigley CC of Dublin.

(BASED) Scottish Daily Express, May 15 th. 1962

'Nessie', sketched by Mrs.E.Christie of Altsaigh L.N. 20 ft. long: one hump: 'enormous wash'.

Model of a huge vertebra found in Lake Winnipegosis, Canada.

(BASED) Winnipeg Free Press Aug 5·61 & Aug 15·62

Lake Manitoba: Photo from boat. Hump 2 ft. high. Snake-like body. Travelling rapidly.

FIG. I

1961 I received a letter from Lt.-Colonel J. D. Blyth, Chelten-
ham, Glos., including an eyewitness account and sketch of
something peculiar seen in a north Canadian lake some fifty
years ago – long before the days of publicity:

Dear Mr. Dinsdale,

I am sending the following extract from a letter which I have
just received, as I think it may interest you although it describes
a happening more than fifty years ago. The writer when a young
man was one of a party on a trek in the wild part of northern
Canada; I don't know what they were doing there, possibly
they were prospecting. Here is what he says:

'When in north Canada, while crossing a divide we came
upon a lake. It was surrounded on all sides save one by precipitous rock cliffs of 30 feet or so. On the fourth side was a swamp.
At the foot of the cliffs were scattered rocks and strewn about
them bones and magnificent antlers – moose, etc. While looking
for a place to get down to them we saw in the middle of the lake
a vast swirl. We assumed the lake was the site of a crater and
that what we had seen was gas. But no! Shortly afterwards there
was another great upheaval and we all five saw a vast dark
olive-coloured object break the surface. No head or tail but
thus – (see Sketch 2) – it had lumps on it and its movement was
slow. It was less than 200 yards from us and clearly visible.
Size – alarming!

'The whole place had a most macabre and unpleasant atmosphere and we left considerably frightened.

'The lake would have been about two miles in diameter.

'Now what was that? Oddly enough later I met a bloke who
described an almost identical experience in South America.'

On further inquiry I found the witness to be a relative of Col.
Blyth – now living in Newlyn, Cornwall – and that he could do
no more than generalize as to the position of the lake, which he
describes as 'approximately 300 miles west of the Hudson Bay
Post at the Forks (Albany and Montreal rivers) and the some
more miles due north' – but such is the immensity of northern

VARIOUS ASPECTS OF
MONSTER HUMPAGE
— as seen off Brazil
from the 'Valhalla', in 1905;

— at Loch Ness, in 1961...

...from shore (Stitt report)

...from the yacht 'Finola' (Lowrie report);

— in northern Ontario;

— and N.E. Siberia in
1964 (Gladkikh sketch).

Sketch 2

FIG. 2

Canada, with its multitude of lakes, many of which are still un-
named, this vagueness is not surprising; and if anything adds to
the pleasantly mysterious aspect of the report.

RUSSIAN REPORTS

In 1962 Moscow radio reported on two separate lake-monster
sightings by geologists and geographers working in a remote
and virtually unexplored area of Eastern Siberia, and to the
southwards amongst the Tien Shan mountains. The *Guardian*
printed the story on 15th February, 1962; under the caption
'SOVIETS GO ONE BETTER: Two Soviet Loch Ness
Monsters . . .', and since that time there have been other references in the Press.

As with most reports of this kind information has been
sketchy, and thus I have been doubly fortunate to get in touch
with a Soviet scientist, at the Moscow Institute of Oceano-
graphy, who has been able to send me authentic information in
exchange for recent data on the L.N.M. – and equally Mr. G.
W. Creighton in this country, who is fluent in Russian, and
interested in this subject too.

The following excerpts are translated by him from Dr. S. K.
Klumov's article in the scientific journal *Priroda* (Nature)
August, 1962.

'In Eastern Siberia there is a huge very scarcely populated
mountainous region with an extremely severe climate, and equal
in area to Belgium. I refer to the Sordongnokh Plateau, which
lies on the Oimyakon Tableland, not far from the Cold Pole (at
Verkhoyansk). Not a single zoologist or botanist has yet visited
this region.

'During the Tertiary Age, so the geologists tell us, this extensive region was relatively low-lying, and sloping off gradually
eastwards . . . but the process of mountain forming cut off the
low-lying area from the Sea of Okhotsk and raised it to a height
of about 1,000 metres. . . . On the newly-formed plateau a few

small rivers were dammed up by collapsing mountains, and there appeared a system of interlinked lakes.

'In July 1953 the Soviet geologist V. A. Tverdokhlebov (translated literally this rather splendid name means "hardbread") leader of a prospecting party, was engaged in geological work on the Sordongnokh Plateau. It was a bright sunny day when he reached the shore of Lake Vorota. There was scarcely any wind. Glancing at the smooth surface of the great lake, Tverdokhlebov and his young companion Boris Bashkatov saw, at a distance of some 300 metres from the shore, some object that was shining brightly in the sun. At first they thought it was a floating empty gasoline drum, but on looking more closely, they saw that the object was – alive! It was swimming rapidly towards the shore, and to the very spot where they were standing. The geologists climbed up higher on the cliff face – to some 15 or 20 metres, and continued to watch it. The animal came closer, and it was already possible to see those parts of it which emerged from the water. The breadth of the fore part of the creature's torso – evidently the head – was as much as two metres (6 feet 6 inches). The eyes were set wide apart. The length of its body was approximately 10 metres (32 feet). It was enormous and of a dark-grey colour. On the sides of its head could be seen two light-coloured patches. On its back was sticking up, to the height of half a metre or so, something which seemed to be in the nature of a dorsal fin and which was narrow and bent backwards. The animal was moving itself forwards in leaps. Its upper part at times appearing above the water and then at times disappearing. When at a distance of 100 metres from the shore it stopped; then it began to beat the water vigorously, raising a cascade of spray and then it plunged out of sight. The animal did not show itself again, although the eyewitnesses carefully scanned the surface of the lake for a further half hour.

'The nearest inhabited spot is 120 kilometres (75 miles) from the lake. Among the local inhabitants – hunters and fishermen – the lakes of the Sordongnokh Plateau, and particularly the biggest of them all, Lake Labynkyr (about 9 miles long and 200 feet deep) have an evil repute. They are convinced that some Monster lives there, which they call a "Devil". Many a time this "Devil" has carried off their dogs when these have jumped into the lake to retreive ducks that have been shot. Once the "Devil" chased a fisherman's raft and the man was able to see that the animal had an enormous mouth and was of a dark-grey colour. In short many local inhabitants have themselves seen it . . .'

Dr. Klumov goes on to consider what the animal may be. A very large fish or amphibian, possibly – or a relic from the fauna of Tertiary times, conceivably; bearing in mind that the area is a 'total nature reserve' as yet uninfluenced by man, and in which large tracts of swamp are covered with a long red moss, which, in his opinion, is the bog-moss of the Tertiary period.

Subsequently, on 21st December, 1964, he sent me a resumé of expedition activity in 1963 and 1964 to Labynkyr and Vorota – but advised that the report from Lake Sary-Chelek in the Tien Shan mountains was probably attributable to cormorants, swimming one after the other, giving the impression 'some long animal similar to a snake'. At any rate, no further reports had been received from that region which could not be explained.

Comments on Labynkyr and Vorota are as follows:

'In 1963 a small expedition visited these lakes. Four members of this expedition observed some object for five minutes at a distance of some 800 metres, which several times emerged from the water, and then submerged. They couldn't photograph it because the sun was setting.

'In 1964 the big expedition consisting of three groups replacing one another visited both lakes. The first group from Tallin (Estonia) arrived at the lake when it was still covered with ice. Among the members of this group there were geologists, geomorpholgists, zoologists and divers. This group in spite of repeated immersions up to 30 metres saw nothing.

'They lived there for two weeks and returned to Tallin. This group was followed by a second from Kuibyshev (town on the river Volga), including eighteen men mainly aeronautical engineers. They saw nothing too.

'The third group which was at the lake for the second half of August was the smallest one. Two of them saw on the surface of the water three rather large round objects which were moving along at a distance of some 100 meters from the shore. The observers were running behind the moving objects along the shore trying to photograph them. They noted that these three objects submerged simultaneously, and emerged in the same way. It is not known whether it was one animal with three humps or three separate animals. I have received no photographs and no more detailed descriptions. These observers live in Riga.

'Recently a new report about some unknown animal in another Yakutian lake has appeared in the newspaper *Komsomol'skaya Pravda* (Moscow) 21st November, 1964. I am enclosing the clipping.'

The article *The Mystery of Lake Khaiyr* is by G. Rokosuev, Deputy Chief of the Moscow University expedition to the lake, which is about 500 miles north-west from Labynkir and 100 miles from the shore of Laptev's sea; reached after a very difficult journey over swampy tundra.

G. Rokosuev writes:[3] 'At Khaiyr settlement (which is about 150 miles inland from the Laptev Sea), Kharchenkov was told that not even hunters dare approach the lake where the creature dwells, that has inspired such fear in the local populace. The basin of the River Omoleya has numerous lakes, all of which have large quantities of fish. Only in this one mysterious lake, so they assured us, there are no fish at all. No wild geese or ducks will alight on its surface. This is a "thermal" lake, that is to say it freezes several days later than the surrounding lakes. According to the geological findings, it lies in the zone of a recent disruption of the Earth's crust. The lake is approximately 600

[3] Translation by Nikolai Vassiliev and Gordon Creighton.

10 This very early print (Stradano, 1580) shows the Indian python under straitened circumstances—although in the background a member of the colony appears to have escaped detection, while in the process of swallowing a goat.

11   The Barra 'long necked' monster carcase; in fact the desiccated remains of a beaked whale, washed up on this Hebridean island coast, July 1961.

metres by 500 metres. Nobody has ever measured its depth. But the natives say it is very deep. Dull sounds have often been heard coming from the lake, and strange splashes have been seen on its surface, which the local people attribute to the Monster, but judging by their accounts it did not seem that anybody had ever actually seen it.

'Quite unexpectedly, N. F. Gladkikh, a member of the biology group, literally stumbled upon the creature. This was how it happened. He had gone down to the lake to collect water, early one morning, and there beheld this creature, which had climbed out on to the bank, and seemed to be browsing on the grass.

'It had a small head on a long shiny neck, an enormous body with bluish-black skin, and an upright dorsal fin. Gladkikh was scared, and at once ran back to wake up the head of the biology unit. But when the members of the unit arrived at the lake with rifles and cameras the beast had disappeared. Only crushed and trampled grass was to be seen. They examined the lake shore carefully, but found no signs that grass had actually been eaten. It was a very calm morning, but they saw waves on the surface of the lake, and thought that these possibly marked the area where the creature had submerged. Back at the camp Gladkikh quickly made a sketch of the animal. (See Sketch 2.)

'Fortunately it was also seen again later, and this time by several people at once, namely the head of the expedition and two other members of the Biology Group. They were looking across the lake when suddenly the head appeared out in the middle of the expanse of water, and then the dorsal fin. The Monster was lashing the water with its long tail and sending out waves all over the lake.

'You can well imagine how astonished we all were by this actual experience which demonstrated the truthfulness of popular legend. At present no one can say what type of animal this is – maybe it is one as yet unknown to science. Perhaps the last of the long extinct Ichthiosauri? I do not know. I am only a geologist.

'Next year, we will organize our base nearer to Lake Khaiyr, and we will try to photograph this creature.'

If the Gladkikh sketch is anything to go by, perhaps it would have been more appropriate to say 'long-necked extinct Plesiosauri': and in this connection an excerpt from *Life Magazine* 22nd January, 1965 cross-refers to the spine-tingling character of the Russian monsters be they from Lake Khaiyr, Vorota or Labynkyr.

A party of explorers, *en route* to Oymyakon, reputedly one of the coldest places on earth, came to hear of one during their travels: 'We had seen incredible things and had heard tales about dining on 20,000-year-old mammoth meat. But the strangest tale of all was about the lake of Labynkyr. Lurking in its depths, we were told, is another Siberian wonder. Some time ago, a group of men who had stopped there saw a reindeer walk into the lake. It disappeared below the surface. Then a dog swam in; it too was swallowed up. Suddenly, shrouded in mist, a black Monster emerged from the lake, *snorted* (my italics) and plunged back. One of the men, a scholar, assured his group that the Monster was a dinosaur.

'We were excited by the tale but our host warned us that nobody would take us to the lake of Labynkyr. What was there, he said, made men's blood run cold . . .'

During the course of the Loch Ness expeditions I have been careful to collect 'odd' stories, and scraps of information which, for one reason or another, lie outside the usual category of evidence. Much of this information is based on hearsay, which can be very unreliable; but some of it is believable because of the circumstances connected with it. One such account emphasizes the carnivorous nature of the beast – or *Beiste*, as it is known in the Gaelic.

Some years ago, a stag was hunted down one of the glens which lead to the northern shore of Loch Ness. In fear it entered the water, swimming out strongly. When some way out it became involved in a sudden swirl.

Changing direction, it headed back to the shore – but on climbing out, over the rocks and shingle, it was seen, quite literally, to be walking on three legs. The fourth leg was missing!

The reason why this account has not been publicized is because the stag was not, I understand, being hunted legally. A recurring situation in the Highlands of Scotland, one may add.

A second story, based on the experience of a single witness, came to me in a letter. There can be no doubt about its accuracy – but I am not sure about its interpretation. Loch Ness is a fault zone, and an underwater shift could possibly cause a noise and disturbance, or the release of a pocket of gas – but this at best provides a poor explanation.

The letter reads: 'I was standing on the edge of the loch (southern shore, close to "Red Braes")[4] cleaning the minnow of the weed, with my rod in the crook of my arm, and with my back to the loch. It was then I heard a "*snort*" from the water which I must confess gave me quite a start. I looked round and just where I imagine the shelf (the submerged ledge which projects out in most places some 20–30 yards from shore) begins, the water was boiling and full of commotion. Bubbles too were coming to the surface, but it was all over in a few seconds and the surface was calm again. I may say that it was a perfect day with not a ripple on the loch, warm and sunny and very mild. Now with regard to the noise, I can only liken it to the sound made by a horse when snorting: whether clearing its nostrils or not I cannot say, although I think the noise made by a horse is caused mainly by a shuddering of the lips. It was, of course, very much louder than any horse I ever heard, and consisted of one "snort" only. I immediately went back to where my wife was sitting and told her of my experience . . .'

Yours sincerely
G. A. S.

(Dated) 16th April, 1962.   Inverness, Scotland.

[4] Brackets enclose my own comments.

If the Russian Monster 'snorted and plunged back', when surprised, could it be that when Mr. Smith's back was turned the L.N.M. behaved in the same manner? If it raised its head above the surface, at a few yards range, it may have been even more startled than he was – and most large air-breathing animals in the wild react suddenly to fear. It remains a possibility.

SWEDISH REPORTS

The first indication that Sweden too is a member of the club, arrived unexpectedly at my house in February 1962 – a letter from a Mr. Gordon To in Stockholm.

' . . . when I was reading your book a few Swedish friends said to me that there is a lake in Sweden called Storsjön (The Big Lake), said to have monsters; also there is a museum close to the lake with exhibitions with traps and such-like equipment from the old days for catching them. Also there are photographs. I will check in the library for you . . .'

True to his word, Mr. To did precisely that and has since sent me a sixty-page booklet on the subject called *Storsjöodjuret*,[5] by Knut Svedjeland, with some really priceless illustrations, and a photograph of the huge circular spring-trap and 'harpuner' devices made to catch the beast in 1894, now on exhibit in the museum at Östersund.

The lake is far north, on the same latitude as Trondheim in Norway – about 14° E by 63° N and must be frozen over for long periods during the winter.

Indeed in one of Karlson's sketches he caricatures a small and unhappy looking fisherman, huddled in furs by a hole in the ice, clutching a long 'harpuner' with a string attached to it! But, despite these ribald overtones there is much in the book to be taken seriously, and thanks to the Curator at Jämtlands läns Museum at Östersund, and the work of his assistant Mr. Björn Rosén, the facts are briefly summarized as follows:

[5] Publishers: S-förlaget Östersund. 1959.

Letter to me dated 12th April, 1965, from the Curator.

'From 1820 to 1898 the Monster was observed twenty-two times, mostly by trustworthy persons, and in our own century the animal has shown itself many times; latest in 1959. In spite of the many variations of the statements of appearance a few traits in common can be put together.

'The length has been hard to determine. The reports vary from $3\frac{1}{2}$ to 14 metres (11 to 45 feet).

'The thickness is estimated at about 1 metre. The shape mostly has been stated to be lengthened, with some humps. As the food may be fish, the animal is not dangerous but can be annoyed, and then shows a mobile, long tongue.[6] The skin is described as slippery and shining in the sun. The colour is stated to be greyish, grey with black spots, in front dark-brown or reddish-brown, possibly greenish, and behind it is grey or light-brown.

'The head is said to be round and smooth like that of a dog, with great eyes. The animal occasionally swims with its head above water.

'The extremities are described as short, stumpy legs or feet, possibly big clumsy fins, possibly long, webbed hind legs. It has great fins of the back or of the head, possibly ears, described as little sails, which can be laid tight on to the neck. These fins or ears have an estimated diameter of 1 metre.

'The speed of the animal is about 75 kilometres an hour (about 45 m.p.h.).

'The Great Lake Monster most often is seen in the middle of summer when the weather is calm and fine, but it also has been observed in storm. Many theories have been started as to the real character of the Monster: a sheat-fish, an Enaliosaurus, a Basilosaurus, or belonging to the Pinnipedia.

'Several expeditions have been fitted out in order to capture the animal, and in 1894 a company was established with the

---

[6] This almost human characteristic, must endear the Swedish monster to everyone!

41

King Oscar II as a member. The traps and harpoons in the Länsmuseum in Östersund originate from the efforts of this company.

> Yours sincerely,
>
> Björn Rosén,   (The compiler).

A further cross reference to the Swedish Monster appears in Ivan Sanderson's typescript on N.L.M.'s (northern lake monsters) in which he mentions Swedish 'Water Cows', and the Lake Storsjon specimen as . . . 'also very large with greenish looking shiny skin, a long thin neck at least 10 feet long, small head, the usual bumps, and a capacity for rushing headlong about the lake at the speed of a motor-boat, leaving a huge wake, and making sudden sharp turns . . .'

This last comment I find interesting, because when I filmed the Loch Ness animal in 1960, it made just such a wake; and an astonishingly abrupt 90° turn to the left, the wash from which can just be seen in a still from the film (Plate 8b in *Loch Ness Monster*): which infers that despite their bulk, these creatures are capable of sudden manœuvres.

Finally, Dublin's *Evening Press*, 4th June, 1965 steps in with a piece of information. No source is given, but it is probably the book *Storsjöodjuret*. It implies that on occasion the Swedish Monster does more than stick it's tongue out . . .

'First reports were published during the middle of the last century, but Swedish folklore tells of the Monster having been seen hundreds of years ago.

'The story first made big headlines about sixty-five years ago, when two girls were attacked by a sea creature[7] as they walked along the shore of the lake. The girls ran for their lives and told an incoherent story of the attack.

'This was the first and only time the Monster was reported to

---

[7] In the original this could be an implied cross-reference to the Norwegian 'Soe Orm' or great sea-snake, evidence for which was collected by Erik Pontoppidan as long ago as 1752, and published in his celebrated book *Natural History of Norway*.

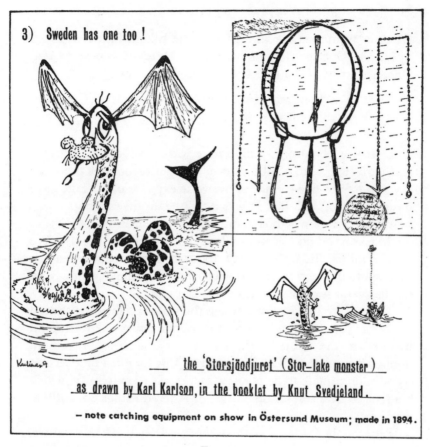

FIG. 3

be aggressive. Most reports speak of it showing no interest in humans. After this incident reports of the creature's appearance aroused national interest, in Storsjon Lake, which covers 176 square miles and is 300 feet deep . . .'

Reference is also made to the attempts to catch the beast in 1894, and a private venture, financed by a well-to-do Östersund widow. She hired a Norwegian whaler and harpoon expert – who spent a year on the lake without catching a glimpse of it.

43

Excerpts from a report submitted to the Inland Fisheries Trust, by three Dublin clergymen: Rev. Matthew Burke, C.C., Daniel Murray, C.C. and Richard Quigley, C.C.

Title: 'The Sighting of an Unidentified Aquatic Creature. Lough Ree, 18th May, 1960.'

1. 'It was about 9.30 p.m. There was no wind, and the lake was perfectly calm. Visibility was still quite good, as the clear sky and mirror-like surface of the wide expanse of the lake gave unusually good lighting. It was a still beautiful evening.

'We were in a row-boat, some 50 or 60 yards off shore from St. Marks wood on the east or Leinster side of the lake. . . . We were scanning the water round about for rising trout when one of us spotted a very strange object which was moving slowly on the flat calm surface, about 80 yards away.

'There were two sections above the water; a forward section of uniform girth, stretching quite straight out of the water and inclined to the plane of the surface at about 30°, in length about 18–24 inches. The diameter of this long leaning section we would estimate to be about 4 inches. At its extremity, which we took to be a serpent-like head, it tapered rather abruptly to a point.

'Between the leading and the following sections of this creature, there intervened about two feet of water. The second section seemed to us to be a tight, roughly semicircular loop. This portion could have been a hump or a large knob on the back of a large body under the surface that was being propelled by flippers. As to the dimension of this section, if a loop, we should say the girth of a large fifteen pound salmon; if, however, a round hump . . . we should put its base at about 18 inches. . . . We would estimate the overall length of the two visible sections, measured along the surface from tip of snout to end of hump, at about 6 feet.

'The movement along the water was steady. There was no

44

apparent disturbance of the surface, so that propulsion seemed
to come from the well-submerged portion of the creature. There
was no undulation of its body above water. It was cruising at a
very leisurely speed, and was apparently unconcerned about our
presence.

'We watched it moving along the surface for a period of two
or three minutes in a north-easterly direction. It was going
towards the shore; then it submerged gradually, rather than
dived, and disappeared from view completely. Another couple
of minutes later it reappeared still following the same course . . .
it reached a point about 30 yards off shore, where it submerged
and we saw it no more. . . .

'Lough Ree is the centre one of the three great Shannon
lakes. There are some parts of it at a depth of twenty fathoms.
Being a limestone lake, there is a rich aquatic life, and trout are
large, three and four pounds being common . . . pike, perch and
eels abound. It must seem strange that there is no other report
which has been published . . . however, there may have been
other occasions when this creature has been sighted, but these
sightings have never been recorded. A serious investigation
might also succeed in assembling further evidence. Legend
ascribes to Lough Ree, in common with several other Irish
lakes the "Piast", a kind of water serpent or dragon. Perhaps
after all the fairy-tales are not so far-fetched!'

2. 'We should like you to accept for the records of the Inland
Fisheries Trust, this addendum to the report we have already
given you. . . . Had we not had this extraordinary experience,
we should not have considered our second sighting worth
reporting, for it was made at much greater distance, and in
somewhat poorer light. In view, however, of our previous experience, we feel that the second one may be significant and
warrants being recorded.

'It was about 9.50 p.m. on the same evening. The surface was
still glassy calm. Looking almost due west, at a distance of
about three quarters of a mile, one of the party observed what

45

seemed to be a long rock projecting a few inches above the water. It seemed to be about the length of a row-boat. Its position as a possible hazard was noted for it was well away from any other rock or land, and might not show up if there were any waves. Looking again in the direction of the rock we were surprised to see that its position had changed. Then checking it against the background of the opposite shore . . . we discovered that it was moving through the water at a steady rate, at about ordinary walking pace. . . . We had it under observation for about ten minutes, before deciding to try and head it off on a converging course. We felt the sound of an outboard motor might scare it, and so we rowed in a quiet manner. Our direction was approximately north. Our view of it was obscured when we passed the small island, just off St. Mark's wood. When we passed this island we found it had disappeared completely, and so we assumed that whatever the creature was, it had dived beneath the surface. We could not help feeling that there was some link of similarity between these two strange appearances.

'One ought not, of course, to assume that the answer to the problem is some completely unknown creature. . . . Nevertheless we are in this case convinced that what we saw was not a pike or otter, or any other fish or animal familiar to us, nor was it some inanimate object such as a tree-branch carried by the current, for there is no current in this part of the lake. . . . We were convinced that what we saw was a living creature of a very exceptional kind and we feel that its identification poses a most interesting problem.'

I first came to hear of the Lough Ree sighting in December of 1962, when I received a letter from Mr. James McM. Ure, Secretary to the British Ichthyological Society, who had spent much time and energy investigating it, and from whose own report on the subject the following extract is taken:

'. . . This single sighting, however, is not the only evidence for supposing the existence of a monster. We must also take into

46

account the many tales of strange creatures which have torn the nets of fishermen, and run off with their lines. I shall recount only three such stories as they are all similar, differing only in superficialities.

'The first experience was had by Mr. Patrick Hanley, when he was fishing in about thirty feet of water outside Bally Bay, a little up the Lough from Athlone. Lough Ree is a limestone lake with visibility rarely extending down farther than about 7 feet, and therefore Mr. Hanley had little chance of seeing the creature which siezed his line. When the creature took the bait, there was no fierce tug, just a hard slow pull, which dragged the boat without any apparent effort towards the middle of the lake. Mr. Hanley decided to cut the line.

'The other two incidents I shall mention were both ex-perienced by F. J. Waters. The first also took place off Bally Bay, where he experienced the same long sturdy pull. . . . Mr. Waters second experience took place on the other side of the lake, near Beam Island, in a depth of 112 feet. In this instant he was fishing for trout with a heavy line, and the creature did not move slowly, but very fast right to the bottom, breaking the line after about 70 feet had come off the spool. The speed of the dive is inclined to go against the possibility of the creature being a giant pike, or other normal fish. Their swim bladders would hardly allow this great change of depth and pressure within a few seconds.

'Both Mr. Hanley and Mr. Waters are experienced fisher-men, and both are certain that the creatures on their lines were *not* giant pike; and they regard the giant eel theory as quite possible . . . (here follows an account of interviews with three other interested people). . . . My visit to Colonel R. of Coosan Point was perhaps the most fruitful. Col. R. has himself seen the Monster. . . . He believes it to be a prehistoric animal of some type, and dismisses the giant eel theory completely. He is a personal friend of Father Quigley, one of the three men and has complete faith in his ability as a naturalist . . .

47

'One phenomenon which I found almost everyone had witnessed, including myself, is one which has also been observed at Loch Ness. It is seen only on a perfectly calm day, and consists merely of a few large waves, like the wash from a large boat, dashing themselves up on the side of the lake, followed again by complete silence. I asked many people about this. . . . The lakeside dwellers have often seen it and wondered at its cause. There were never any boats around at the time. . . .

'As a footnote to the above, it is quite possible that the Lough Ree Monster is a member of *Pythonomorpha*, or Sea Serpents. Since both Colonel R. and Father Quigley are convinced that the creature they saw had flippers, it may be that the Monster is a descendent of these creatures, even although *Pythonomorpha* were marine. They belonged to the Upper Cretaceous period, and were not much less than forty feet long, and are also more likely to be in existence than the Plesiosaurs and Ichthysaurs, which preceded them.'

Bearing in mind Father Quigley's reference to the 'Piast', which 'Legend ascribes to Lough Ree, in common with several other Irish lakes' – the next clue is interesting. I came upon it by chance when following up a reference from another Irish correspondent, Major. H. C. Butler, who wrote: 'In Joyce's *Irish Names of Places*, page 190, the following paragraph occurs: "We find one mentioned by Adamnan as infesting Loch Ness in Scotland" . . . in the same paragraph other monsters are mentioned, but these all relate to Ireland. St. Adamnan was Abbot of Iona in A.D. 679.'

Having already dealt with Adamnan's biographical account of Columba's experience with a water-monster at Loch Ness, in A.D. 565[8] I did not expect to find anything new, but it is always advisable to follow up clues as a matter of principle. After some delay I obtained the book. It was one of three volumes published at the turn of the century, containing the

---

[8] *Loch Ness Monster*, page 34.

most astonishing mass of information on Irish names, places, traditions, folklore myths and legends.[9]

At first glance I could find no such reference on page 190 in any of the three volumes, and nearly gave up the search, but in reading Chapter 5 of Volume I *Fairies, Demons, Goblins and Ghosts* I ran into it on page 198 – and experienced that breathless moment which comes occasionally to all researchers – who meet the unexpected, and recognize a 'find'. To the archaeologist it may be the fragments of a vase perhaps; to the palaeontologist a fossil bone, individually without shape, but when fitted together with other parts constructing the form of something recognizable; linking the past with the present.

This is what I read . . . 'Legends of aquatic monsters are very ancient among the Irish people. We find one mentioned by Adamnan as infesting Loch Ness in Scotland. In the life of St. Mochua[10] of Balla, it is related that a stag which was wounded in the chase took refuge on an island in Lough Ree; but that no one dared to follow it "on account of a horrible Monster that infested the lake, and was accustomed to destroy swimmers". A man was at last prevailed to swim across, "but as he was returning the beast devoured him".'

'O'Flaherty has a very circumstantial story of an "Irish Crocodil" that lived at the bottom of Lough Mask; and in O'Clery's *Calendar* (page 145) we read about the upper lake of Glendalough – "They say that the lake drains in its middle, and that a frightful serpent is seen in it, and that from fear of it no one durst swim in the lake." And in some of the very ancient tales of the *Lebor-na-hUidhre* we find heroes encountering enormous lake serpents.

'This legend assumes various forms in individual cases, and many are the tales the people can relate of fearful encounters

---

[9] *Irish Names of Places* by P. W. Joyce (1901), Vol. 1. Longmans Green and Co.

[10] St. Mochua founded a monastery at Balla in the early part of 7th century.

with a Monster covered with long hair and a mane. . . . Several
lakes in different parts of the country are called Loughnapiast, or
more correctly *Loch-na-peiste* each of which is inhabited by a
demoniacal serpent; and in a river in the parish of Banagher,
Derry, there is a spot called Lig-na-peiste (Lig, a hollow or a
hole), which is the abode of another . . .'

It is interesting to note at this point that Loch Ness, Lough
Ree and Lake Okanagan each have a legendary reputation for
water monsters which are dangerous, and that in more recent
times the Storsjön animal has shown signs of 'aggressiveness'.
The Russian account of the Monster in lake Khaiyr in 1964
seems to indicate it has a nasty disposition too – and if the
sketch by N. F. Gladkikh is accurate (No. 2) – and I see no
reason why it should not be – then it should be treated with
respect, by those who pursue it; at least until they find out more
about it!

Correspondence on the subject of Irish water monsters has not
been limited. The extract following being from a letter written
30th June, 1961, by Mrs. Cicily M. Botley of Tunbridge Wells . . .

'Since yesterday I had occasion to visit the library of the
Folklore Society, I took the opportunity of copying out the
relevant part of an account of the sighting of "monsters" in
Lough Nacorra near Croagh Patrick.
'The observer was a Mrs. A. V. Hunt of Ardmoyle House
Co. Tipperary: also a friend and two men then working on the
chapel. The year was not given; it was June in perfect weather,
the lough was quite calm:
' "Suddenly the surface of the water was disturbed by a huge
black shape that rose and swam the length of the lake in what
appeared to be a few moments. Other similar shapes appeared,
and these weird things kept playing about, diving and swimming like a lot of seals. The lake is between two to three miles
long and from the height on which we were, and in comparison
with the cattle, the creatures looked bigger than any house we

could see; even with the aid of binoculars we could not distinguish any details at that distance . . . we called to the men who were at work on the chapel to come and watch. After a short time the creatures disappeared, one by one, and the lake resumed its former tranquil appearance." '[11]

In two letters written 4th May and 3rd June, 1964, by Mr. Patrick J. N. Bury, Waterford, Eire, other references appear: 'Cleevaun Lough in the Wicklow hills is another lake where a "Piast" is said to dwell. An Englishman who went to swim in it was warned about the beast. He threw his dog in before venturing in himself, and it vanished in a swirl. . . . There is also an account of a great "Piast" in Lough Mask in County Mayo that devoured a man many years ago. . . . In your book you mentioned the Redskin's pictographs[12] – but you did not mention our Pictish pictographs (the pun is unavoidable). They show some clearly recognizable creatures, and one that can be described only as a "swimming elephant" . . .'

Mr. Bury then gave me Museum references, and a list of other Loughs in Ireland from which reports of monsters have emanated, including Loughs Ree, Dub, Neagh, Muck, Bran, and Bray, again in the Wicklow hills, supported by a clipping from the 'Mailbag' column of the *Evening Press* 17th June, 1963, which reads:

'On Whit Monday a friend and I had a most unusual experience at Lough Bray in the Wicklow Mountains. We have since mentioned it to others and have been greeted with incredulity . . . it is therefore in the hope that someone may be able to offer an explanation that I write, as we are absolutely certain of what we saw on the evening in question. . . . Soberly and without exaggeration we are convinced that we saw a creature which could well be described as a Monster. Looking

[11] From *True Irish Ghost Stories*, p. 6 by Seymour and Neiligan, published in 1926. (This event took place before the First World War.)

[12] Refers *Loch Ness Monster*, p. 181, Lake Okanagan history.

down into the lake, which was perfectly clear in the evening sunlight we saw a large hump like the back of a rhinocerous emerge from the water. Ripples spread out to each side of it and then a head something like a tortoise only many times bigger broke surface. It came up about three feet above the surface, moved slowly around and swam forward a few yards. As it did so the body was more clearly revealed, circular and not less than 10 or 12 feet in circumference. It was a dark greyish colour. Suddenly and silently the creature seemed to dive and smoothly vanished leaving an agitated swirl of water. We saw it for not less than three minutes.

'Comparing our stories we found them to be identical to a surprising degree, although my friend thought the head was more like that of a swan.

'We would like to know if anyone else has had an experience of this kind at the lake and we are informed that there has been at least one other story of this kind. There may be a natural explanation, which we would be obliged to obtain as it was a disturbing sight which still affects us.'

L.R. Dublin 2.

There are in fact two Lough Brays – identified as Upper and Lower, over ten fathoms deep, and situated in lonely rugged country at 1,459 feet and 1,228 feet above sea-level respectively; about 10 miles south-west of Dublin bay. Both lakes are small and lozenge shaped, the largest being Lower Bray some $\frac{3}{4} \times \frac{1}{2}$ miles at most; and both drain individually into the short Glencree River.

It is hard to imagine any large animal surviving in either lake, should it live on a diet of fish – but as the report is so clear, and recent; and the lakes so small, a boat search with echo-sounding gear could help to resolve the issue.

SCOTTISH HIGHLAND REPORTS

These fall under two headings, concerning – (a) Loch Ness, and (b) Other Highland lochs, and the Western Seaboard area.

So much has already been written about the first, I intend to comment only on its historical and legendary background as an introduction to three 'on-shore' reports, in letter form.

(a) *The 'Mighty Chasm of Glenmore'*, or the Great Glen as it is commonly known, follows the line of the fault stretching from west to east across the Highlands of Scotland. It has, since prehistoric times formed a natural channel of communication, with fortified positions springing up along it. Fort William; Fort Augustus; and a line of castles have marked the pages of history with Scottish and English blood, spilled in ferocious Clan battles, and the Wars of Independence.

Perhaps the most famous of these is Castle Urquhart, which stands today in mellow ruin on the site of a prehistoric fort, on the northern shore of Loch Ness. Through the barbarous years of medieval history it came under siege on more than six occasions, before crumbling into decay in the early eighteenth century.

Founded on a spur of rock it commands a view which, legend would have us believe, was once of forest and pasture, and the homes of people living in the sheltered depths of a valley through which a majestic river flowed . . . 'in which was found every fish good for the food of man. Although the people were many peace and friendship prevailed. The women plied the distaff, and their homes and children they did not forsake; and when the men did not hunt the boar in the forest, they chased the deer in the mountain, or tended their cattle on the plain.

'There was a spring in this happy vale which was blessed by Daly the Druid, and whose waters were ever afterwards an unfailing remedy for disease. The well was protected from pollution by a stone placed upon it by the Druid, who enjoined that whenever the stone was removed for the drawing of water, it should then be immediately replaced. "The day on which my command is disregarded," said he, "desolation will overtake the land." The words of Daly were remembered by the people, and became a law among them: and so day followed day, and year gave place to year.

53

'But on one of these days a woman left the child of her bosom by the fireside and went to the well to draw water. No sooner did she remove the stone than the cry reached her ear that the child had moved towards the fire. Rushing to the house, she saved the infant – but forgot the word of the Druid, and failed to replace the stone. The waters rose and overflowed the vale, and the people escaped to the mountains and filled the air with lamentation, and the rocks echoed back the despairing cry – *The lock 'nis ann! The loch 'nis ann!* (There is a lake now).

'And the lake remained, and it is called Loch Nis,[13] to this day.'

This charming story, recorded in English by Willaim MacKay was thought to be of purely mythical origin until 1893, when the Highland Railway Company put down a bore hole at a point some 29 feet above ordnance datum level. Sunk to a depth of 320 feet, it passed through various strata of sand, gravel and boulders – but at 163 feet pierced a 13 foot belt of clay, furnishing evidence of a deep pre-glacial channel in which flowed a great river, at the mouth of the valley of the Ness.

W. H. Lane in his booklet supporting the Amphibian theory makes use of this fact in tracing the ancient river systems existing at the time, when Scotland was part of a continental area continuous with Ireland on the south-west, and Scandinavia.

Across this area the rivers drained south-eastwards, combining to form a Grand Trunk River, which flowed over the present floor of the North Sea, before uniting with ancient Rhine, and discharging into the Atlantic Ocean.

At the time of rift which formed the Great Glen, extending farther in both directions than it does today, the rivers to the north-west of it were beheaded, causing their waters to pour down the fracture in a river, which would form a tributary to the Grand Trunk River.

On the banks of this 'magnificent Fracture River' lived primitive man, and with the coming of the period of glaciation –

---

[13] Loch Nis, so written in Gaelic; pronounced Loch Neesh.

the last ice-age, these people and the local fauna would have moved away, following the course of the river – and similarly, with the recession of ice centuries later, their decendents could have returned.

In 1726 a fossil specimen of a type of amphibian, allied to the existing giant salamander was recovered from Upper Miocene strata at Basle on the Rhine – and, W. H. Lane maintains that 'There would appear to be no reason why this type of amphibian should not have continued on through the Pliocene into the post-glacial era. There was no physical obstacle to prevent an amphibian of the giant salamander type from ascending the Grand Trunk River and penetrating the post-glacial basin of the Ness.'

This is an interesting and ingenious theory, but the fact remains that Loch Ness was an arm of the sea, a relatively short time ago, and, as the chapter following will show, there is a distinct similarity between reports obtained from it and those obtained from the open sea: but with regard to details of appearance we can do no better than to refer to the comments of witnesses – particularly if these describe the 'beastie' out of water:

Letter dated 11th September, 1962, from Mr. D. J. A. Briggs of Wimbledon, London.

'. . . a friend of my father's, a Mr. E. H. Bright can remember seeing what he thought to be the Monster when he was about eight years old (he is now ninety).

'He remembers meeting his cousin walking by the shore near Drumnadrochit when suddenly they saw the Monster appear from the near-by woods, which were about 100 yards away. It "waddled along" to the edge of the loch aided by its four legs, entered the water and sank rapidly, leaving a tremendous wash. They both ran home, he to his grandparents' home. Half scared but excited he told his grandfather of his experience. He described it as having a long neck like an elephant's trunk with a small head similar to that of a snake, being of a dark-grey colour and generally looking like a large elephant. After relating all this his grandfather laughed and suggested he had been drinking a "wee droppie" hoping that it would pacify him a little. Later several three-pronged footprints were found by him and other people in the same spot where he had seen the Monster. After a short time his grandfather admitted that there had been talk of a so-called Monster in the past, but it was never discussed by the people of the village. He told me that a friend of his, a Jimmy Hossack saw the Monster when he was a young man. He would be about 120 years old if he was alive today.

'Mr. Bright said he would never forget the experience . . .'

Letter dated 25th June, 1961, from Mr. Edward P. Smith of Selmeston, Sussex.

'. . . in 1939 I did hear a very curious story. I had motored round the loch by the southern shore and finished up by having tea at the Foyers Hotel. There were tables on the lawn, and one of these was occupied by an old Scottish lady who, I gathered, lived in Aberdeen and happened to be holidaying in Inverness where she had lived as a child. She must have been quite seventy, and gave me the impression of absolute honour and good faith.

'We got into conversation and I made some jocular reference to the Monster, and she told me she and her chauffeur had seen it only that afternoon. They, too, had been driving along the southern road . . . when they had noticed an upturned boat somewhere near the shore. Imagining an accident, they had stopped the car and descended to the lake edge, which is nothing like as grown up as it is now, to see if they could help – only to watch the "upturned boat" shoot off down the loch and eventually sink. That was a perfectly normal sighting in those days, but she went on: "I've seen it once before out of water. When I was a wee girl, my two brothers and I shared a governess with a family living at Dores. We were driven out in a gig each day from Inverness and fetched every evening. One hot summer day – we took our lunches with us – my brothers and I picnicked on one of the northern slopes not far from the old graveyard. We had nearly finished our meal when we heard a noise and, looking round, saw coming down the slope behind and towards us an enormous and extraordinary animal, bigger than an elephant, but about the same sort of colour. It had a head perched on a relatively slender neck, and it turned from side to side and seemed to peer at us, passing us a few yards to one side, and waddling down to the lake where it entered the water and disappeared. It had a long tail. Of course we were a bit frightened, and frightfully interested. When we got home that night we could hardly wait to tell our father. He listened, and then ordered us up to our rooms. A few minutes later he came up and caned us all. 'Now,' he said, 'I want you to understand that I'm not whipping you for telling me a fairy story; but for telling me a fairy story and pretending it is the truth.' "

'I never learnt my old informant's name, and she must have been dead these many years; but, on my honour, that is what she told me. I shall never forget it and I believe it, because her description of her father's reaction rings so astonishingly true. If I am right about her age, it must have taken place in the very late 1870's.

'My old friend and Parliamentary colleague, the late Sir Murdoch MacDonald, M.P. for Inverness, Ross and Cromarty, often told me about his sighting of the Monster; but that is fully related in Mrs. Whyte's book. . . .'

Both these letters record evidence at secondhand, but the similarities are obvious and they back date the Monster's on-shore activities by quite a few years – from the middle twenties, in fact, when Mr. Albert Cruickshank saw the beast at night on the northern shore. From an historical point of view they are interesting too, as is the reference made in the Scottish *Press and Journal* 29th July, 1964, by David James who wrote: 'The most interesting bit of new information obtained this year (thanks to a New Zealand correspondent) is that the seventh edition of Daniel De Foe's *Tour Through the Whole Island of Great Britain*

57

(volume 4) contains an account of the "Leviathans" frequently disturbed by General Wade's men blasting the military road from Dores to Foyers in 1726.'

This is the same road across which the Monster was seen to pass more than two hundred years later, in broad daylight. . . .

Letter to Mr. F. W. Holliday dated 16th December, 1936, from the late Mr. F. T. G. Spicer, a Company Director of Todhouse Reynard and Co. Ltd. Berkeley Square, London.

'In reply to yours of yesterday, it was on July 22nd, 1933, that my wife and I were motoring along Loch Ness between Dores and Foyers when we suddenly saw a trunk-like thing come out of the bracken from the hillside on our left. We were about 200 yards away, and as it crossed the road we could see this trunk was really a very long neck which moved very rapidly up and down in curves, that were 2 or 3 feet in height from the ground. We did not see any feet. . . . There is no doubt he came down from the hillside and when he was broadside on he took up all the road; which I have had measured, and it is 20 feet wide. He was elephantine in colour, and before we reached him he had disappeared into the loch, which was only 20 feet down on our right.

'I got out of the car and could see the traces of where he had gone through the bracken, but there was no sign of him in the water. I might say it was a lovely summer's day. The creature was quite big enough to have upset our car. Apparently he could not move very fast, and if he had stopped I should have done likewise, as there was no room to turn our car round in the narrow road.

'The neck moved very rapidly and the body followed in jerks. . . . I have been to the spot many times since but have never been fortunate enough to see him again, as it is a million to one chance of so doing . . .

'In December of that year I broadcast to twenty million people from the B.B.C. and have letters from all over the world. . . . I have been ridiculed a good bit but I believe most people

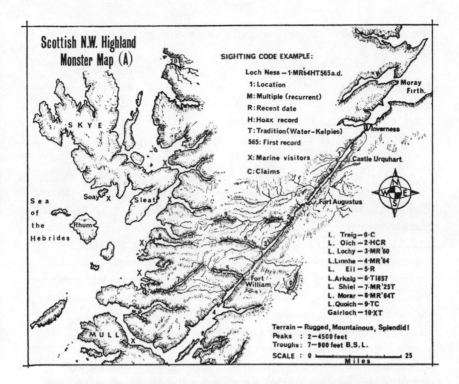

Scottish N.W. Highland
Monster Map (A)

SIGHTING CODE EXAMPLE:

Loch Ness — 1·MR64HT565a.d.

1: Location
M: Multiple (recurrent)
R: Recent date
H: Hoax record
T: Tradition (Water-Kelpies)
565: First record

X: Marine visitors
C: Claims

SKYE

Moray
Firth.

Inverness

Castle Urquhart

Sea
of
the
Hebrides

Soay   Sleat

Rhum

Fort Augustus

L. Treig — 0·C
L. Oich — 2·HCR
L. Lochy — 3·MR'60
L, Linnhe — 4·MR'64
L. Eil — 5·R
L. Arkaig — 6·T 1857
L. Shiel — 7·MR'25T
L. Morar — 8·MR'64T
L. Quoich — 9·TC
Gairloch — 10·XT

Fort
William

MULL

Terrain — Rugged, Mountainous, Splendid!
Peaks : 2—4500 feet
Troughs: 7—900 feet B.S.L.
SCALE : 0 ———————— 25
                        Miles

think there is something there now, as it has been seen many
times since in the loch. As far as I'm concerned I do not mind
what they think, only I would assure you that there is no doubt
it exists ... and I hope the day is not very far distant when you
and I shall be able to see a good photograph of it and then we
shall know what it really is ...

Yours, etc:

'P.S. I estimated the creature's length to be 25 to 30 feet.'

(b) Other Highland Lochs, and Western Seaboard Area:

Looking at Sketch Map A the line of the Great Glen extending to the south-west of the Ness contains the waters of Oich,
Lochy, and Linnhe, which is a sea loch; and that branching
almost due west from these Arkaig and Eil point slender fingers
at Shiel and Morar. Off the immediate coastline the Sound's
of Mull and Sleat, and the Kyle of Lochalsh, and farther west

59

the Isle of Soay, all have a history of sightings, of one sort or another.

Starting with Loch Oich, which is very small there is the recent case of 'Wee Oichy', the 'Monster' reported and pictured by the *Scottish Daily Express* on 8th July, 1961. The story behind this undoubted hoax (or the one to be had from the grape-vine) is that a group of notorious practical jokers built a self-propelled Monster, and set it afloat with the object of fooling the public, then allowing the story to grow for a week or two, they would lay claim to it – amid *paroxysms of laughter*. The plan succeeded in that the contraption was seen and photographed, and described seriously – but then had to be abandoned, because a piratical group of students intervened, claiming the Monster as their own; so spoiling the fun.

This was but one of many hoaxes enacted over the years, which have done much to amuse the public, and confuse the issue. Some have been ingenious, others merely absurd providing, if nothing else, the comic relief which finds a place in every human drama, however complex.

Farther to the westwards of Oich there exists an entrancingly beautiful lake called Lochy. Some ten miles in length, and over four hundred feet deep it has on rare occasions produced evidence; and so too has Linnhe, which forms the tidal entrance to the Great Glen fault . . .

Letter dated 18th September, 1961, from Mr. Eric Robinson, Owston Ferry, Doncaster.

'I write to you in all good faith, and hope you will accept my evidence. . . . Our first monster was seen on the afternoon of 21st June, 1954, ploughing along the surface of loch Linnhe in calm water; with no boats in the vicinity. Speed 30–35 m.p.h. Three humps showing slightly above water-line followed by the outstanding feature, the terrific churning of water at the rear of the creature as caused by the propeller of a boat when under way. Time in sight about two minutes. No binoculars available. Creature headed towards entrance of Loch Leven; it was reported by Kinlochleven fishermen a fortnight before in their own waters. . . . Six years later our second sighting took place in Loch Lochy, where we were staying in a private caravan above the shore about 200 yards from Glenfintaig House. Time approx 7.25 p.m. 15th July, 1960. Monster first seen as what appeared to be two stationary waves. Got binoculars and then realized it was a live creature. Started to move in a southerly direction then the huge back came up out of the water and commenced to roll its body over and over.[14] My friend and my wife both watched through the binoculars and we definitely saw a fin or paddle on the side of it's body as it turned. Underside of the body was a lighter colour. Waves broke on the shore from the turmoil it caused, and we were amazed. Estimation 2–300 yards from shore. We really thought at one point it was going to land. . . . Size of back was 15 to 20 feet, and should say total length would be 30 to 40 feet, according to the gap between humps when first spotted . . . nine other witnesses besides myself saw this creature in the loch. At least three were sceptics before! '

Constance Whyte, on page 131 of *More Than a Legend* notes that the late Dom Cyril Dieckhoff,[15] of St. Benedicts Abbey, obtained evidence for monsters in Lochy, and also Quoich, due north of Arkaig – which in turn enjoys a long-standing tradition for 'Water Kelpies'. Indeed, in 1857 in his autobiography *Memoirs of an Ex-Minister* the third Earl of Malmesbury wrote: 'October 3rd : This morning my stalker and his boy gave me an account of a mysterious creature, which they say exists in Loch Arkaig, and which they call the Lake-horse. It is the same animal of which one has occasionally read accounts in the newspapers as having been seen in the Highland lochs, and on

[14] This behaviour is characteristic of the L.N.M. on occasions: described as a 'fantastic creature, rolling and plunging over and over' by Mr. John McKay and his wife, of Drummadrochit, who watched it 22nd May, 1933.

[15] Brother Dieckhoff became interested in this subject, and undertook a great deal of research, assisted by his knowledge of Gaelic. His records remain at the Abbey, Fort Augustus.

the existence of which in Loch Assynt the late Lord Ellesmere wrote an interesting article; but hitherto the story has always been looked upon as fabulous. I am now, however, really persuaded of the truth. My stalker, John Stuart, at Achnacarry has seen it twice, and both times at sunrise in summer on a bright sunny day, when there is not a ripple on the water. The creature was basking on the surface; he only saw the head and hind quarters, proving that its back was hollow, which is not the shape of any fish or seal. Its head resembled that of a horse. It was also seen once by his three little children, who were all walking together along the beach. It was then motionless about thirty yards from the shore and apparently asleep. They at first took it for a rock, but when they got near it moved its head, and they were so frightened they ran home, arriving in the state of greatest terror. There was no mistaking their manner . . . and they offered to make affidavit before a magistrate. The Highlanders are very superstitious about this creature. They are convinced that there is never more than one in existence at the same time, and I believe they think it has something diabolical in its nature, for when I said I wished I could get within shot of it, my stalker observed very gravely, "Perhaps your lordship's gun would miss-fire." '

In the book *September Road to Caithness* by 'BB' published[16] in 1962 reference is made to Loch Eil and the appearance of a most peculiar object. On the morning of 17th October the author walked along the shore admiring the landscape . . . 'with every detail of mountain and shore bathed in brilliant light. I was watching some mallard paddling about among weedy rocks at the end of a little promontory when there appeared out of the calm water exactly opposite me a large black shiny object which I can only compare with the blunt, blind head of an enormous worm.

'It was, I suppose, some 50 yards from where I was standing, and it kept appearing and disappearing, not moving along,

[16] Publishers: Nicholas Kaye Ltd, London.

but rolling on the surface. The water was greatly disturbed all round the object. It had a shiny wet-looking skin, but the head (if head it was) was quite unlike a seal's and had no face, or nose, no eyes. It rose quite a long way out of the water, some three feet or more, before sinking back . . .'

Turning and racing back to his van for his binoculars, the author returned only to find a swirl on the water with loud crying gulls hovering over it.

Considering that Loch Eil is an extension of Linnhe, and that curious pole-like objects have been seen to rise above the surface of Loch Ness, generally thought to be the neck of the Monster, with the small head continuing the line of it, the *Observer*[17] report stating that – 'On 22nd June (1964), Mrs. Preston of The Grange, Tadcaster, Yorkshire saw a head and neck in the salt-water Loch Linnhe at a range of 25 yards, identical in character to many of those described in Loch Ness' is worth noting.

Whether or not these objects characterize the heads and necks of immature specimens is debatable, because in the really big animals the head appears to be distinct, when seen at close quarters.

Farther to the southward, Loch Lomond produced some disturbance in the late summer of 1964, a large humped back being seen by a Mr. Haggerty, a Helensborough butcher and his wife on 22nd September: and according to a British Rail magazine a Mr. Sandy Watt, and his fireman Bob Wilson working the 4.35 p.m. freight train from Yoker to Crainlarich emerged from a tunnel above the lake to see a huge object swirling along – 'bigger than a long boat and moving fast – just like a torpedo'.

If these reports are accurate, they are very difficult to explain, because although Lomond has a legendary history I am not aware of any other sightings in recent years – whereas in Shiel

[17] *Observer*, 27th December, 1964. Article by David James entitled 'Fine Weather Monster'.

and Morar to the northward, old history is supported by contemporary fact, in the appearance of Monsters known to the local people by nickname. In the latter case on 20th May, 1964 *a' Mhorag* exposed three large humps, together some 30–40 feet in length to Mr. Alec Patmore (a Company director) and his wife Carol, in perfect visibility and a flat calm – duly reported by Scotland's *Sunday Post*, 31st May, 1964.

The question of humps, or 'humpage' versus simple back sightings is very much a puzzle, until reading an eyewitness account of a transition . . .

Letter from Miss Helen Stitt, of Belfast, Ireland.

'. . . There were eight of us. Mum, Dad, Brother, Sister, Uncle, Aunt, and my girl-friend Sandra.

'On the evening of 21st July, 1961, we camped beside Loch Ness about eight or nine miles from Inverness. The loch was silent and calm, only to be broken by the odd little fish which jumped out of the water to catch the hovering flies. My father was preparing his rod for a quiet evening's fishing, when we noticed quite a large disturbance in the water. From the spot rose a large oval-shaped object, *which formed slowly* (my italics) into four clear distinct humps. The four humps then swam across the water . . . nearly to the edge, and disappeared.

'The humps appeared to be all the same shape (see Sketch 2) and were dark-grey or black. In all I think the length would have been 50–60 feet. . . . Now none of us can dispute the existence of the Loch Ness Monster. It is a true saying – seeing is believing.'

Marine reports from the Scottish Highland west coast owe much to R. T. Gould in his *Case for the Sea Serpent*, in which sightings are recorded for Mull, Sleat and Lochalsh – but in recent times the Island of Soay pinpoints an off-shore report, first mentioned by Gavin Maxwell, in *Ring of Bright Water*. The animal was seen from a boat at a few yards range, and having now interviewed one of its two occupants, Mr. Gavin, an

64

engineer on holiday at the time I can include his account with assurance. It serves to provide an introduction to the next chapter – 'Salt Water Serpents'.

On 13th of September, 1959, Mr. Gavin was fishing for mackerel from a small boat, in company with Tex Geddes,[18] who lived on the Island of Soay and knew the local waters well.

In the distance he spotted a black object, moving on the calm surface – but it was not the back of a killer whale, a group of which they had seen a little before. It approached, and at Tex's urgent request Mr. Gavin sat absolutely still in the boat. The animal passed within 15–20 yards. It would have weighed about five tons . . .

'At the water-line the body was 6 to 8 feet long. It was hump-shaped rising to a centrally-placed apex about 2 feet high. The line of the back was formed by a series of triangular shaped spines, the largest at the apex and reducing in size to the water-line. The spines appeared to be solid and immobile – they did not resemble fins. I only got a lateral view of the animal, but my impression was that the cross-section of the body was roughly angular in shape. Apart from the forward glide I saw no movement.

'The neck appeared to be cylindrical, and at a guess about 8 inches in diameter. It arose from the water about 12 inches, forward of the body. I could not see where it joined; about 15 to 18 inches of neck was visible. The head was rather like that of a tortoise with a snake-like flattened cranium running forward to a rounded face. Relatively it was as big as the head of a donkey. I saw one laterally placed eye, large and round like that of a cow. When the mouth was opened I got the impression of large blubbery lips and could see a number of tendril-like growths hanging from the palate. Head and neck rose to about

[18] Author of a book on harpoon fishing for basking shark, Mr. Geddes was qualified to identify any large sea animal in the area. He was completely nonplussed.

a height of 2 feet. At intervals it went forward, and submerged. It would re-emerge, the large gaping mouth would open (giving the impression of a melon with a quarter removed) and there would be a series of very loud roaring whistling noises as it breathed. After about five minutes, the beast submerged with a forward diving motion – I thought I saw something follow the body down. It later resurfaced about a quarter of a mile farther out to sea and I then watched it until it disappeared in the distance. (I have heard that the crews of two lobster boats, fishing north of Mallaig have also seen the animal – much to their consternation.) . . . I would mention that when I saw the beast it was a beautiful bright day and the sea was perfectly calm.'

Mr. James Gavin lives at 46 Bucknells Drive, Bricket Wood, Herts, England – and comments in his letter that of the various explanations put forward by the experts . . . 'in my opinion, none of these theories account for what I saw'. One such concluded the Monster was a large iguana lizard from South America.

3

SALT WATER SERPENTS

JOHN ASTON, in his book *Curious Creatures* quotes from the statements of Olaus Magnus, Archbishop of Uppsala in 1555 . . .

'All fishermen of Norway are agreed that there is a Sea Serpent 200 feet long and 20 feet thick that lives in caves and rocks near Bergen. . . . He hath commonly hair hanging from his neck a cubit long, sharp scales, and is black and hath flaming, shining eyes. He puts up his head on high like a pillar.'

In this chapter a number of eyewitness reports of sea monsters appear, the majority of which seem to describe an animal known historically as the 'Great Sea Serpent' – about which much has already been written:[1] and which, in all probability is the marine progenitor of the Loch Ness Monster, and its kind in other freshwater lakes.

Descriptions are so similar there can be little room for doubt on this point – although the issue is confused from time to time by reports of other unidentified sea animals which are automatically classified as sea serpents; one of which, at least, fits the title. It has the appearance of a gigantic snake, without limbs, fins or appendages, but its colossal head in no way compares with the 'Nessie Type' of Monster, which has been reported over a period of three hundred years from the seas and

[1] Books of Ref: *Natural History of Norway* (1752), Erik Pontoppidan. *Romance of Natural History* (1860), Philip H. Gosse, F.R.S. *The Great Sea Serpent* (1892), Dr. A. C. Oudemans. *The Case for the Sea Serpent* (1930), R. T. Gould. *Le Grand Serpent de Mer* (1966) Dr. Bernard Heuvelmans.

oceans – particularly the New England coast of America, the rocky shores of western Canada, Iceland, northern Scotland and Norway – and the fact that it has not yet been officially classified is no bar to its existence, or even the possibility that it may turn out to be an air breathing animal.

The Giant squid, or 'Kraken' as it was known, was thought to be of purely mythical origin until quite recent times – and perhaps this unique distinction will be lost to the G.S.S., when it in turn is received within the category of scientific zoology.

The argument that an air-breathing animal must frequently be seen at the surface, is not valid, as proved by the case of the False Killer whale (*Pseudorca crassidens*) which was known from pleistocene fossils, but which had never been recognized by whalers. Up until the turn of the century it was 'known' to be extinct; but then several shoals stranded themselves on Scottish coasts, and elsewhere – indicating how little we know about the waters that surround us.

But whatever Science may think about the 'Great Sea Serpent' – mistaken in name though it may be, it can do no harm to record what eyewitnesses have had to say about this strange and sometimes terrifying beast.

One of my first clues appeared in a letter from Anthony Oliver at the B.B.C., whom I had met during a showing of the 1960 'Nessie' film. He said that while looking through some very old back numbers of the *Illustrated London News* he had come across a report as long ago as 1856!

In due course, after searching through the I.L.N. archives, I found the report, but recognized it as one of the many treated by Gould in his 1930 publication – in which he comments: 'Ever since the *Dædalus* case, the *Illustrated London News* has shown a praisworthy readiness to give space to similar reports. Between 1848 and 1877 . . . for example, it published ten such . . .'

But, as Cmmdr. Gould's book is now so long out of print this very clear evidence bears repeating.

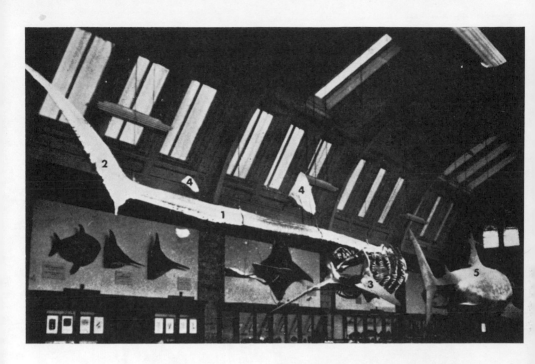

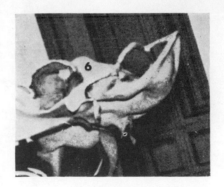

12 This photograph indicates how the rotting remains of a
Basking shark can end up looking like a 'Sea-Serpent'. The
massive lower-jaw and gill frames fall away leaving the Spine (1)
continuing out to tip of Caudal fin (2), Pectoral fins (3) and 1st and
2nd hump-like Dorsal fins (4). The skull (6) now looks like a small
head attached to a long neck, and body, with fore-limbs and
cow-like tail—quite different to the tubby Basking shark (5) so
well known to fishermen.

13 The comments included with Brian McCleary's sketch read: "Sighted off Pensacola, Florida, March 24th 1962: About 15 ft. protruding from water . . . Oval green eyes, and visible nostrils. Head . . . more like snake than fish, or any other marine animal. Made hissing noise, and was carnivorous."

Illustrated London News, 3rd May, 1856. Letter to the Editor under the heading 'Another Sea Serpent'.

'Sir,

'We beg to hand you the enclosed sketch of a sea serpent we had the good fortune to sight on 30th March last.

'*Imogen*, from Algoa Bay, towards London. Lat. 29° 11′ N. Long. 34° 36′ W. Bar. 30·5; calm and clear. About five past eleven a.m. the helmsman drew our attention to something moving through the water, and causing a strong ripple about 400 yards distant from the starboard quarter.

'In a few moments it became more distinct . . . and showing an apparent length of about 40 feet (above the surface of the sea), the undulations of the water extending on each side to a considerable distance in its wake. Mr. Statham immediately ascended to the maintopsail-yard, Captain Guy and Mr. Harris watching the animal from the deck with a telescope.

'After passing the ship about half a mile, the serpent "rounded to", and raised its head, seemingly to look at us . . . and then steered away to the northward . . . frequently lifting its head. We traced its course until nearly on the horizon, and lost sight of it from the deck about 11.45 a.m.

'No doubt remained on our minds as to its being an immense snake, as the undulations of its body were clearly perceptible, although we were unable to distinguish its eyes. The weather being fine and the glassy surface of the sea only occasionally disturbed by slight flaws of wind we had a perfect opportunity of noticing its movements.

'In conformity to your regulations we enclose our references and remain, Sir, your obedient servants – James Guy, Commander; J. H. Statham; J. B. Harries and D. J. Williamson, Passenger.'

Accompanying this report were four sketches – one as seen through the telescope, and the others as seen with normal vision, showing a continuous length of back but with many bumps on it. Two show a longish head uplifted.

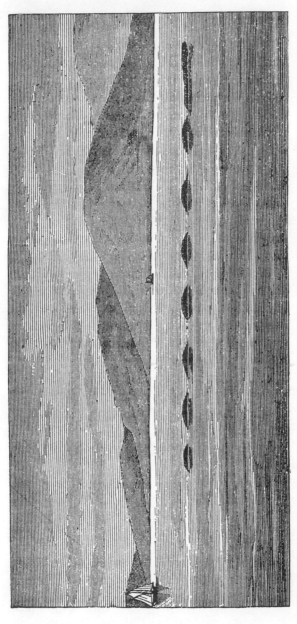

FIG. 4. 'Sea-serpent as seen in the Highland loch in 1872' from the book *Animal Life* by Frank Buckland, M.A. Seen repeatedly from a boat in the Sound of Sleat by Revs. David Twopenny, John Macrae and his two daughters. Closest range 100 yds.: Estimated length 90–100 ft. . . . 'Many of the Norwegian accounts compute it to be considerably longer. . . . There is scarcely a probability that it is a serpent . . . as it was approaching I plainly saw the sea running off its back. . . . It appeared to be basking, and often moved slowly, but sometimes with great rapidity, and when at the most rapid rate these convolutions disappeared. . . . M. F. was frightened out of her wits . . .'

SHETLAND ISLAND INCIDENTS

Scalloway, Shetland Isles, 24th July, 1961. Excerpts from a letter:

'Dear Mr. Dinsdale,

'Being interested in sea monsters for many years past . . . I am just waiting for that photo that will make history!

'Sea monsters have been seen here in Shetland at different times; notably the 1881 *Bertie* Monster, and the 1903 *Adelong* Monster. Reports of sea serpents were also received from two ministers, in the Sullum district of Shetland: Rev. Nobel Scott and Rev. Blackwood (Congregational ministers of Sullum 1891–98 and about 1920 respectively).

'The *Bertie*, a boat of 45 foot keel, was fishing 90 miles southeast of Bressay on the east side of Shetland. There were six of a crew and as they had been fishing for two days their hold was full. It was afternoon, the weather was fine and the lines, set the previous morning, were being hauled. While thus engaged the men noticed a large hump appearing on the surface not far distant. They imagined at first that it would be a whale, for they came across these frequently.

'Shortly afterwards, however, two other similar humps became visible, and the appearance of these put the idea of a whale out of the question. As they continued to watch the shoulders of the creature rose above the surface. These were rounded and had a fin on each side.

'They next saw the head coming into view – only the upper part was visible, and it seemed to be covered with a growth resembling seaweed, which trailed in the water on each side.

'The eyes could be seen very distinctly. These were extremely large and their glare gave the object an exceedingly fierce look. The creature headed straight for the boat, and as the men feared it would foul the lines they tried to frighten it off. One of the crew who had a rifle put in a double charge of powder and two balls. He fired at close range but the bullets were seen to glance off the huge slimy body (note slime covered body, like that seen later by the *Adelong*). Ballast stones were thrown as well.

'The men's frantic efforts only infuriated the brute. It raised its great tail and thrashed the water with a deafening noise, and at this stage it dived when quite close alongside, and the wash set up by the enormous body set the boat on her beam ends. A man named Williamson, who related the story to the writer (Mr. John Nicolson) was hauling a line at the moment and was pitched backwards into the hold, which fortunately was full of fish. Another member of the crew was also thrown into the hold, while the Skipper, Goudie, narrowly escaped being sent overboard.

'The boat righted itself, but the boxes of fish, oars and other gear on deck went over the side. After this experience it was considered unsafe to remain longer in the vicinity. The lines were cut and the mainsail hoisted but owing to the light wind little headway was made and the Monster ranged alongside for a distance – the crew estimated that it was considerably longer than the boat. It was only when darkness fell that they lost sight of their unwelcome follower.'

Williamson, who related the details to Mr. Nicolson,[2] said the recollection of it remained with him like the memory of some frightful nightmare. The story is of course a true one.

'On May 30th, 1903, the crew of the Shetland fishing boat *Adelong*, when fishing off Scalloway on the west side of Shetland, saw with amazement a sea monster about 30 feet long rising out of the water a short distance from the boat. On its head it had what looked like a horn and a large flipper-like appendage. It came quite close to the boat before submerging. Ten nets were destroyed. It appeared to be covered with a thick mucus substance.

'Yours etc.

(Signed) W. J. Williamson.'

[2] Author of *Resting Chair Yarns* – a collection of Shetland Island stories.

In later correspondence Mr. Williamson said he would try
and get in touch with a surviving member of the *Adelong* crew,
who lived in another part of the Shetlands – and in due course
he did, through an intermediary, but with an entirely negative
result: which prompted him to comment – 'I seem to remember
that there is an old Celtic belief that things of this kind should
never be spoken of, or it would bring bad luck. This may be the
case here . . .'

But if superstition enters into it, then the story of the *Adelong*
Monster runs parallel to one of the most detailed and extraordinary sea-serpent accounts on record – that concerning
H.M.S. *Hilary*,[3] an armed merchant cruiser of 6,000 tons,
sunk by a German submarine in the Atlantic on 25th May,
1917.

Her commander, Captain F. W. Dean, R.N., subsequently
wrote a full account of the occurrence which was first published
in *Herbert Strang's Annual*, 1920, and later with some added
detail by Gould.

Paraphrasing, it seems that when the *Hilary* was in distant
sight of the Icelandic mountain peaks one brilliant and calm
morning in May of 1917, the lookout reported something large
on the surface.

Thinking it might be a submarine the captain raced to the
bridge only to find that it was in fact a living creature, though
apparently not a whale. Bearing in mind the constant need for
anti-submarine gun practice his first reaction was to order up
three of his 6-pounder gun-crews; but before opening fire he
decided to have a closer look.

The ship was turned about, and in due course passed the
creature on the starboard side at a range of about thirty yards –
it appeared to be quite unperturbed – 'The head was about the
shape of, but somewhat larger than that of a cow, though with
no observable protrusions such as horns or ears, and was black,
except for the front of the face, which could clearly be seen to

[3] Formerly of the Booth Line, her loss was recorded in Parliamentary
Paper No. 200 of 1919.

73

have a strip of whitish flesh, very like a cow has between its nostrils. As we passed, the head raised itself two or three times, apparently to get a good look at the ship. From the back of the head to the dorsal fin no part of the creature showed above water, but the top edge of the neck was just level with the surface, and its snake-like movements could be clearly seen. (It curved to almost a semicircle as the creature moved its head round as if to follow us with its eyes).

'The dorsal fin appeared like a black triangle, and when the creature was end on, this fin was seen to be very thin and apparently flabby, as the upper part turned over sometimes like the top of a terrier's ear when cocked. The fin was estimated to be 4 feet high[4] when in the position highest out of the water . . .'

Subsequently the Captain obtained estimates of length from the First Lieutenant, F. C. P. Harris, R.N.R., the Navigator and the Officer of the Watch; 'from which it may fairly be assumed that the true length of the neck was probably not less than 20 feet; and assuming that the dorsal fin would be just behind the junction of neck and body, the total length of the creature would be about 60 feet.'

Having had a good look at the beast, the *Hilary* left it astern, then at a range of 1,200 yards turned about and opened fire. The first and second gun-crews straddled the target, but to everyone's surprise failed to disturb its 'equanimity'. The second round from the third gun scored a direct hit however, causing at once a furious commotion which, said the Captain, 'reminded me more than anything else of a bather lying on his back in smooth water and kicking out with all his force to splash the water, only of course on a vastly greater scale. It continued perhaps for three seconds, and then stopped, and we saw no more of the creature . . .'

In some measure this act of cruelty was justified by the need for gun practice – as proven by events, because at 7 a.m. on the second or third day following the *Hilary* stopped a German

[4] For comparison see *Loch Ness Monster*, p. 130, and also Plate 17.

torpedo, and sank, though not before the crew had taken to the boats.

Picked up shortly afterwards by a patrol drifter, the Captain noticed a small brown hand-bag being passed aboard, which was surprising because the ship had settled fast, and there had been no time to pack up personal belongings.

Questioning his First Lieutenant, Charles M. Wray, Captain Dean later found out more about the hand-bag, and the odd circumstances connected with it.

At the time of the sea-serpent episode the Officer of the Watch was a young man, brought up at sea by a Captain with a wide knowledge of sailors' superstitions – in which he firmly believed – and when the order was given to enter details of the gun practice in the ship's Log, he had made a vehement appeal against mentioning the sea serpent. Overruled, he had been heard to say: 'Well, that makes it a certainty anyhow – we shall never reach port again' – and when relieved of the watch he returned to his cabin, and packed up his valuables in the small brown hand-bag, ready for the coming disaster!

That briefly is the story of the *Hilary*, and as it was originally published by her skipper, a Royal Naval Captain, there is no reason to doubt its accuracy, despite the fact that confirmation in the ship's Log was lost at the time of the sinking. Destruction of essential ship's documents to avoid capture would have been automatic – these usually being thrown overboard in a weighted bag.

THE 'VALHALLA' INCIDENT

The excerpt following is from the contents of *Three Voyages of a Naturalist*[5] – being an account of many little-known islands in three oceans visited by the steam auxiliary yacht *Valhalla* of 1,700 tons, by Michael John Nicoll, a naturalist. It is from the report given to the British Zoological Society of London, 19th

[5] Publishers: Witherby and Co., 1908. (British Museum Library reference copy. No. 7002 e 22.)

June, 1906, and later published in its 'proceedings', on 10th October, page 721. It reads:

'At 10.15 a.m. on Thursday, 7th December, 1905, when in latitude 7° 14' S. longitude 34° 25' W., and in a depth from 322–1,340 fathoms, Mr E. G. B. Meade-Waldo and I saw a most extraordinary creature about 100 yards from the ship moving in the same direction but very much slower than we were going. At first all we could see was a dorsal fin, about 4 feet long, sticking up about 2 feet from the water; this fin was a brownish-black colour and much resembled a gigantic piece of ribbon-seaweed. Below the water we could distinctly see a very large brownish-black patch, but could not make out the shape of the creature. Every now and then the fin entirely disappeared below water. Suddenly an eel-like neck, about 6 feet long and of the thickness of a man's thigh, having a head shaped like that of a turtle, appeared in front of the fin. This head and neck, which were of the same colour above as the fin, but of silvery-white below, lashed up the water with a curious wriggling movement. After this it was so far astern of us we could make out nothing else.

'During the next fourteen hours we went about twice, and at about 2 a.m. the following day . . . the First and Third mates, Mr. Simmonds and Mr. Harley, who were on the bridge at the time, saw a great commotion in the water. At first they thought it was a rock awash about 100 to 150 yards away, just aft of the bridge, but they soon made out that it was something moving and going slightly faster than the ship, which at that time was doing about 8½ knots. Mr. Simmonds hailed the deck, and one of the crew who was on lookout saw it too. Although there was a bright moon at the time they could not make out anything of the creature itself, owing to the amount of wash it was making, but they say that from the commotion in the water it looked as if a submarine was going along just below the surface. They both say emphatically it was not a whale, and that it was not blowing, nor had they ever seen anything like it before. After they watched it for some minutes it "sounded" off the port bow, and they saw it no more.

'This creature was an example, I consider, of what has so often been reported, for want of a better name, as the "great sea serpent". I feel sure, however, that it was not a reptile that we saw but a mammal. It is of course impossible to be sure of this, but the general appearance of the creature, especially the soft, almost rubber-like fin, gave one this impression. . . .'

Reference to the animal as a mammal is interesting, because it supports the current theory put forward by two famous zoologists that the 'great sea serpent' may in fact be a type of gigantic long-necked seal, or *Pinniped*, as opposed to a reptile; but I feel one should also note the head, described 'like that of a turtle'. (See Sketch 2.)

THE 'SANTA CLARA' INCIDENT

A recent *Associated Press* report describes a collision between the Greek ship *Santa Clara* and a serpent-like Monster, on 30th December, 1947, 118 miles east of Lookout Cape (34° 30′ N., 76° 30′ W.).

The Captain's account of what happened runs as follows:[6]

'It was a clear sunny day. Suddenly John Exelson (third mate) saw a head like a snake's head sticking up out of the water about 10 yards from the ship on the starboard side. His shout of astonishment drew the attention of two other officers. Amazed, all three watched it until it disappeared astern.

'The Monster's head was about 30 inches in breadth, 2 feet thick and 4–5 feet long. The body was cylindrical, and about 3 feet thick. When the creature was abreast of the Captain's bridge, they could see that the water was red over a radius of 30–40 feet. The visible part of the body was about 34–36 feet long. It was to be assumed that the reddening of the water came from the creature's blood, it having been cut in half by the bows of the ship. From the time that the creature was first noticed until it disappeared, it was writhing in agony.

[6] Not verbatim: as translated from the Russian account.

'Its skin appeared to be dark brown, and smooth. No fins nor hair nor protuberances were seen on its head or neck or other visible parts of the body.'

Dr. S. K. Klumov refers to this encounter in his article in the Soviet journal *Priroda*, August 1962, and concludes that the creature was probably a gigantic marine eel thought by some to exist, due to the capture of a 6 feet eel-larva by the Danish Oceanologist Antoni Brunn, in the South Atlantic, in February 1930. The lava of the ordinary eel is some 2–3 inches in length, producing an adult of 3–4 feet; and if the growth proportions remain the same a 6 foot lava should produce an adult 60–70 feet in length.

Another cross-reference appears in the April 1964 edition of the U.S. magazine *The Lookout*, in an article by Ivan Sanderson, who took the trouble to interview the ship's officers. He provides a more detailed account: 'Under a clear sky, vessel on course, winds light, and calm sea, a crew member forward sang out to the officer on the bridge that there was an object straight ahead. It was large enough to cause damage. . . . However, it was too late to avoid a head-on collision that, while happily doing no damage to the ship, sent such a shudder through her from stem to stern it brought others on deck at the double. Whatever had been hit was caught athwart the prow for a few moments and then broke free and drifted by to starboard only a few feet from the hull. As it did so it came almost directly under the gaze of all on the bridge, and others on deck below.

'This object was a very large animal from which blood in enormous amounts was pouring into the wash. About 30 feet of its spindle-shaped, glistening body was above water, and this tapered at one end into a narrow but not too long neck on which was an enormous tapering triangular head stated by all witnesses to have been at least 3 feet across above the eyes. The creature passed astern and was sucked into the wake where it thrashed about amid blood-red foam, until it finally sank. The ship was stopped but nothing further was seen.'

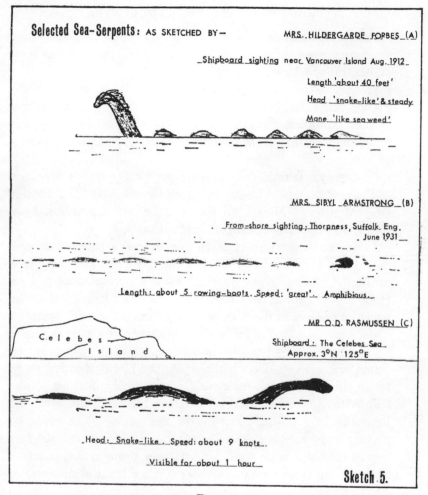

FIG. 5

This description, based as it is on conversation with actual witnesses seems to rule out the giant-eel theory, because an eel would not be expected to have a definably separate neck, from the rest of its serpentine body. But, as the animal was clearly of unknown species no one can be sure about it.

ROBERT LE SERREC'S ENCOUNTER

Another remarkable report which may possibly relate to a similar type of animal comes from the Great Barrier Reef of Australia, which stretches endlessly for some 1,250 miles; in places as much as 300 miles in width. It concerns the French traveller-photographer Robert le Serrec, and a young Sydney skindiver, Henk de Jong, who approached a gigantic snake-like creature from underwater, attempting to capture it on film.

The story was reported convincingly by *Everybody's Magazine* of Sydney, on 31st March, 1965, under the title 'The Barrier Reef Monster' – giving full space to Le Serrec's personal account, and the circumstances surrounding it.[7]

It appears that Robert le Serrec, his wife Raymonde and their three children, veterans of some five years of roving in a converted 70-foot fishing yawl found themselves encamped on Hook Island (about two miles from Hayman Island) after the wreck of their boat the previous June. They had with them an 18-foot motor-launch. In early December the tail end of a hurricane had swept the island deluging it with unaccustomed water, and on 12th December, 1964, the family decided to go across the bay to wash their mildewed clothing under a waterfall. With Raymonde at the tiller, her husband and Henk de Jong checking diving gear in the cockpit and the children playing on its roof, they ran across a huge dark object lying in a lazy curve just underwater. At first they thought it was a tree but drawing nearer they could see a huge head at one end of what appeared to be a supple-looking body, some 70 feet in length.

It lay motionless in the shallow water, and with the engine reduced to idling speed the boat was circled around it cautiously. Said Robert le Serrec: 'My heart pounded harder than it had ever done before. I must admit that I felt afraid. If the Monster

[7] Excerpts are included here with kind permission of the Editor, Robin Brampton, *Everybody's Magazine*, 54 Park St. Sydney, Australia: having also the Author's approval.

had been in aggressive mood, or had simply moved clumsily, our frail launch would have been smashed to pieces.'

The children at first did not appear to be upset by it, but on hearing the word 'snake', became frightened and started to make a noise. They had been taught to be afraid of snakes on the island. It was thought wisest to return them to land. The return trip took some fifteen minutes but the Monster had not moved away. There was clearly a large white mark on its body, like a big wound . . .

'This time we really got to close quarters. We saw two little whitish eyes peering from what looked like the body of a giant snake. Henk got into the dinghy and we filmed him circling the Monster. Still the beast did not move. I decided to leave Raymonde on the boat with one movie camera and go underwater with Henk to examine and film the creature. . . . The fact that we could see what appeared to be a big wound in the Monster's body made us think it could be dead. . . .'

Slipping into the sea, armed with a protective device fired by a shot-gun cartridge – which was obviously useless against such a great creature, the two men found that when in the water, the plan did not seem quite so attractive. . . . 'Behind the glass of his mask Henk's eyes seemed much bigger than normal. He seemed to ask, "Do you think it really worth it to film the Monster?" I hesitated myself, then pride won. With extreme caution I swam forward, making as little noise as possible with my flippers . . . underwater, things were a little murky. It was only when we got to within 20 feet of the serpent that we could see its head clearly. The head was large – about 4 feet from top to bottom – with jaws about 4 feet wide. The lower jaw was flat like like that of a sandfish. The skin was smooth but rather dull, brownish-black in colour, the eyes seemed pale green, almost white.

'The skin looked more like that of a shark than an eel. There were no apparent scales. Nor did we see any parasites around. We supposed the flexible tail would have shaken any off. There were no fins or spines, nor were there any apparent breathing openings – although there must have been some. Perhaps we didn't see them because our attention was focused mainly on the creature's menacing mouth – the inside of which was whitish. The teeth appeared to be small. A fragment of some dark substance hung from the upper row of teeth – possibly part of a fish. As the Monster was lying on the sandy bottom, we could not see the colour of its belly. The creature was about 70 feet long. Behind the head the body was about 2 feet 4 inches thick and remained that way for about 25 feet, then it gradually tapered to a whip-like tail.

'The general colour of the body was black with 1 foot-wide brownish rings every 5 feet – the first starting just behind the head. The skin was smooth but dull.

'I started the camera, and the head rose from the sand. The mouth opened menacingly several times. Moving with effort, the front of the great creature began to turn towards us – we were filming from one side – and, after filming for a short while longer, I made for the surface with Henk at my side.

'We swam frantically towards the boat – Raymonde had been so upset at seeing the Monster start towards us that she had stalled the engine . . .'

Back in the boat with the engine restarted, a search was made for the beast, which had by now disappeared into deep water, and during the next few days local beaches were examined in the hope it might have been washed up dead. The great wound in its side had been clearly seen by both men when underwater: 'It was about 5 feet long and gave the impression of having been torn by teeth. The hole seemed to have almost reached the spine. Our theory is that the huge creature had been struck by a ship or a submarine. With its spine damaged, and constantly plagued by fish and sharks attacking the raw flesh wound, the Monster probably sought shelter in the shallow waters of Stonehaven Bay to escape from its enemies.

'At no stage did we try to capture the serpent. We didn't even think about it. Nothing less than a cannon would have paralysed or killed it.

'And this is apart from the fact that we had no desire to harm the Monster – all we wanted to do was study and photograph it.'

Some time later, after very careful thought Robert le Serrec decided to release his astonishing photographs, and tell his story – not unmindful of the fact that ridicule could spoil his reputation as a serious photographer. But his moral courage, it seems, matched the physical variety shown when he and Henk de Jong coolly entered the water to get a closer look at the beast – and has been justly rewarded by the attention of scientists in Australia, France, Britain and America – few of whom can really doubt the authenticity of his discovery, which may relate to a giant unknown type of eel, or perhaps the 'sea serpent' of legend. In due course he intends to publish a book about his experiences, entitled *The Great Adventure of the Saint-Yves D'Armor*.

Research by the staff of *Everybody's Magazine* has turned up some other evidence in support of the Barrier Reef Monster, claimed to have been seen more than thirty years ago. Writer Jim Oram produced an article in the 26th May edition entitled 'Mystery Monster of Our North' in which he describes the experience of Mr. Boyd Lee, a well-known Barrier Reef fisherman, and a friend. . . .

'The two men watched the giant turtle floating on the surface of the lagoon, its immense flippers idly waving. It was the largest turtle they had ever seen. And there was something else about it which drew their attention. The turtle's head was looking down into the water, bobbing from side to side as though it was expecting something to happen.

'Seconds later something did happen. In the words of one of the men "A mighty head, that resembled a giant snake, came out of the water and struck once, but only once, at the turtle. Then the turtle and the vast head that had engulfed it disappeared. That turtle must have weighed 500 pounds." "We didn't investigate," he later told a friend. "We made off at the double, that darn thing was capable of picking any of us off the deck of the boat." ' (See also Appendix Note J).

Commenting on the incident in his book *Fangs of the Sea*, author Norman Caldwell had this to say about it – 'Lee's tale sounded so fantastic I felt like grinning. But, I thought of the type of man Lee is. He is not above a leg-pull – but not about his fishing; he takes that too seriously. It is more to him than a living ... it is his life. Boyd Lee is not the man to spin fish stories.'

Again, in August 1934 a Queensland newspaper published a report in which a Mr. H. Hurst and two others sighted something large on the surface of Bowen Harbour, North Queensland. It was about 30 feet long, and on being approached lifted a large turtle-like head about 8 feet out of water. The body was like 'a huge armoured hose'.

Mr. Hurst and his crew members did not like the look of it at all, and having no rifle on board made for shore.

Later three separate parties of fishermen farther north, near Townsville, reported seeing it on the same day. One man told the local newspaper: 'Its head resembled a huge turtle more than anything else, and was slightly arched. Farther along three smaller dark objects were seen, giving the appearance of a Monster of the sea with a series of humps.'

Lastly, a film producer, Mr. Robert E. Steele spotted something long and sinuous and made a sketch of it – describing it in the following terms: 'Twenty-five feet long; a snake-like head with fins on either side, very small eyes, a tail more like an eel than a snake, the body about 12 inches in diameter, no particular fangs or tongue showing, and the body an impressive lime-green colour tinged with brown about the fins.'

With the exception of Mr. Hurst's report these accounts do not relate to a 'Monster' approaching the size of that photographed by Le Serrec – but the first description of 'a mighty head, that resembled a snake' could well be applied to any one of his pictures.

Some idea of the fearsome size of the creature can be obtained

— 5 ft. wound.

BASED ON ROBERT LE SERREC'S
PHOTO'; GREAT BARRIER REEF,
AUSTRALIA, DEC. 12 th. 1964.

Animal lying in 8 ft. of water
Length about 70 ft.

14   Quotation from *Sud Pacific* magazine: 'Les Photos du
Monstre-mystere de Hook Island . . . Quant aux instances
scientifiques, elles se sont manifestees par la voix du Dr. F. H.
Talbot, conservateur de la section Poissons au Museum
d'Australie, qui a declare: "Extraordinaire! Il (le monstre) est
totalement different de toutes les autres creatures marines que
connait la science . . ." '

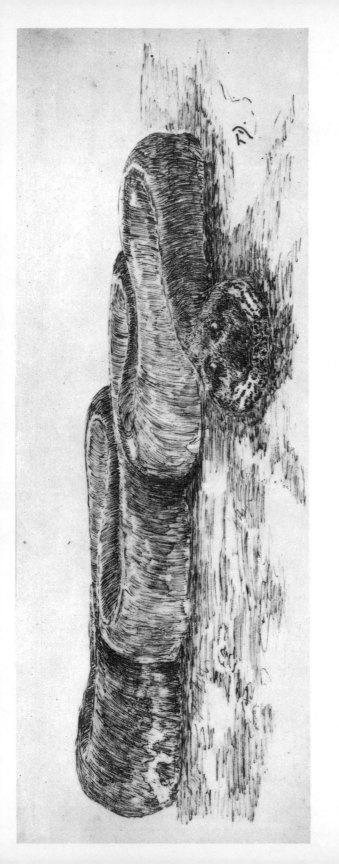

15 'Satan's Serpent'. Is this the 'frightful beast' described by Father Victor Heinz, and other witnesses? The Great Serpent of Amazon legend? My drawing is based on a minute study of the photo' published by the Brazilian newspaper *Dario de Pernambuco*, 24th January 1948, purporting to show such an animal, killed with a machine-gun near Manaos, on the Amazon. Its diameter was 30 inches, and 'it measured no less than 40 metres', 130 feet! Estimated weight was 5 tons. Known as the *sucurijú gigante*, or *cobra grande* or *Tunguru*, in certain areas it is held in superstitious dread by forest Indians. The picture is accurate in dimension and detail, but there is some alleviation of the deep shadows present in the original. Features of note are the lack of distinct markings on top of the body; the mottled underbelly; the impression of immense size; the fact that the body is clearly *greatest at the 6th convolution*.

from Plate 14, the outline of which is traced from a clear photo-graph published by *Sud Pacific Magazine*. Allowing for perspec-tive, the small dinghy gives a fair impression of scale, which is important – but it is in the mysteriously beautiful colour pic-tures taken from just a few feet that details become evident. The eyes, and the great whitish wound in the body can easily be distinguished.

The July 1965 edition of America's *True Magazine* published two of these photographs on good paper, in colour, and the article by Ivan Sanderson is in keeping with the standards set by this excellent periodical.

He considers the various aspects of the case, carefully, in-cluding that of a hoax – and comes out unreservedly in favour of the Monster being a live animal of very unusual character.

He does not think it can be a mammal, because there is no limbless mammal known, either living or fossil, nor does he think it is a reptile or amphibian for various other technical reasons – and although the case for a giant unknown type of eel seems quite a good one, Sanderson observes: 'I don't think it is an eel exactly. There are about 350 species of living eels but none of these are completely limbless or lack at least some exter-nal signs of a breathing apparatus. However, there is a strange group of fishes, known as the *Synbranchidae*, that are completely limbless and which have only rudimentary internal gills. They breathe mainly through the mucous membranes of the throat and have two small slits under the throat for the eviction of the water that they take in through the mouth. . . . These odd creatures are popularly known as "Swamp Eels" and are found mostly in fresh water in South-east Asia, Africa, Central and South America. But there is one deep-sea species. I will tenta-tively suggest that Le Serrec's animal might be a member of this group. The *Synbranchidae* are a very ancient and primitive form of fish and it is possible that a giant form may have evolved in the waters of the Pacific. The animal shown in the photo-graphs matches neatly what a giant *Synbranchid* might look like . . .'

85

These comments come from a man holding a Cambridge B.A. in zoology, with some thirty years of experience in collecting expeditions, the world over.

THE 'TAIYUEN' INCIDENT

The *Daily Telegraph*, 15th June, 1961 : Letter to the Editor.

'Sir

'There was a Monster similar to that of Loch Ness in the Celebes Sea, south of the Philippines. I and my family and a whole boatload of passengers and crew on board the s.s. *Taiyuen*, saw it running parallel to the ship half a mile away to port in clear sunshine on a summer's day in fine weather.

'The creature was dark-skinned, with a head similar in proportion to a snake's, and a tapering neck thickening as it neared the water by about half as much again as the part immediately behind the head.

'The neck disappeared below water level, but two humps followed, evenly spaced by the water in between the three visible parts. These were followed by a barely visible "wake", stretching for possibly the length of a cricket pitch.

'This creature swam parallel with us for about half an hour and then veered half-left away from us to the west, completely disappearing in a similar period. Inasmuch as the *Taiyuen* was steaming about ten knots it could be said the creature maintained this speed as well. We excitedly questioned the captain about it at lunch, but he would not talk beyond mumbling that such things were often "seen hereabouts".

'Yours, etc. O. D. Rasmussen
'Tonbridge, Kent.'

Upon request Mr. Rasmussen sent a very good sketch, included in the composite picture 'Selected Sea Serpents' (5).

MRS. SIBYL ARMSTRONG'S SERPENT

Letter in reply to an indirect request for information:

Penn, Buckinghamshire, 9th July, 1961 – 'My sister Mrs. Hamilton has told me you would like to have my account of the creature I and two other people saw off the east coast in June 1931 – rather a long time ago I'm afraid.

'I had rented a bungalow for a month at Thorpness in Suffolk, built on the edge of a low sandy cliff – with nothing between us and the sea. The weather had been set fair for some days and the evening we saw the creature was a particularly clear and brilliant one – not a cloud in the sky and the sea dead calm – it was about 8 p.m. – the beach deserted.

'Our governess, the cook and I were eating supper in the sitting-room, which had french doors opening on to the beach with, of course, a full view of the sea. I was looking vaguely at the view and noticed what I took to be a man's head swimming. I remarked he was bathing late but as I said it I saw this head was coming at a great speed and was much too big for a man's head. I went outside for a better view and saw there was a great length of a snake-like body behind. I exclaimed in surprise and the other two came out to see – we were all astonished – forgot the sleeping children and ran along the cliff trying to keep up with it and see all we could. There was then at the Aldeburgh end of the beach, a large sandbank which I was told afterwards was a ¼ mile out, but I do not think it could have been so much – people used to swim out and you could distinguish them by their bathing dresses if brightly coloured. Anyway, when the monster got level with the sandbank which was now between it and the deep sea it turned and drew itself up on it. It was now with its back to us. It went over the crest and on reaching the water on the far side raised up its front part and beat on the sea with enormous oyster coloured *fins* (I suppose) making such a volume of spray . . . it made me think of a swan beating the water with its wings – meanwhile the length of its body was across the sandbank with the tail end still in the water on the beach side – it then ceased beating on the sea and the whole body was pulled over. It was incredibly long. I don't remember what the tail end was like – it all happened so quickly, but whereas in the water it looked black, when on the sandbank it was a tawny sandy colour. It was a marvellous sight . . . and the agility with which the Monster crossed the sandbank makes me realize they are not completely helpless on land.

'The next evening I looked most carefully at fishermen's rowing boats coming along to collect lobster pots at approximately the same distance out, and came to the conclusion the Monster was about five times as long – I hope you will not think this is an incredulous story, but I do promise you it is exactly what I saw.

'In October 1938 I saw an account by the vicar of Southwell in *The Times* of an exactly similar creature seen by him, twelve fishermen, and two ladies at the same time on the same afternoon, but there was no sandbank there for it to come out on to. I have tried to draw what I saw, but am no artist . . .'

One of Mrs. Armstrong's drawings appears in Sketch 5. In answer to further questions she said that she was so astonished by the spectacle she did not think of trying to measure the animal's girth, but that when crossing the sandbank the rear portion was well in view . . . 'and thinking carefully about it I should guess it as having been about four times as wide as a man bather[8] on the sandbank. Perhaps I did not say enough about the enormous volume of water which it was beating up – it was terrific – no wave breaking on the sandbank in a storm could have gone so high, and now as you have asked me about size, I should think the front part raised up with fins beating must have been five or six times as high as a man – I do hope you won't think this ridiculous, but that is what it must have been, the whole animal was incredibly *vast* – I remember too

[8] I am of average build and measure about 20 inches across the back with arms at my sides.

that its skin, which I described to you as a tawny colour, was mottled looking like a toad's – certainly the colouring would have made it hard to see had it been lying on the sea-bed . . .'

THE DUNCAN REPORT

Extract from Sydney's newspaper *The Sun-Herald*, 30th September, 1962:

'Brisbane, Saturday. Queensland's marine biologists are fascinated by the report this week of a sea monster off Brisbane's Moreton Bay. One of them said he would not by any means describe the report as "rubbish". Mr. Robert Duncan, sixty-eight, reported the "dreadful looking Monster" playing idly on the surface of the ocean off Bribie Island. Mr. Duncan has lived at the island resort for fifty years and is held in high repute.

'He said: "I was standing on the sand-dunes near my house which is about 200 yards from the ocean beach. I saw something breaking the surface of the water. I hurried inside to get my binoculars. What I saw was something out of a nightmare. I just couldn't believe my eyes. On the water I saw a dreadful looking creature with a body like a whale but with a long neck just like a swan. It was very fat and well developed. Two fins jutted out from each side of its long neck. The Monster also had fins down near its tail and the tail was like a fish's. Its body was a greyish-whitish colour. The skin was smooth with no scales and very shiny."

'Queensland ichthyologists say Mr. Duncan's report is just one in a series over many years of Monsters off the Queensland coast . . . recalling the ancient coastal aboriginal legend of a sea creature called the "Moha Moha" . . . reputed to frequent the ocean near Fraser Island, off Maryborough . . . Queensland's most authentic mystery Monster of the sea, recorded in 1890 has become a text-book item, and is still unexplained. Miss Lovell, a schoolteacher on Fraser Island reported sighting the creature in shallow water near the island's northern tip. She and four other witnesses made out a statutory declaration . . . claiming the Monster had a long neck, a big head and wedge-shaped, fish-like tail (*also*) "a great dome-shaped carapace like a turtle's back". . . . This report is documented in a classic book on the Great Barrier Reef by W. Savile Kent. Queensland officials have been struck by the similarity in the descriptions by Miss Lovell and Mr. Robert Duncan.'

Miss. S. Lovell's account appears in detail in *The Great Barrier Reef of Australia* (pages 332–7) published in 1893, and is also treated at length by R. T. Gould in *The Case for the Sea Serpent* in 1930 – but as it seems to relate to some unknown and almost unclassifiable species of marine animal, I have included it under the *Oddities* section in the chapter following.

MRS. HILDERGARDE FORBES' ACCOUNT

Milton, Mass. U.S.A. 24th July, 1962 – another letter:

'. . . I am one of the lucky people who have seen a "Sea Serpent" and since I have never before recorded the event, will write what I can remember . . .

'It was August, 1912, and I was on a steamer bound for Skagway, Alaska. We were passing along the east coast of Vancouver Island when I saw my Monster. He was going south so I saw him in direct profile. His speed struck me as neither fast nor slow. I cannot now say how near he was but I could see him clearly and remember thinking, if only I had binoculars I could see every detail. I tried very hard to figure out his length and settled on about 40 feet. This is how he looked (see Sketch 5).

'He was definitely snake-like; head raised and steady all the time he was in view; this was several minutes; dark but not black; his mane seemed like seaweed; did not see eye, mouth, etc.; he had a number of "humps" (probably five to seven) which seemed to rise and fall as he moved. I did not get the impression that he had a large body and don't remember how he disappeared, probably just passed out of sight. Oddly enough there was nobody else on deck at the time – either passengers or crew – and I failed to convince anybody that I really had seen anything.

'Some ten or fifteen years later I read in a Boston newspaper (quoting some west-coast paper) an account of a couple who were honeymooning in a small sailboat. They went ashore and, as the girl sat on a rock alone, a beast that sounded much like my friend came and laid his head on a rock near by. It seemed she was not amused. I vaguely remember that their encounter was at Chatham Bay on Vancouver Island. Surely this rugged coast is just the place for a Sea Monster . . .

'Yours, etc,

'(Mrs.) Hildergarde B. Forbes.'

Mrs. Forbes is quite right about the rocky coastline being just the place for a sea monster. It is. In fact Vancouver Island's resident sea serpent acquired a nickname some years ago – the 'Cadborosaurus'; on which much information exists in the files of local newspapers.

FLORIDA TRAGEDY

In the May 1965 edition of *Fate Magazine*, there appears an extraordinary story, under the heading 'Escape from a Sea Monster', by Edward Brian McCleary.

It concerns the experience of five young skin-divers off the Florida coast in 1962, as recounted by their only survivor; and as the details of this appalling tragedy include a large unknown aquatic animal, similar in appearance to that described on many occasions in the past, and by Mr. W. J. Hutchison in particular[9] in the Bay of Meil, 1910, I immediately wrote to the editor about it: who referred me to the editor of the American magazine of the same name, which first published the article.

[9] See *Loch Ness Monster*, page 200.

In due course I got in contact with Mr. McCleary, who sent a clear and concise report of what actually happened, together with permission to quote from his magazine account.

Under the circumstances I do not think anyone would make up such a story. This is what he wrote:

(Letter to me dated 23rd July, 1965, from Mr. E. B. Mc-Cleary, 125 Saint Mary's Street, Fort Walton Beach, Florida, U.S.A.):

'On the 24th of March, 1962, off the coast of Pensacola, Florida, a "skin-diving" accident occurred. I was the lone survivor of the five on the trip. We were in an Air Force rescue raft bound for a sunken ship a few miles off the coast. Midway out, we were caught in a storm and dragged out to sea. When the storm cleared, we were in a dense fog, therefore not knowing our position or the direction of shore. We, or rather I was later informed, were 5 miles out. After sitting for about an hour, we began to hear strange noises, rather like the splashing of a porpoise or other large fish. Accompanying the noise was a sickening odour like that of dead fish. The noise got closer to the raft and it was then we heard a loud hissing sound. Out in the fog we saw what looked like a long pole, about 10 feet high, sticking straight up out of the water. On top was a bulb-like structure. It bent in the middle and went under. It appeared several more times getting closer to the raft each succeeding time. Many people, at this point, do not understand why we abandoned the raft . . .

'What happened to us is that we became terror stricken; in an open raft in a March fog miles off the coast with an unknown terror lurking near us. The wisest thing to do would have been to stay in the raft, but we were too terrified to think clearly. Now that I am safe I still wonder if I should have stayed.

'After we were in the water we became split up in the fog. From behind I could hear the screams of my comrades one by one. I got a closer look at the thing just before my last friend went under. The neck was about 12 feet long, brownish-green and smooth looking. The head was like that of a sea-turtle except more elongated, with teeth (I am not positive of this. It looked of if there were teeth on the gums). I did not see any fins, although there appeared to be what looked like a dorsal fin when it dove under for the last time. Also, as best I am able to recall, the eyes were green with oval pupils.

'I finally made it to the ship, the top of which protruded from the water, and stayed there for most of the night, early that morning I swam to shore and was found by the rescue unit.

'That is the best I can give you of the story, in brief. I hope that what I have told you will be of some help, even in a small way.'

Fate Magazine comments that Edward McCleary was born in Brooklyn in 1946, and moved to Walton Beach with his family in 1961. Now a pre-medical student in a Florida college, he had been diving for three years at the time of the tragedy.

This fact may help to explain the abandonment of the raft, because expert skin-divers are not afraid of the water, and with fins can cover distances quickly – and the reaction to mortal fear can, in my own experience, result in an almost uncontrollable desire to escape.

In the magazine account, McCleary describes this part of the story in greater detail . . .

'I've never seen anything like that in my life. What do you think it was?' I whispered.

'Maybe it was an oarfish. I've heard they look like snakes,' Warren answered.

'Oarfish don't stand straight up,' Brad said.

'Maybe it's a sea monster,' I suggested. Everyone looked at me in silence. We all had been thinking the same thing. I was just the first to say it.

'The silence was broken once again by something out in the fog. I can only describe it as a high-pitched whine. We panicked. All five of us put on our fins and went into the water. Patches of brown crusty slime lay all over the surface. I began to swim and kick spasmodically. I felt a small current under the surface and hoped it would carry me in the direction of the shore. "Keep together. Stay behind me and try for the ship," I yelled.

'Eric and I were swimming together. The rest were together behind us. We made pretty good time at first. Our fear was indescribable . . .'

Subsequently four of the party perished – and I feel Mr. McCleary has been right to omit the details in his letter; because the facts cannot be proven.

Certainly, I have never been in any doubt as to the potential danger faced by those who swim in waters inhabited by these animals, which must be fish-eating carnivores – and although the fresh-water variants typical of the Ness seem to pay little heed to boats, having seen one of them I would never bathe in the lake – and whenever possible try to warn others not to do so either. But, at the present time it is difficult to get people to take the matter seriously. Perhaps, Edward McCleary's letter will have a more noticeable effect, particularly because of the report obtained from Inverness, 30th July, 1965, which reopens the question of 'access to the sea'. (See Appendix, Note I).

NEW ENGLAND COASTAL SIGHTINGS

Sunday Standard Times, New Bedford, Mass., U.S.A., 17th May, 1964.

'. . . Last week's sighting was the first in the area since 1957 when the crew of the scalloper *Noreen* reported they had seen "something with a very large body, weighing perhaps 35 to 40 tons, whose alligator head rose 26 feet in the air".

'Six men were on deck when "something" reared up from 40 fathoms of water off the starboard quarter and began "to show an inquisitive interest in the ship. He had a large body and a small alligator-like head," the *Noreen*'s Log reads. The body was shaped somewhat like a seal and there was a mane of bristly hair or fur, which ran down the middle of his head.

' "He would surface the upper part of his body, and glide out of the water, with the lower part remaining submerged. The portion visible measured about 40 feet in length . . . at no time did the whole body show. He stayed on surface no longer than forty seconds at a time. You could hear the heavy weight of his upper body when he dove below, creating a large splash and subsequent wake. He surfaced four times in twenty minutes during which we were trying to stay clear of him."

'The Captain decided to change course, and when he did the creature surfaced again. The Log reads: "he rose off our starboard bow, keeping the same distance from us. The Captain then ordered the drags to be brought in, turned the boat and steamed at full speed to the west away from the queer fellow." The *Noreen* steamed for about twenty minutes before she set her drags again; the final notation in her Log reads: "That was the last we saw of him, which made us all happy." '

Where possible I have tried to keep sightings in date-of-occurrence order, the next report coming from the dragger *Blue Sea*, as published in the *Standard Times*, New Bedford, 14th May, 1964. The encounter took place in the cold Atlantic off Nantucket:

'. . . members of the crew of the dragger *Blue Sea*, say they spotted a curious-looking creature Tuesday afternoon, about 30 miles south of Round Shoal Buoy. "At first we thought it was a buoy, and then a whale," engineman Alf H. Wilhelmsen said. "We started out after it. When we got close enough for a good look we could tell it wasn't a whale. Bjarne Haugen said he'd never seen anything like it in his life, and he's been at sea for a long time. . . . Captain Jens Wilhelmsen, who was below deck at the time, said the men described the 'Monster' as black in colour, and at least 50 feet long. "It was more than half the length of the boat . . . and the *Blue Sea* is nearly 80 feet long," he calculated.

'The body of the creature had several humps, and there was a blow-hole in the top of the alligator-like head. . . . It seemed

95

to "skim along the top of the water", and for a while kept pace about 50 to 100 feet to starboard, at about 8 miles an hour. . . . Alf said, "It came towards us, swung along and then moved parallel to us. It left a wake in the stern, like it had a propeller, and it *blew air out of the hole in its head*." (My italics: see page 19).

'Captain Jens said both men on deck "got the shivers" when they got near the creature, even though it "never appeared hostile". After pacing alongside the dragger for about five minutes the thing "simply turned its head north and swam away". The serpent, all told, was within sight of the boat for about a half-hour.

'Captain Wilhelmsen, a fisherman since 1939 said he had no reason to doubt the story of the crew members.'

Later, all three men reported the encounter to an official of the U.S. Bureau of Commercial Fisheries upon landing in New Bedford.

On 22nd May, 1964 the *Standard Times* reported that another New Bedford dragger, the *Friendship*, had encountered an 'unclassifiable' creature about 40 miles east-south-east of Great Round Shoal Buoy.

One of the crew members, Mr. Thomas Keeping said:

'It was not a whale, or anything else he and three shipmates had ever seen in their years at sea. The dragger circled it twice to get a good look, and had it in view for about fifteen to twenty minutes. The body was deep blue or blackish and "where the neck joined the body was irregularly scalloped." It was thought to be about 30 feet long, and 'it had a light-grey dorsal projection, triangular in shape and rounded on top. This was about 4 feet long and meaty looking. On the back were two blow-holes, pear shaped or oval . . . and as we circled we could see that where the mouth area might be was a very light colour.'

Captain Albert Pike described it as 'weird looking, with barnacles on its sides'.

If these two encounters relate to the same animal – and it

seems reasonable to assume they do in view of the coincidence of dates, and location, then the description of 'blow-hole' orifices on the back could be mistaken – because as it was heard to breathe through the top of its head, it could hardly do so in a second place as well!

Certain of the long-necked Plesiosaurs, which became *totally adapted* for life at sea had nostrils on top of their heads – which, in appearance were not unlike those of small alligators: but equally true is the fact that evolution of sea-going mammals has produced blow-holes in much the same place.

From the encounters described in this chapter it seems to me there really are two basic types of 'Great Sea Serpent'. One is genuinely of serpentine form, and the other can sometimes appear to be, with its long serpentine neck, and the top of its body and tail showing above water, with or without a protrusion of humps of varying shape.

Both animals grow to stupendous size, and when seen at close quarters can be quite terrifying: but in neither case will the mammal versus reptile, or for that matter fish or invertebrate theories be resolved until specimens are killed or captured – or possibly a small piece of living tissue recovered from them for chromosome analysis.

4

MYSTERY, MONSTER, OR
MERMAID?

WE all love a good mystery!

During the course of correspondence and research into the subject of aquatic monsters generally I have found the clues to several; and in the span of this chapter have tried to arrange them so that the reader can examine the details, and draw his own conclusions – which will probably be different to my own.

The main body of information stems from a completely varied collection of letters, newspapers, magazine articles and books, and in sifting through these I have surprised by the apparent volume of Monster Lore, or legendary history: to say nothing of the more obviously factual accounts of unknown aquatic animals, of colossal size.

The first of these is brief enough. It refers to the remains of some vast creature washed ashore in Alaska in July 1956, and provides a fair example of the type of report which appears from time to time, which could either be of scientific interest, or a mistaken or garbled account of something quite ordinary. Extract from the *Daily Mail Yearbook*, 1957 (page 74):

'Mystery Monster: A giant hairy Monster, with 6 foot tusks was washed ashore on the coast of Alaska in July 1956. The carcase which was more than 100 feet long and 15 feet wide, had crimson flesh. Its origin and species were a complete mystery. Experts said that it fitted no known description of prehistoric beasts and that the 2-inch reddish-brown hair which covered the thick decaying hide excluded any relationship to whales.

'The Monster was discovered by a veteran Alaskan hunting guide, and was apparently washed ashore during a gale in the Gulf of Alaska. Explorers who flew northward to view the carcase said the Monster had a huge head measuring 5½ feet across, with eye sockets 9 inches wide and about 42 inches apart. Its teeth were 6 inches long and 5 inches wide at the base.

'Clusters of ribs extended 6 feet from the spinal column, and the moveable upper jaw, a solid tusk-like bone protruded several feet beyond the end of the fixed lower jaw.'

This is a strange account by any standard. In the first place the animal compared in size to the Blue whale, which is the largest animal known, and yet the experts discounted it being any sort of a whale. But who were these experts? What were their qualifications I wonder – and if the carcase really was so extraordinary why have we not heard more about it since? These are reasonable questions, but they are difficult to answer so long after the event, so whatever we choose to make of it, the story depends on its accuracy as reported.

The great length of the beast – the reddish-brown hair – the huge eye sockets appear to fit the 'sea serpent' specification in some measure, but equally the description of the head and upper jaw would seem to rule it out.

The strange jaw makes one wonder whether the carcase might have been that of a very large Sperm whale – upside down, with the long-toothed[1] lower jaw appearing on top; but it hardly seems probable, because despite the ruinous jumbled state of some carcases when they come ashore, they are generally recognizable for what they are. And besides, Sperm whales

[1] The Sperm whale or Cachalot is the largest of the toothed whales. Teeth are in the lower jaw in irregular numbers and measure some 8 inches by 3 inches in diameter.

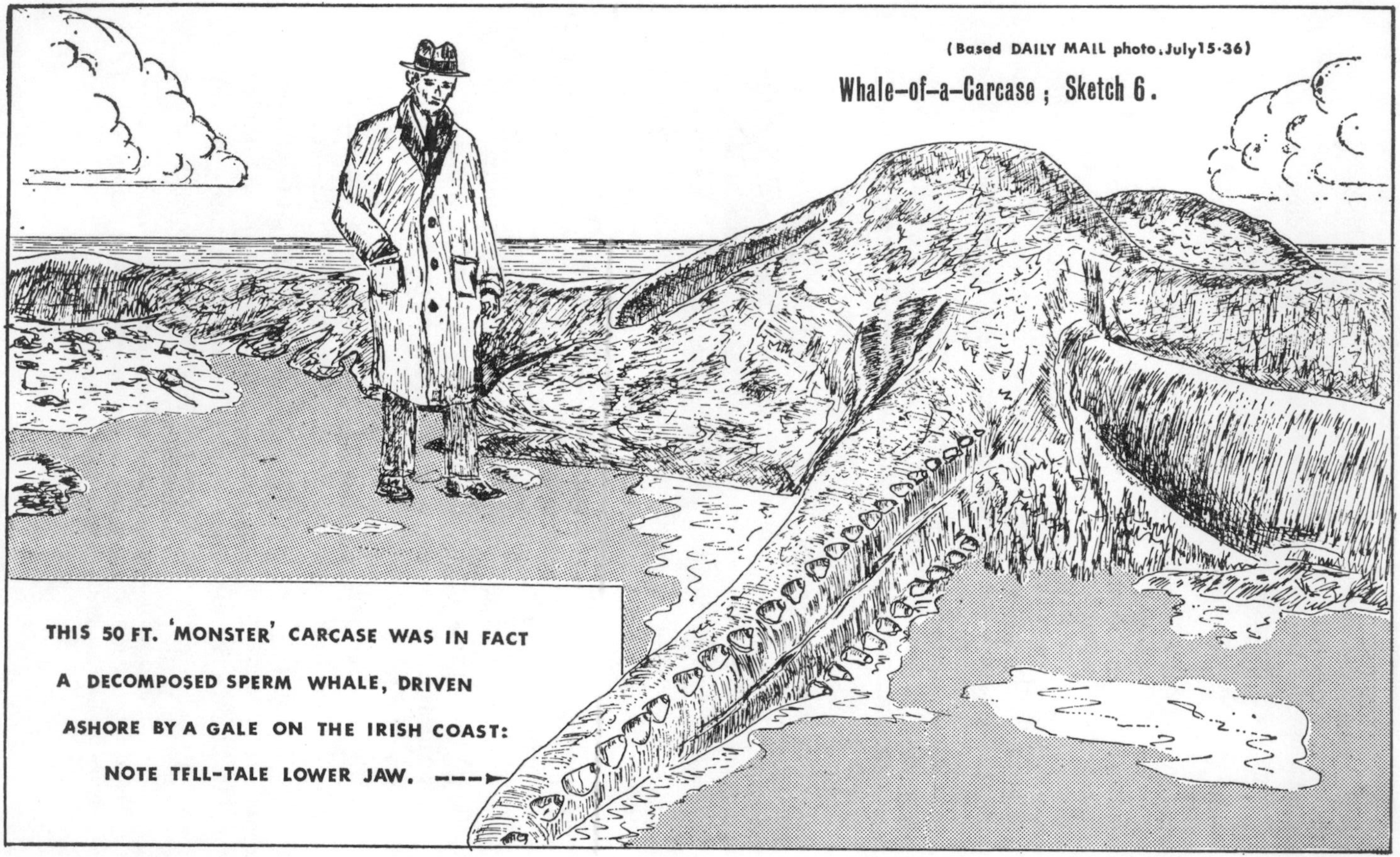

(Based DAILY MAIL photo, July 15-36)

Whale-of-a-Carcase ; Sketch 6.

THIS 50 FT. 'MONSTER' CARCASE WAS IN FACT
A DECOMPOSED SPERM WHALE, DRIVEN
ASHORE BY A GALE ON THE IRISH COAST:
NOTE TELL-TALE LOWER JAW, ----➤

FIG. 6

rarely grow to more than 60 feet, have surprisingly small eyes and are without hair.

Sketch No. 6 shows one of these creatures in a much decomposed state, but with the tell-tale lower jaw giving the clue to its identity.

MONSTERS OF THE TASEK BERA

Roughly in the middle of the Malayan Peninsula there exists a great lake, which is deep in places and filled with curiously wine-coloured water. Plant growth is prolific, and the Tasek Bera, as part of the lake is known is surrounded by tall beds of reeds. It is a remote place, peopled by the Semelai of aboriginal stock, and up until the period of terrorism which plagued the area in the early nineteen fifties, very little was known about it.

Stewart Wavell, author of the book *The Lost World of the East*[2] first visited it in 1951, gaining a ride in an army helicopter. Recognized as an expert in jungle craft, and something of an explorer he was interested in tribal music, and customs – and quickly became friendly with the local headman, who introduced him to the more secret of these.

He was intrigued by a curious legend which explained the origin of the lake, involving a traditional figure called Nagaq – an old man, who, it was said, had caused the lake to be formed centuries before by making a hole in the ground with his staff, from which a flow of water had arisen, drowning all but one or two of the inhabitants.

Wavell inquired why it was the old man was called Nagaq, because he knew the word 'Naga' referred to some kind of a dragon. Reluctantly, the headman admitted a connection, stating that Nagaq today was the term for a giant cobra – and that great serpents of this description lived in the deeper parts of the lake. He said that a fully-grown serpent was as tall as a palm tree. It had a big head like a snake – and a long neck

[2] Souvenir Press, London. 1958.

which thickened near the water, where it was fully 6 feet wide. Sometimes the tail could be seen, but never the body, which remained under water.

Warming to his story he added that the serpents had never been known to attack a man, but that on one occasion a Semelai had been accidentally swallowed when asleep in his canoe. Waking up inside, disturbed by the sudden rush of water he hacked his way out with his *parang*, emerging from the tip of the Monster's tail!

Laughing self-consciously when telling this part of the story, the headman then became more serious . . . 'one thing I have not told you,' he said, 'the serpents have horns on their heads; not hard ones, but soft and small!'

Much amused Wavell returned to civilization, and with the passage of years his recollection of the Semelai and their curious stories slowly faded. The chance of returning to such a remote place was slim – but, something then happened which served to prompt his memory, and decided him to go back and look for the legendary serpents himself.

Returning from the Tasek Bera an officer of the Malay police had an extraordinary tale to tell. Bathing one afternoon at a place close to a projecting headland, where the water was clear and deep, he suffered a fearful shock. Looking back towards the shore, at a distance of about 40 yards he observed the massive head of a snake rising above a fifteen-foot clump of Rassau palm. Its body was enormously thick, smooth, and the colour of slate; and behind it he made out 'two upper contour curves' rising above the surface, which seemed to be a part of the creature. In panic he raced for his boat, and rowed away, but on glancing back he could see the Monster still – watching unperturbed.

Wondering whether the great serpent had been an illusion, caused by some trick of light, or the life-like branch of a tree or some other natural object, Wavell questioned the local Chief of police as to the character of the witness, and was told – 'This officer is utterly reliable and has a fine record. He

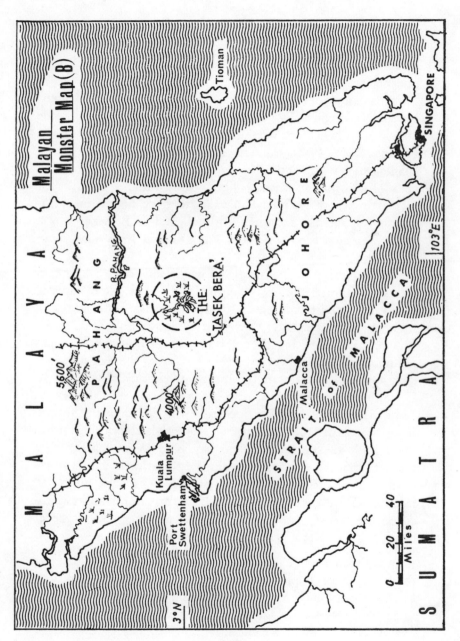

doesn't exaggerate normally and I should accept his word every time. But as for the Monster, I must say it's a bit of a queer story.'

Preparations for an expedition went ahead. Wavell had heard enough to convince him it was worth the effort, which in the absence of a helicopter would mean a journey by canoe up the Pahang River, through miles of untracked jungle. It was a challenge in itself, and while in progress another interesting piece of information came to light. No less than four different natives to whom he talked claimed to have heard an extraordinary sound the monsters emitted. Rarely heard it was a great echoing screech of noise, but different from that of an elephant.

Arriving at last at the headland where the police officer had seen the Monster, the party stopped for a little before moving on to re-establish contact with the Semelai. After days of watching unsuccessfully Wavell decided to go back to the headland before setting off on the homeward journey. He was disappointed and had given up hope of seeing the monsters in a lake so much overgrown by enormous clumps of vegetation. He settled down to watch, with his tape-recorder at the ready. Time passed, but then, unexpectedly, the silence was shattered by a quite extraordinary noise . . . 'A single staccato cry from the middle of the lake chilled my blood with fear. It was a snort: more like a bellow – shrill and strident like a ship's horn, and elephant's trumpet, and sea-lion's bark all rolled into one. I was momentarily petrified then frantically switched on the recorder and waited for the next cry – but it never came . . .'

In 1962 an R.A.F. party of enthusiasts made the journey to the Tasek Bera, hoping to find out more about the monsters, but as no word of their success has been published, it seems they also failed to solve the mystery. But certain it is that Stewart Wavell believes there is something tangible behind it.

THE HUNT FOR THE BURU

In this account a large expedition is involved, which bravely plunges into territory about which little is known even today. The hunt, as the title of the book suggests, is for a legendary creature called the 'Buru' described by primitive tribesmen in terms which suggest it may have been a type of surviving saurian – but let me introduce the subject by quoting from a letter:

19th October, 1961.
Dear Dinsdale,

The Hunt for the Buru, by Ralp Izzard was published in 1951 by Hodder and Stoughton. As this book is scarce I thought I would give you a very brief outline of what it contains. The creature in question can hardly be the same as the sea serpent; but it really does look as though a long-necked saurian type of reptile exists, or did exist within historical times in Northern Assam, so the matter may be pertinent to your own researches.

Here are a few facts:

1. About the end of the last war, C. R. Stonor and J. P. Mills visited a tribe called the Apa Thani in a remote upland valley in Northern Assam, and learned that these people had a tradition that a number of large water animals used to live in a large swamp in the vicinity. They called it the 'Buru' – pronounced as in 'cuckoo' and meaning 'Monster' (the word is clearly akin to the Urdu word 'burra', pronounced as in 'currant' meaning 'big') and said that their ancestors had long ago drained the swamp for cultivation, and killed the Burus, which were now extinct.

2. The Apa Thanis point out three burial sites where the last three Burus were buried.

3. General description of the Apa Thani Buru:

(*a*) Length about 12–14 feet and 'long shaped'.

(*b*) Head about 20 inches long, and elongated into a great snout, flattened at the tip. The eyes were behind the snout.

Teeth, 'flat like those of a man', except for a pair in the upper and lower jaws, which were large and pointed 'like those of a tiger or boar'.

(c) Neck about 3 feet in length, and could be stretched out or drawn in.

(d) Body was roundish, 'the breadth of a man's arm and body across the back' and with a girth such as a man could just put his arms around.

(e) Tail, rounded and tapering and about 5 feet long. Not very pointed. It was fringed at the base, with broad lobes which ran the whole length on either side springing from the dorsal surface of the tail.[3]

(f) Legs, about 20 inches long, with claws on the feet and looked like the forefeet of a burrowing mole. (Against this another informant said, 'it had no legs, the body was like a snake!')

(g) Skin, like that of a scaleless fish. There were no hairs, but three lines of short, blunt spines ran down the back and along each side.

(h) Colour, dark blue, blotched with white, and a broad band of white ran down the belly.

(i) Habits, it lived entirely in the water (fresh) and never came to land. It used to put its neck up out of the water, and make a hoarse bellowing noise. It is believed it did not eat fish, but 'lived on the mud'. Harmless to man. Nothing known of its young or breeding habits, though one informant said there were no eggs, and the young were born alive.

4. So much for the Apa Thani Burus – simply a tradition of an extinct creature – with nothing tangible today, except perhaps the three skeletons, lying under the mud of the old swamp.

5. Later on, Stonor heard an extraordinary account from another tribe, the Daflas, of a swamp valley many miles from the other where the Burus were said to still be in existence. This place was called *Rilo*.

[3] Refer Sketch No. 7.

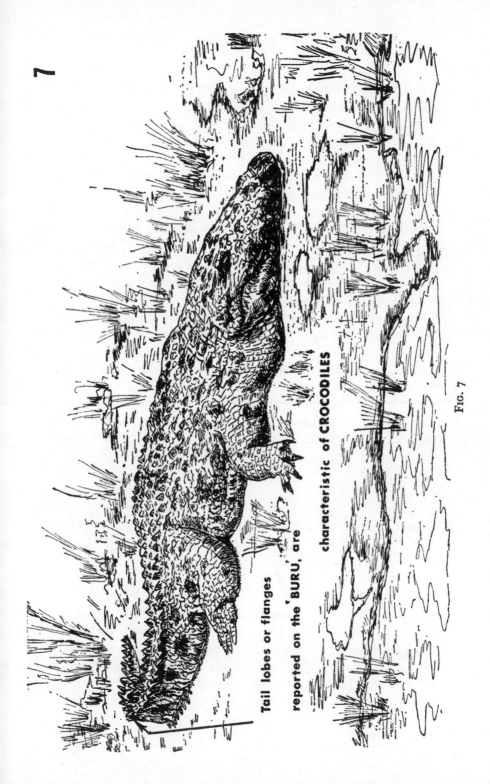

7

Tail lobes or flanges

reported on the 'BURU', are

characteristic of CROCODILES

Fig. 7

6. In 1948, Stonor, Izzard and Hodgkinson, with a large number of porters, visited Rilo, but failed to find the Buru (the same word was used by the two tribes, in spite of the difference in language). The swamp in question was supposed to fill with water between May and September, and become a lake; but this actually did not happen, and the Burus, which were believed to be hibernating, never appeared.

The Rilo Buru had a rough general description similar to the other, was about the size of their domestic buffalo and – according to most informants – had small horns. Scores of Daflas at Rilo swore they had seen them frequently, right up to the previous season: so the Englishmen had to return completely mystified.

Conclusion: It seems doubtful (though possible) whether the Buru exists today. But if it once did, the question is what was it? Some have thought it may have been a type of primitive crocodilian. But, though crocodiles are found in the Brahmaputra, the two Buru swamps are many miles over mountainous country from that river. And as Stonor pointed out in a recent lecture to the Fauna Preservation Society, crocodiles only exist in warm waters, while both Rilo and the Apa Thani valleys have much colder climates. It remains an enigma!

Sincerely,
Morton Marrian.

Shortly after receiving this letter, Marrian kindly lent me his copy of the book. I was absorbed by it; and carefully examined the accompanying map, which was a small section cut from an aeronautical chart. At first I had some difficulty in placing it, due to the large scale effect, but on consulting the new (and splendid) *Times Atlas* I was able to produce a map showing roughly where the Dafla hills are situated, and also the place called Rilo, which is hidden amongst the mountains in the vast and virtually unexplored territory now claimed by both China and India. It lies in fact right in the middle of this 'disputed territory', and in consequence it seems unlikely that any further

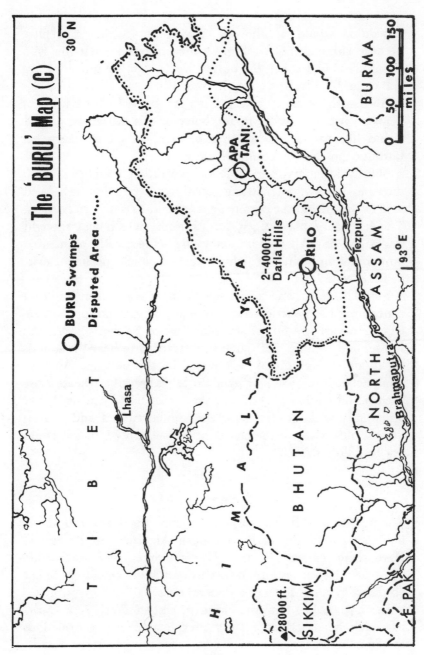

The 'BURU' Map (C)

○ BURU Swamps
Disputed Area ......

30°N

N

BURMA

150

100

50

0

miles

APA TANI

TIBET

Lhasa

HIMALAYA

2-4000ft.
Dafla Hills

RILO

Tezpur

93°E

ASSAM

NORTH

Brahmaputra

BHUTAN

28000 ft.

SIKKIM

E.PAK.

expedition would be allowed to visit it – which is a pity, because although the book gives the impression that the Rilo Burus are now defunct, the burial sites at Apa Thani valley are known and might prove worth excavating.

And so the mystery of the Buru stands, with little hope of being solved, but before taking leave of this intriguing book I would like to refer to another passage, which will serve as introduction to the section following.

Shortly after arriving at Rilo, expedition members fell to discussing tales of other strange creatures, reputed to have been seen in Assam and the remote area beyond its northern borders. The legendary black tiger, for example, which was thought might one day fall to a hunter's rifle – the grossly pigmented opposite of an albino, or 'white' tiger of which specimens exist in India today.

But of the yarns and stories spun none was stranger than that concerning the experience of two tea-planters, hunting at the edge of a vast swamp, near a place called Sadiya . . . 'As the sun set one evening, both men were startled to hear the sounds of a ponderous animal wallowing in the swamp. As they approached they were amazed to see a reptilian head raise itself on an endless neck above the reeds. Both men fired, but apparently without effect, for the animal turned and heaved its vast bulk away to the centre of the swamp whither it could not be followed.'

THE MYSTERIOUS BEAST

For this inquiry it is necessary to leave the East, and travel half-way round the earth to South America: to Paraguay. Here, some years ago a young Englishman enjoyed the free life of a true adventurer, and in traversing this enormous continent obtained material for half a dozen books.

In 1954 C. W. Thurlow-Craig published *Black Jack's Spurs* in which he describes a truly inexplicable occurrence. This briefly is his story:

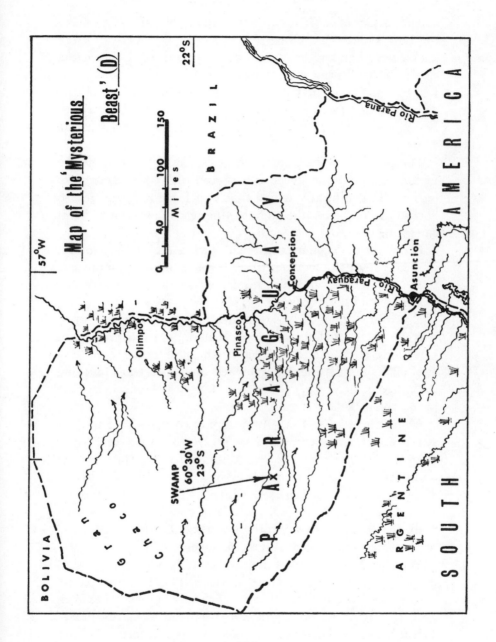

After a tour of service as an officer in the Royal Navy, during the First World War, Craig set sail for South America to seek his fortune. Landing in Argentina, he first worked on a cattle *estancia* before journeying north from place to place, and job to job, arriving ultimately in Paraguay – and it was during the course of this journey he came to hear of the 'Mysterious Beast' – a more or less fabulous creature which lived in the swamps.

The Beast, it was said, was a type of snake, as thick round the middle as a horse, but twice as long and with a poisonous spike on its tail. The head was like that of a large dog, and it also barked like one – but the oddest thing was the way in which it caught its prey.

It did this by suction, combined with a dash of hypnotism. It would spy its quarry, entice it through hypnotic influence, then by breathing in apply the deadly suction, against which nothing could stand for very long.

Not overly impressed by this description, Craig proceeded northwards only to find the story repeated, though with different variations. He began to wonder whether the 'Beast' might not, after all, have some foundation in fact – and later, when ranching in Paraguay, he was to witness something which may even have been caused by it!

About three miles from the junction of the Alto Paraguay River and a tributary, the Rio Jacare, or Alligator Stream there is a crossing called El Paso Limpo. Here the water is clear and deep, and some forty yards across. At one side of it there is an incongruous landmark; a white tombstone. Inscribed in English it commemorates the death of one Thomas, a Welshman, the younger of two brothers working for the Port Ranch, which Craig was later to run as manager.

One day Thomas had been sent to the Paso Limpo to collect cattle, which a young Paraguayan called José, had rounded up on the far side of the river. Thomas first sent his own horse over, and then stripping off his clothes prepared to swim after it. When half-way across he . . . 'gave one yell of terror and disappeared in a huge swirl of water, thrown up by something very big indeed'.

In due course a launch was sent up from Pinasco to investigate. The river bed was grappled for two hundred yards in each direction, and submerged obstructions cleared with dynamite. Nothing was found, no flesh, or bones, or clothing: and this added to the mystery, because it was known that alligators (which normally attack on the surface) generally hide their prey under some log or crevice until suitably decomposed.

Speculation ran riot. The local Indians and Paraguayans swore the 'Mysterious Beast' lived in the waters of the pass; but others thought a giant catfish or manguruyú had swallowed the unfortunate Thomas. These fish grow to an enormous size, weighing half a ton or more, and are voracious scavengers – and there are unconfirmed reports of specimens attaining a length of 18 feet.[4] In his book *Spinners Delight*, Thurlow-Craig describes an incident in which a Labrador dog was taken by a manguruyú in such a manner, while retrieving a shot duck in a river near Asuncion. An event witnessed by several people – but on that occasion the tail of the great fish broke surface, giving the clue to its identity.

Some time later, in 1930, during an afternoon siesta, the ranch-hand José broke in on Craig in a great state of excitement . . . 'Don Carlos,' he shouted, 'the Beast is again at the Pass . . . I was putting those young steers across when the rearmost one was seized from underwater and vanished, even as Senhor Thomas vanished. There was a great wash when he went down, but I could not see what took him!'

A second report from José, the solitary witness, made some people believe he had invented the whole affair – but those who knew him thought differently.

Time passed, and again the excitement died down, but some months later it became necessary to swim a whole herd across

[4] Major Percy Fawcett, the explorer wrote in his memoirs: 'In the Paraguay River there is a freshwater shark, huge but toothless, said to attack men and swallow them if it gets the chance . . .'

the waters of the Pass, to avoid the threat of flooding. Craig was made responsible, and after swimming a thousand head across the river without mishap, disaster struck once more; but this time there *were* several witnesses . . . 'the third and last sweep accounted for ten stragglers. As we were putting them over the last animal, a three-month-old calf that was swimming strongly behind its mother suddenly gave a great bawl, and was pulled under. I was within twenty yards of that calf, together with José and old Rufino, my foreman. We saw no fish, no alligator, nothing but a great swirl of water . . .'

This was to be the last disappearance while the author was still with the Port Ranch, but the story does not end here – not quite. About eighteen months later, at a place some 60 miles to the west of the Alligator River, when herding a small group of cattle in company with a couple of local Indians, one of them happened to remark that a few leagues distant there existed the 'Swamp of the Beast' – which was a very bad place to go. Intrigued, Craig went in search of it, though unaccompanied; both Indians having suddenly found more urgent business to attend to. It was not far away, and well worth the visit. A peaceful place about a mile across, surrounded by tall papyrus but with deep clear water in the middle. It was full of water-fowl; discounting the tale that in the haunt of the Beast 'nothing lived'.

Riding slowly round it, scores of animal tracks could be seen leading to the water – but as Craig made his way forward at a leisurely pace he came across something which dispelled his mood of complacency . . . 'not the Beast, but a track such as I had never seen before, made by something either going into or coming out of the water, nearly 3 feet wide and about 6 inches pressed into the firm mud. It might possibly have been made by a great snake, 35 feet long or thereabouts . . . it had not been made by a big alligator, either, for there were no claw marks on either side. At that moment the mule took fright; and so did I . . . we left that place!'

Now, what could it have been, this 'Mysterious Beast'? What

type of powerful carnivorous animal could have snatched a fully-grown man, and then a steer, and a calf? – leaving only a great swirl of water to mark their disappearance.

There seem to be three possibilities – a large alligator which had learned to attack from underwater: a gigantic manguruyú or catfish: or the Mysterious Beast, whatever that might really be. To be honest I have yet to be convinced that an alligator cannot attack from underwater, because I have seen a crocodile take a waterbird in this fashion, though it surfaced to swallow it, and as the Rio Jacare was full of alligators from which it gained its name, we cannot rule them out entirely. However, it should be remembered that the local people who lived amongst these rivers infested with alligators (or Caimans, to be more exact) did so on the basis of practical experience, which is usually the best type of experience.

The manguruyú theory, improbable though it must appear is interesting – particularly because of the episode of the Labrador dog, which seems to establish it as a possibility; although the idea of a catfish swallowing a man and a young steer does seem a bit incredible.

This is the theory, however, to which Craig subscribes because of an experience he had some time after the event, when he witnessed and actually shot a type of armoured catfish as it was crossing from one pool to another. It appeared to be sculling its way across the mud on its pectoral fins – completely out of water. He felt that if a catfish $2\frac{1}{2}$ feet long could behave in such a manner, a very much bigger one might do so too, and thus explain the amphibious nature of the 'Beast' described by Indians who claimed to have seen it: but before accepting any view I would like to introduce another theory, in explanation.

South America is the home of some of the largest snakes found on earth. The boa constrictor and the giant anaconda, closely related to that other enormous snake, the python. They are constricting snakes, which kill their prey by flipping coils of their bodies about it and squeezing it to the point of asphyxia, before swallowing the animal whole.

Boa constrictors have been known to reach 18 feet in length, and there have been claims and counter claims to the largest anaconda. Snakes of 29 feet have certainly been killed, and there are persistent rumours which infer that anacondas of vastly greater dimensions exist; 40, 60 and even 80 feet in length! In his remarkable book *On the Track of Unknown Animals*,[5] Dr. Bernard Heuvelmans devotes the best part of a chapter on the Giant Anaconda, and presents some interesting evidence. One account describes the experience of an Englishman in 1907; the famous Major Percy Fawcett, sent out to survey virtually unexplored territory separating the borders of western Brazil, northern Bolivia and Peru. The Royal Geographical Society of London sponsored this expedition, during which Fawcett shot a colossal anaconda.

The account appears in his personal memoirs: It seems that while drifting slowly down the Rio Abuna River the triangular head of an enormous serpent broke surface near the boat. The creature swam for the shore and began to emerge. It was of a tremendous length, and disregarding the shouts of fear and warning from his native crew, Fawcett raised his rifle, and sent a ·44 soft-nosed bullet into it, breaking its spine some 10 feet below the head. The animal writhed and twisted, and great tremors ran up and down its body.

Stepping ashore he approached the reptile, though with a certain apprehension. As far as he was able to measure some 45 feet of body lay out of the water, and about 17 feet within it – a grand total of 60 feet or more! But, surprisingly it was no more than a foot thick at its widest part. Attempts were made to cut a piece out of the skin, but due to the frightening muscular contractions were not pressed home. In the Major's own words: 'A penetrating fetid odour emanated from the snake, probably its breath, which is believed to have a stupefying effect, first attracting then paralysing its prey. Everything about this snake was repulsive. Such large specimens as this may not be common, but the trails in the swamps reach 6 feet

[5] Rupert Hart-Davis, 1958.

in width and support the statements of Indians and rubber
pickers that the anaconda sometimes reaches an incredible
size, altogether dwarfing that shot by me. The Brazilian bound-
ary Commission told me of one killed in the *Rio Paraguay* (my
italics) exceeding 80 feet in length!'

I find his last statement interesting because the Rio Paraguay
is the river into which the Alligator River flows. Furthermore
the reference to the fetid breath of the snake first attracting and
then paralysing its prey – bears a striking resemblance to the
semi-hypnotic performance attributed to the 'Mysterious
Beast' – though as Heuvelmans points out, it is in fact a quite
mistaken hypothesis, even accepting that the breath of carnivores is often foul in the extreme.

The theory I would like to put forward, therefore, is that the
disappearances in the Alligator River may have in fact been
caused by an enormous snake. The water at the 'pass' was some
12 feet deep, and as snakes swim in a series of graceful lateral
undulations one might well have snatched its prey without being
seen: and the idea of a 60 or 80-foot carnivorous snake taking a
man is not by any means absurd. There are of course tales of
pythons and boa constrictors swallowing whole sheep, and deer
complete with horns, but although these are sometimes exaggerated it is a matter of record that on the island of Salebabu
(Talaud Islands) a fourteen-year-old Malayan boy who was
killed and swallowed by a 17-foot reticulate python. This
account appears in a very recent book called *The Giant Snakes*[6]
by Clifford H. Pope, which provides a wealth of information on
the natural history of giant constricting snakes – the anaconda,
the boa constrictor and the largest pythons, of which there are
four distinct species. Mr. Pope is an authority on reptiles and as
he owned a pet python, called Sylvia, has been able to study
these coldly expressionless animals at first hand. There is a
section in his book which deals with reports of attacks on man,
from which the following excerpt is taken:

[6] Publishers: Alfred A. Knopf, New York 1961, and Routledge and
Kegan Paul, London.

'More recently, Rolf Blomberg recounted the fate of a thir-
teen-year-old boy who disappeared while swimming at the
mouth of Yasuni River, a tributary of the Napo River of Peru
and Ecuador. Friends saw bubbles rising where the ill-fated
boy had disappeared; one of them dived, only to find what he
thought was the body of an anaconda. A day and night of
constant search by the victim's father revealed the reptile lying
half in and half out of the water. It had disgorged the lost boy,
and was dispatched with five shots from a rifle. From this same
source comes the story of a man who was killed by an anaconda
while swimming in the Napo – also Kirt Severin adds an
"authenticated attack"; A man was pulled into a river by an
anaconda while he was watering cattle, the snake seized his
legs, coiled round him as he stood in the water, pulled him in
and drowned him.'

It is difficult for a layman to conceive even a very big snake
swallowing a human being – and from a technical point of view
it is unlikely, because contrary to popular belief the process of
constriction does not usually crush the bones of the body. In
most cases only enough force is employed to suffocate, and both
the shoulders and pelvic girdle of a man present a major
obstacle. However, if a 17-foot python could swallow a boy of
fourteen (the body was later removed from its interior) it seems
reasonable to suppose a much bigger specimen could swallow a
fully grown man.

Sketch No. 8 shows how the snake coils itself about its unfortunate prey preparatory to swallowing it – and although the
effect is repulsive, it portrays yet another adaption in nature
which is altogether marvellous. It also explains why zoo snakes
are usually fed at night; though meals of this kind are surprisingly infrequent! Clifford Pope says these big snakes have the
ability to live for two and a half *years* without food. An example
occurred in Frankfurt in Germany, where a female reticulate
python fasted some 570 days; resumed regular feeding for a
time, and then fasted another 415 days before eating again.
This extraordinary feat is explained by the animal's ability to

AN INDIAN PYTHON CONSTRICTING ITS PREY.

Sketch 8.

FIG. 8

really 'stoke the furnace' with one gigantic meal. For example, research has shown that if a 17-foot, 70-lb. python swallows a 20-lb. pig it supplies itself with more than 400 times its daily energy need – which (if I may be a little childish) must prove something of a bore for the constrictor.

In contrast to these cold scientific facts, and my sketch, which is based on a photograph, the delightful picture appearing on Plate 10 shows the python in entirely different circumstances.

The print is an original, one of a series of grotesque and barbaric animal pictures by *Stradano*, in 1580 – and if due allowance is made for artistic licence, the whiskers and other appendages the snakes are recognizable – if only because one of them can be seen in process of swallowing a goat (in the background).

119

The Latin inscription reads . . . 'India produces a huge serpent with vigorous body, which driven by hunger lies lurking in the water. It emerges, hangs down from a shady tree, uncoils and seizes a beast: but is killed with clubs and flames.'

But to return to South America and its stories of serpentine monsters – Dr. Heuvelmans reports on another type of aquatic snake; of such staggering dimensions as to appear quite unbelievable – which seems altogether different from the anaconda.

Lorenz Hagenbeck, one-time director of the Hamburg Zoo, and son of Carl Hagenbeck, the famous animal collector, appears to have been convinced of its existence – for the good reason he knew two Roman Catholic priests who had seen the creature. Fathers Frickel and Heinz – the latter describing his experience in no uncertain terms:

'During the great floods of 1922, on May 22nd at about three o'clock to be exact, I was being taken home by canoe on the Amazon from Obidos; when suddenly I noticed something surprising in midstream. I distinctly recognized a giant water-snake at a distance of some 30 yards. To distinguish it from the *sucurijú*, the natives who accompanied me named the reptile *sucurijú gigante* (giant boa), because of its enormous size.

Coiled up in two rings the monster drifted quietly and gently downstream. My quaking crew had stopped paddling. Thunder-struck, we all stared at the frightful beast. I reckoned that its body was as thick as an oil-drum, and its visible length some 80 feet. When we were far enough away and my boatmen dared to speak again, they said the monster would have crushed us like a box of matches, if it had not previously consumed several large capybaras.'[7]

Questioning his boatmen afterwards Father Heinz was told that a similar snake had been killed south of Obidos, on the river bank, while swallowing a capybara. Later, when opened up it was found to contain four more of these huge rodents (an

[7] Dr. Bernard Heuvelmans: Eng. Trans. *On the Track of Unknown Animals* (1958), p. 293.

adult measures 2–3 feet in length and stands 18 inches at the shoulder) – and near by two large round excrements were found, full of animal hair and with a bone from an ox's foot sticking out of one of them!

It is difficult for an impartial observer to read this chapter without concluding that there really must be some kind of gigantic water-snake, or unknown animal living in this area. On the strength of much inquiry Hagenbeck even put an estimate on its size: Length – up to 130 feet. Diameter – 2ft. 6 ins. at the widest part. Weight – about 5 tons. Colouring – dark chestnut, the belly mottled with dirty white. Eyes were exceptionally large; made more terrifying by luminescence, which appeared distinctly as a bluish light on the water surface at night.

While on an expedition, Father Frickel, a Franciscan priest from Oriscima had approached to within a few paces of the head of one of these creatures, lying out of water. He stated that its eyes were 'as big as plates'.

Apart from verbal evidence two photographs purporting to show this 'giant boa' were published in a Rio de Janeiro newspaper – and during his researches Father Heinz was able to gain assurance that the negatives had not been tampered with. These photo's show two different snakes, one killed in 1933 and the other in 1948. The first was so huge four men were unable to lift its head; and the second measured 115 feet – according to the reports. Both snakes had been killed with machine-guns.

Paul Gregor in his recent book *Amazon Fortune Hunter*[8] makes reference to the killing of another gigantic snake by a Brazilian army patrol at a place called Amapa, near the borders of French Guiana, in 1954 . . . 'the reports of the O.C. Northern Region claimed that this particular snake measured 120 feet; double the length of the one seen by Fawcett!' . . . and there is a second and in some ways confusing account in this book of some

[8] Published 1962, Edition Pensee Modern, Paris, and Souvenir Press, London.

awful aquatic Monster, which came close to upsetting his canoe, and although dramatic in style it gives the impression that he had a real and quite terrifying experience.

Travelling down a tributary of the Amazon in a canoe, with two native guides, Paul Gregor heard tell of the 'Controller'; an apparently legendary water-monster, living in a certain place, which would not allow anyone to pass at night. Ridiculing the thought he forced onwards, but was soon to witness the appearance of a bluish light moving on the surface – the sight of which petrified his two companions, who promptly turned the canoe and made for shore. Later the same night, the author, who was inwardly more afraid of an attack by his crew than the Monster, forced a resumption of the journey virtually at gunpoint.

Sliding over the inky water, he began to regret this hasty action, because he distinctly heard the sound of something large squelching about in the mud – and then a fearful stench of decomposition assailed his nostrils. For a while attention was diverted by a squall, which nearly capsized the boat, but when it abated the Monster closed in upon them . . . 'Within ten yards I saw what I can only describe as a "thing". There were two gaping holes in the darkness, two round glittering holes about 18 inches apart; they were dark blue, with flashes of brick red; as large as the fist of a child'.

There was also a peculiar loud clicking noise, and the sounds of stertorous breathing. Almost paralysed with fear Gregor switched on his electric torch . . . 'I saw what appeared to be a small floating island of grass emerge from the water. Immediately afterwards I realized that this was not grass but a mane of long hair,[9] such as one might find on a great horse covered with mud . . . I stared with mesmerized attention, I could make out a gigantic body, round and glacis . . .'

Galvanized into action Gregor siezed his Winchester, and

[9] If this is a correct observation it would seem to classify Mr. Gregor's Monster as similar in type to the marine animal first described by Olaus Magnus – and not the *sucurijù gigante*!

firing like a madman emptied the 17-shot magazine at point-blank range. The Monster submerged in a whirl of foam . . . 'an enormous flail lashed the water in fury, making the canoe spin round on its axis . . .'

So ended the encounter: the experience of which seems to have had a lasting effect upon the author, though he admits he still does not know what to make of it.

Stories like these are difficult to assess, at second or third hand, and however much we would like to believe in them it is necessary to weigh the evidence carefully before jumping to conclusions: but with this object in view, and the *sucurijú gigante* more specifically, I would like to add some information which came into my hands unexpectedly.

On the 10th of May, 1964, I received a letter from Mr. G. W. Creighton, M.A., F.R.G.S., of Rickmansworth, Herts, in which he said: 'Herewith my notes and two precious photos. This material embodies all I know or have heard or read about the giant snakes . . . the photos will certainly be of interest, but is there anything that can be made of them that is reproducible?'

Examining the enclosures I found his notes, entitled 'Giant South American Water-Serpents' to contain much factual and legendary information on the anaconda – and two newspaper photographs allegedly of the *sucurijú gigante*, together with translated inscriptions.

At first glance I could see that the pictures would not reproduce a second time (the minute dots resulting from the news-print screening process prevent this) – but felt that with a little patience I could probably convert them to pen and ink line-drawings using a technique applied in engineering drawing, which is precisely accurate.

Results can be seen on Plate 15 and Fig. 9; and, with regard to the inscriptions Mr. Creighton writes:

'While I was stationed as H.M. Consul at Pernambuco, from 1947 to 1950 the first picture appeared in the *Diario de Pernambuco* of 24th January, 1948. . . . The text beneath the 'photo reads:

"SUCURIJÚ WEIGHING FIVE TONS. The snakes of Brazil's interior have given rise to innumerable tales and legends, in which they appear with monstrous proportions, swallowing bullocks entire with even greater ease than the city dweller eats his cheese sandwich. Only recently, the Rio de Janeiro Zoo acquired a specimen which reporters described as 'monumental' in size. This was a boa constrictor (giboya) 8 metres in length.

"Well, here in this picture our readers can see a giant anaconda (sucurijú) captured alive on the banks of the Amazon. It is engaged in its siesta after having pulverized a steer, the horns of which animal were hanging from its mouth, which was dilated to an unimaginable degree. A band of Indian half-breeds managed to put a rope round the creature and bring it into Manaos, towed by a river tug. There it served as an object of popular curiosity, until a burst of machine-gun fire put paid to the monster.

"The snake weighed five tons, its diameter was 80 centimetres (31·5 inches), and it measured no less than 40 metres (131 feet.)

"The photograph was received here yesterday by air from Manaos, and we owe its reproduction in our pages to the kindness of Senhor Miguel Gastão de Oliveira, manager of the Banco do Povo to whom the picture had been sent by one of his brothers who resides in Manaos, the capital of the state of Amazonas."

'The second photograph appeared in the newspaper *A Provincia do Pará* (Province of Pará) for 28th April, 1949, and was specially secured at my request by H.M. Consul at Belém (Pará) as the attached letter shows. This picture shows a snake floating in a river, with river bank and buildings beyond, but it is a pity that no attempt has been given to provide a yardstick by which it can be measured.

'A PROVINCIA DO PARÁ' 28th. April 1949

—'Não será esse monstro a legítima "cobra-grande" da legende ?'

(Is not this monster the genuine "Great-Serpent" of legend ?)

FIG. 9. The newsprint photo on which this pen-sketch is based gives a better impression of buoyant rotundity, which leads me to believe the snake-like object is the body of a dead 'sucurijú gigante', floating belly uppermost. Length was estimated at well over a hundred feet. The original picture is remarkably clear.

'I have never shown these pictures to any naturalist, or indeed anybody in England, so have no idea what a photographic specialist would say about them, or what deductions he could make. The text beneath the second picture reads as follows:

"THE 'GIANT SERPENT' DOES IN FACT EXIST! Inherited from the Indians, and deeply rooted in the minds of the population of the Amazon Valley, there is found everywhere, throughout the interior of Amazonia, the certainty of the existence of the 'Giant Serpent'. We civilized folk consider the tales told by the Indian as being like the many tales told of El Dorado; mere popular superstition and hearsay. But he, the Indian, 'knows' that the Giant Serpent exists, and tells us incredible things about his vast body the size of a boat, his head the size of a paddle, and his vast ferocious eyes that light up the river like beacons. That there is some truth in what the Indian says is more than abundantly proved by the sensational photograph which we reproduce above. It shows a gigantic sucurijú, said to be about 45 metres long (147 feet), floating on the Abuna River (Territory of Guaporé, Brazilian western frontier) where the photographer, Senhor Joaquim Alencar, took it by surprise The negative which we have had the opportunity to examine was developed here in Pará yesterday, and a copy passed to us Is not this monster the genuine 'Great Serpent' of legend?"'

Is it indeed! That is a question to which many people would like to know the answer, but when first examining Mr. Creighton's photographs I concluded that both were of different snakes to those reportedly photographed before, despite the coincident date of 1948 for one of them – because as Heuvelmans states, the other snake photographed in that year came ashore and hid in the old fortifications of Fort Abuna in the Guaporé territory.[10] It was also said to measure 115 feet, as opposed to the 130 feet of the 1948 Manaos specimen.

[10] This is nowhere near Manaos, which is near the conjunction of the Rio Negro, and the main flood of the Amazon, about 800 miles from its outlet.

But whatever their origin both pictures deserve the closest scrutiny, and in poring over them I came to certain conclusions – which in turn relate to particular features in each picture.

Obviously, the pictures are either genuine, or faked – because at such short range there can be no question of mistaken identity – they are both of *snakes* – or facsimilies of snakes, and if this is so the case for faking simply becomes resolved in terms of:

(*a*) Planting a live or dead snake of known species, and faking its surroundings to produce a false scale effect, or:

(*b*) Disguising the corpse of a known snake to make it look different, or:

(*c*) Employing model snakes, made up to suit the imagination, and/or photographing drawings of snakes, and surroundings.

Examining each photo in turn I noticed that in one the snake's surroundings were so blurred they contributed nothing to scale effect, whereas in the other they were perfectly clear but valueless as a yardstick – the building on the far shore being too distant. And yet in both pictures the *impression* gained is that the snakes are of great size. To produce this effect outside of nature without introducing some sort of yardstick means that our faker is a man of astonishing subtlety, and artistry – because he has successfully and deliberately avoided using the one tool available to him to create an impression of size – which is comparison.

Considering the other faking alternatives, I would rule them out one by one. For example, there are features in the 'on land' photograph which (if you know anything at all about the anatomy of snakes) knock out the possibility of a disguised body, or a model, or a picture of a snake, on similar grounds of unbelievable subtlety – and this leaves only one remaining alternative: 'the planting of a live or dead snake of known species ...'

The problem of comparing all the known types of snake with that shown in Plate No. 7 is not too difficult, despite the fact there are some 2,300–2,400 different snakes – because these fall into distinct groups; and if representatives from the viperids, the crotalids, elapids and colubrids are examined it is apparent that with the exception of the very big constricting snakes in the latter group – there is no real similarity – and even in this group the comparison is superficial.

One of the first things that struck me when looking at this photograph, was that although the beast appeared to have an enormous blunt-snouted head of giant-snake type it was altogether different to that of the anaconda, boa constrictor and python. For one thing it had eyes which were much too large, and a great bag of a mouth, the mottled white markings on which were unlike those on the anaconda, which in old age sometimes develops jowls beneath the lower jaw.

Furthermore, the irregularity or 'lumpiness' of its body was positive proof of it being very big, because in all smaller snakes the body is remarkably regular: this characteristic applies only to the giants – if we disregard the case of the recently swallowed meal.

Another thing: in the photograph at the *sixth* convolution the body is at its visible greatest – whereas on the largest of known snakes, the reticulate python, skeletal rib-structure is clearly at its greatest at the *fourth* convolution, as shown in Plate No. 16.

This suggests to me that the snake in the photograph is indeed of hugely greater dimensions than any known snake, and that in consequence the second clearer photograph of it supposedly floating on the Abuna River should be examined with equal concentration.

Here again the impression of great size is gained, and also inanimacy – the long line of the body, with both extremities tailing off below water lies without a ripple on the oily surface – its distinct white and darkly-blotched markings accentuate its buoyant rotundity – and it is this feature which makes one stop to think. Surely no snake would have a specific gravity so low? Because in the middle the body is floating more than half out of water. The S.G. of an anaconda cannot be much less than 1, which is that of water, and thus it could not possibly float in this manner.

But if the markings are different to other snakes (and they certainly are) they partly fit the description of the sucurijú, which is said to be chestnut brown, with its belly mottled a dirty white.

Could this buoyant part in the picture be the upturned belly of a sucurijú? – A dead sucurijú, floating on the surface, with the long internal cavities of its body inflated? *It fits the picture* – which I would otherwise have to reject on the grounds of too much buoyancy. Furthermore, the extremities in the picture do not float at all – they lie below water – which one might expect to be the case. The weight of the head, (and release of gasses formed at that end through the mouth) and the 'solid' part of the extreme tail could cause this.

If this is indeed a sucurijú, it has to be a dead one, floating upside down on the current of the Abuna River – which is an interesting hypothesis, because when looking back through the data on photographs, I found what could be a co-relationship. Dr. Bernard Heuvelmans records[11] that . . . 'The second photograph was taken in 1948. The snake, which was said to measure 115 feet in length, crawled ashore and hid in the old fortifications of Fort Abuana in the Guaporé territory. It needed 500 machine-gun bullets to put paid to it. The speed with which bodies decompose in the tropics and the fact that its skin was of no commercial value may explain why *it was pushed back in the stream at once*.'

The italics are mine – because although the photo of the snake floating on the river was published by *A Provincia do Pará* at Belém (more than 1,000 mile away, at the mouth of the Amazon) on 28th April, 1949 – there is nothing to indicate *when* it was taken: and if there is in fact any coincidence of dates between the taking of this photograph and the one at Fort Abuna at some time in 1948 – it is possible they could both be of the same snake.

If so, it would corroborate my theory, and Dr. Heuvelmans' record – and incidentally show that estimates of length are

[11] *On The Track of Unknown Animals*, Part Four, Chap. 13.

usually in excess of the actual, because the snake on shore was said to be 35 metres (115 feet), and would presumably have been measured after being killed, and the body seen on the river estimated at 'about 45 metres' (147 feet).

Efforts to obtain more accurate information on these dates have not as yet proved successful, so the matter remains undecided: but with regard to the pictures of these two snakes, after very careful examination, and thought, I have come to the conclusion that the original photographs are genuine and as far as it is possible to tell unretouched,[12] and I believe too that they show the '*sucurijú gigante*', which is in truth an excessively rare and unknown species of constricting snake, of titanic – one might say Satanic appearance and size – which is occasionally to be found in that immense area of scarcely explored tropical wilderness through which flows the mighty Amazon and its tributary rivers.

I would hazard a guess too, that after the successful conclusion of operations at Loch Ness, zoologists will be more prepared to admit to their continuing state of fundamental ignorance, in this field, and join together in pursuit of it, which, with world communications as they are could become a matter of no small scientific, and human interest.

THE 'OSBORNE' LEVIATHAN

'In June 1877 the Lords Commissioners of the Admiralty received official reports from officers of the Royal Yacht *Osborne*, relative to a large marine animal seen off Sicily; the documents were forwarded to the Right Hon. R. A. Cross, Secretary of State for the Home Department, who did me the honour to request my opinion on the matter . . .'

So reads the opening paragraph from a chapter written by the great zoologist Frank Buckland, in 1882. It is from his book *Notes and Jottings from Animal Life*, and refers to one the oddest

[12] Retouching of photographs in a newspaper is sometimes a necessary procedure if a good reproduction is to be obtained.

and best documented marine Monster sightings on record. One might consider it to be a classic case, because it describes a creature of unknown species of gigantic size, and stems from an accurate and reliable source.

Commander Pearson of the *Osborne* in forwarding accounts of the three officers who saw the beast wrote: 'I myself saw the fish through a telescope, but at too great a distance (about 400 yards) to be able to give a detailed description; but I distinctly saw a seal-shaped head, of immense size, large flappers, and part of a huge body.'

Lieutenant Haynes wrote: 'On the evening of June 2nd the sea being perfectly smooth, my attention was first called by seeing a ridge of fins above the surface of the water, extending about 30 feet, and varying about 5 or 6 feet in height. On inspecting it by means of a telescope at about one and a half cable's distance, I distinctly saw a head, two flappers, and about 30 feet of an animal's shoulder. The head, as nearly as I could judge, was about 6 feet thick, the neck narrower, about 4 to 5 feet, the shoulder about 15 feet across, and the flappers each about 15 feet in length. The movements of the flappers were those of a turtle, and the animal resembled a huge seal, the resemblance being strongest about the back of the head. I could not see the length of the head – but from its crown or top to just below the shoulder (where it became immersed) I should reckon about 50 feet. The tail end I did not see, it being under the water – unless the ridge of fins to which my attention was first attracted, and which had disappeared by the time I had got a telescope, was really the continuation of the shoulder to the end of the body. The animal's head was not always above water, but was thrown upwards, remaining above for a few seconds at a time and then disappearing. There was an entire absence of "blowing" or "spouting". I herewith enclose a sketch (A) showing the view of the ridge of fins, and (B) of the animal in the act of propelling itself by its two flappers.'

Lieutenant Douglas M. Forsyth wrote: 'At five p.m. on the 2nd inst. while passing cape St. Vito, north coast of Sicily, I

10

THE 'OSBORNE' LEVIATHAN

Sketch (B)

As seen through a telescope by officers of the Royal Yacht. June 1887.

Head to visible base of 'shoulder'—50 ft. Body width—15 ft. Fins — 15 ft.

Fig. 10

observed a large black-looking object on the starboard quarter, distant about two cables; and on examining it with a telescope, I found it to be a huge monster, having a head about fifteen or 20 feet in length. The breadth I could not observe. The head was round and full at the crown. The animal was slowly swimming in a westerly direction, propelling itself by means of two large flappers or fins, somewhat in the manner of a seal. I also saw a portion of the body of the animal, and that part was certainly not under 45 or 50 feet in length.'

Mr. Moore the engineer, also wrote a few lines confirming that he had seen the ridge of fins with the naked eye; but not the body. He said they extended for about 40 feet, and were 7 or 8 feet in height, as far as he could judge.

Armed with these clear and quite authentic reports, Frank Buckland sought the written opinions of Professor Owen, Mr. A. D. Bartlett of the Zoological Gardens, Captain David Gray of the whaling ship *Eclipse*, and a Mr. Henry Lee; and in due course sent these to the Lords of the Admiralty, together with his own.

Reading through them one cannot help being struck by the contrasting attitudes of the two naturalists, Bartlett and Owen; both competent and famous men. In his reply Professor Owen disposes of the four officers' statements in just a few lines, which suggest that at the distance they could well have been mistaken, and that as the observations were made by those not conversant with natural history, he could not form any opinion worth recording! He goes on to say, 'there are no grounds for calling it a "sea monster" ', but ends up by drawing attention to the (then) Admiralty Manual of Scientific Enquiry, which describes with uncommon good sense what action should be taken, and what notes recorded when 'an object is seen afloat, and attracts notice by its magnitude or other peculiarity . . .'

All things considered Owen's reply is something of a 'stone waller', whereas that from Mr. Bartlett is much less dogmatic. In a long and carefully worded letter he weighs all the pros and cons and concludes that he is 'unable to identify the figures and description with any known animal. With the dimensions given, it is most conclusive – in fact, proof postive – that no known species of animal was seen, the dimensions being so extraordinary that they admit of no doubt that the creature is entirely unknown to naturalists . . . not only do I accept as true the statements made to the best judgement and belief of the parties who have made them, but doubtless from time to time other strange sights have presented themselves, and have remained unrecorded for fear of derision and misbelief; but this, as seen at 400 yards on a clear day, appears so perfectly easy of observation that I cannot doubt the correctness of the statement in sketch (B).'

There is more to Mr. Bartlett's letter, and in support of it Mr. Henry Lee's opinion is very similar. Amongst other things he says: 'The witnesses are trustworthy as to character, and competent by training and experience. The Officers of Her Majesty's Navy are incapable of combining together to officially and intentionally promulgate falsehood' (which is certainly one way of putting it!).

Next, in turning to the opinion of Frank Buckland, we find a third approach . . . 'Possibly I may be wrong, but my theory is that the phenomenon was caused by three of four basking sharks swimming in a line one behind the other – the dorsal and caudal, or tail fins of these huge fish projecting above the surface of the water . . .'[13] Developing his argument further, Buckland points out that when talking to the well salted Captain Gray he obtained the opinion that . . . 'the appearance in the second figure given by the officer of the *Osborne* closely

[13] This possibility is borne out by Thomas Helm in his recent book *Shark*, Robert Hale (1962), in which he states . . . 'one of the most peculiar habits of the basking shark, which has unquestionably been responsible for some of out better sea-monster stories, is that of swimming in tandem. No one knows why, but often three or four of these giants will fall in behind a leader, with each pressing his snout to the caudal fin of the one in front. As they move slowly across the surface of the sea, they appear as a monster. . . . It is easy to understand how an untrained observer might mistake such a sight for a single creature.'

represents a Greenland whale going away from the spectator. The whale, however, has not the power to bring up his fins as represented; neither are they of the same shape or half the size. . . . I have seen the movements of the Greenland whale, the Rorqual, and the Nordcaper, or Hunchback, below water as closely and distinctly as I could wish, and none of them use their fins in propelling themselves. . . . I have frequently seen whales *showing* their fins, but at those times they were lying on their sides, or rolling over and over. We constantly see the Nordcaper off Peterhead during the herring fishery season. I have noticed them within a quarter of a mile of the shore lying on their side thrashing with their long fins . . .'

Thus, in combining his own opinion concerning basking sharks, and that of Captain Gray involving whales, Frank Buckland concludes . . . 'It is quite possible, therefore, that among a shoal of Basking sharks in the Mediterranean a whale should appear rolling over and thrashing with its fins, which would afford a not improbable explanation of the phenomenon observed.'

But, however probable or improbable this may appear to the reader, before arriving at a conclusion it is as well to consider yet another opinion, which is different again. It is that of a certain Commander MacDonald of the fishery cruiser *Vigilant* – which could be of particular interest to naturalists . . .

'Sketch A, with its ridge of nine fins, said to be about 30 feet long, I take to be a fair representation of a small shoal of ca'ing or Bottle-nosed whales (they are not unknown off Cicily). I have frequently seen a similar ridge of fins, and quite as uniform, extending not only 30 feet, but 300 yards and more. With respect to Sketch B, I have several times witnessed what I believe was an explanation of it.

'Every variety of whale known on the coast of the United Kingdom, when about to pair, swim slowly in pairs shoulder to shoulder for some time; and when going away from the observer the dorsal fins appear lying over at an angle of 45°, swaying slightly up and down. When in this position, both whales may be mistaken for one of great breadth, the dorsal fins resembling side flappers; and when the head of one is slightly elevated above the other, it might fairly produce the impression conveyed by the sketch, especially on a person who saw the phenomenon for the first time.'

This explanation is perhaps the most technically interesting, and provides a plausible alternative to that of Frank Buckland, but, like his, it does not entirely fit the picture.

For example: the men who saw the animal described a definite head like a seal 'about 6 feet thick' – and also a neck, which was thinner. They said the movements of the flappers were like those of a turtle – and there was an entire absence of blowing or spouting.

Now, by no stretch of the imagination can a whale, or two whales together, produce the impression of a head like this, or a neck of any sort – and even mating whales have to breathe occasionally – and while the dorsal fin idea is certainly ingenious, surely no one could mistake these fins flopping over at 45° for 15-foot flappers, used in *propelling* the whole enormous mass through the water 'somewhat in the manner of a seal'?

My own suggestion is that the officers of the Royal Yacht *Osborne* described an animal which is still unknown to science, and which normally swims below the surface. Furthermore, that its appearance may have been caused by the attack of *predatory*[14] sharks, or whales. This conclusion, is prompted by an account which appeared on page 199 of my last book, concerning Mr. Bill Hutchison's experience off the Orkney Isles, in the year 1910.

In his statement, Hutchison reported seeing . . . 'a school of whales . . . leaping clear out of the sea' . . . a few moments before the horse-like head and 18-foot serpentine neck of some strange, unknown animal reared above the surface. After des-

[14] Neither Basking sharks nor Bottle-nosed whales are predatory in the sense they attack large animals – whereas other species of shark and Killer whales certainly do – and are noted for the size of their dorsal fins.

cribing the encounter, and the reaction of the boat-crew to it he went on to say: 'Although I have spent a lifetime at sea I have never seen whales jumping as they did; or seen a creature like this one. It is known, however, that whales will jump out of the water to get away from Killer whales – and for this reason I think the creature was following them either to attack, or from curiosity, when we came on the scene . . .'

But, if the explanation I have put forward originates from Bill Hutchison's experience, in the case of the *Osborne* sighting the characters must be reversed – with the strange-unknown-animal acting as the quarry!

ODDITIES

In this section I have assembled a collection of reports and stories which are not so well documented as those preceding, but which serve as exercise in attempting to find a solution: although in one or two cases there can clearly be no solution to evidence which is frankly, inexplicable.

Oddity No. 1: From the *Orcadian* newspaper, 9th September, 1937.

'Sea Monster near Pentland Skerry – Sea Breaking White as on Submerged Rock'

'After the relief to the Pentland Skerries on Friday word was brought ashore that a sea monster had been seen in the vicinity of the Skerries. In a letter, Mr. John R. Brown, occasional lightkeeper, wrote:

"Mr. Scot was speaking last night about a Monster that had been seen about Fair Isle. To tell the truth I never believed much in Monsters myself, but I saw something today resembling nothing I have ever seen before.

"It was about noon when we were working down at the landing at the East End that on chancing to look out to sea I noticed the sea breaking white as on a submerged rock. As I knew there were no rocks at that particular spot, I watched for a little and presently a great object rose up out of the water – anything from 20 to 30 feet and at an angle of about 45°. It was round-shaped and there appeared to be a head on it, but as it was about half a mile from the shore I could not be sure.

"I called the attention of the other two men but unfortunately before they got their eyes on the spot it had disappeared again, though both of them saw the foam it had made. We watched for a considerable time but it never appeared again.

"I have seen what fishermen call a killer whale's fin rise high out of the water, often, but the fin of a Killer resembles the sail of a boat and is easily recognized whereas this object was definitely round-shaped. I am sorry that it did not appear again . . . it would be interesting to have any further news." '

The Pentland Skerries are a tiny group of islands approximately midway between John O'Groats, the most north-eastern tip of Scotland, and South Ronaldsay, the southernmost island of the Orkney group: they lie about 5 miles from each. (Sketch Map E, page 186.)

Oddity No. 2: In the 21st July, 1961 edition of the *Shetland Times*, an article appeared under the heading 'Did the Mermaid Exist?' It concerns a clear, handwritten statement thought to have been made by one Arthur Nicolson J.P., of Lochend, in the early eighteen hundreds: found recently by Lady Nicolson amongst an assortment of old papers and documents. It reads:

'In the presence of Arthur Nicolson of Lochend, J.P. – William Manson, Daniel Manson, John Henderson, residing in Cullivoe in the parish of North Yell, who being solemnly sworn deposit – That, in the beginning of the month of July last, they at the deep-sea fishing from 30 to 36 miles from land, and about midnight took up a creature attached by the back of the neck to a hook, which was about 3 feet long, and about 30 inches in circumference at the broadest part, which was across the shoulders. From the navel upwards it resembled a human being – had breasts as large as those of a woman. Attached to the side were arms about 9 inches long, with wrists and hands like those of a human being, except that there were webs between the fingers for about half their length. The fingers were in number and shape, like those of a man. The little arms were close on the outside of the breasts and on the corner of each shoulder was placed a fin of a round form which, when extended, covered both the breasts and the arms. The animal had a short neck, on which rested a head, about the length of a man's but not nearly so round; and somewhat pointed at the top. It had eyebrows without hair, and eyelids covering two small blue eyes, somewhat like those of a human being – not like those of a fish. It had no nose, but two orifices for blowing through. It had a mouth so large that when opened wide it would admit a man's fist. It had lips rather thicker than a man's of a pure white colour. There was no chin, but they think the lower jaw projected a little farther than the upper one. There were no ears. The whole front of the animal was covered with skin, white as linen, the back with skin of a light-grey colour, like a fish. From the breasts the shape sloped towards the tail, close to which was only about 4 inches in circumference. The tail was flat, and consisted of two lobes which, when extended, might be 6 inches together in breadth, and were set at right angles with the face of the creature: it resembled the tail of a halibut. The animal was very nearly round at the shoulders. It appeared to have shoulder bones and a hollow space between them. The diminution of size increased most rapidly from the navel, which might be 9 inches below the breasts. There was between the nostrils a thing that appeared to be a piece of gristle about 9 inches long, and which resembled a thick bristle. There was a similar one on each side of the head, but not so long, which the animal had the power of moving backwards and forwards, and could make them meet on top of the skull. When the men spoke the animal answered, and moved these bristles, which led them to suppose that the creature heard by means of them. They did not observe what sort of teeth the creature had, nor the parts of generation. There was no hair upon any part of its body which was soft and slimy.

'There is an old opinion among fishermen that it is unlucky to kill a mermaid and therefore, after having kept it in the boat for some time, they slipped it.

'All of which is truth, so help me God.'

This strange and surprisingly detailed account of a 'mermaid' puzzled me when first reading through it, because although I knew the legend was supposed to stem from the dugong (which is a very peculiar sea-going mammal) I did not see how this description could match up with it. However, as I really knew very little about dugongs, the obvious course was to try and find out more about them – and also the history of the mermaid legend, which goes right back into antiquity.

Nosing through book-shops and libraries I found two books – but although the first seems to provide a partial explanation, the second introduces evidence the nature of which is in itself mysterious.

The books in question are *Mammals of the World* by Hans Hvass, and *Sea Enchantress* by Gwen Benwell and Arthur Waugh. This is what the author of the first book has to say about the dugong and others of its tribe – under the generic heading *Sirenians*:

'The Sirenians or sea cows are at first sight rather similar in appearance to the whales, the body is streamlined and almost hairless, the fore limbs are paddle-shaped, and there are no external hind limbs. . . . The eyes are small and there are no external ears, but the muzzle is large with crescent-shaped nostrils, which are only open when the animal is breathing. The thick lips have long sensory bristles. . . . When suckling the young the female holds it between her front limbs. These rather peculiar animals are said to have given rise to the stories of mermaids, although some authorities consider the latter are more likely to have been seals. The Sirenians are divided into three families: the manatees, the dugongs and Stella's sea cow. . .

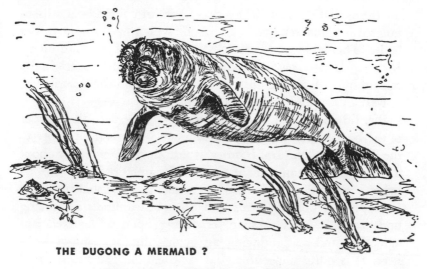

THE DUGONG A MERMAID ?

....THEN MERMEN DESERVE OUR SYMPATHY.

11.

FIG. 11

'The dugongs have a slightly forked tail fluke, and even less hair than the manatees . . .'

This descriptive account of the Sirenians is interesting, but it does not fit the 'mermaid' in one or two respects. For example none of these animals is thought to inhabit the water surrounding the Shetland Isles. Neither manatees, dugongs nor Stella's sea cow (which is now extinct) have ever been reported near these waters, as far as I know.

Furthermore, it is difficult to believe that such a hideously ugly creature as the dugong could be mistaken for the mermaid captured by the fishermen, which had 'wrists and hands like those of a woman'. But whatever the explanation, there is no doubt they did think it was a mermaid, because in reading through the book *Sea Enchantress* I was delighted to find a cross-reference to this very occurrence: on page 118 . . . 'Scotland provided another mermaid in 1833, when six Shetland fishermen reported that they had found one entangled in their lines

off the island of Yell. They drew her into their boat, disen-
tangled her and removed the fishook which had caught in her
body. The incident is described in Dr. Robert Hamilton's
History of Whales and Seals, published in 1939, but was originally
related by a Mr. Edmondston, whom Dr. Hamilton describes as
'a well known and intelligent observer' . . .

Mr. Edmondston had discussed the episode with the skipper
of the boat in person, and was so much impressed he wrote to
the Professor of Natural History at Edinburgh University about
it, and said, 'Not one of the six men dreamed of a doubt of its
being a mermaid,' and ended by saying . . . 'the usual resources
of scepticism that the seals and other sea animals appearing
under certain circumstances operating upon an excited imagination and so producing an ocular illusion, cannot avail
here. It is quite impossible that six Shetland fishermen could
commit such a mistake.'

Reading more about the history of the mermaid and her kin,
which goes back a long time in history – perhaps as much as
seven thousand years, to Babylonia – I found sailors' superstition
closely linked with it: and understandable if one pays heed to
the writings of Olaus Magnus more than four centuries ago,
who warned . . .

'There be monsters in the sea, as it were imitating the shape
of a man, having a dolefull kinde of sounde or singing, as the
Nereides. There be also Sea-men of an obsolute proportion in
their whole body: these are sometimes seen to climbe up the
ships in the night times and suddenly to depresse that part
upon which they sit; and if they abide long, the whole ship
sinketh. Yes (saith he), this I adde from the faithful assertions
of the Norway fishers, that when such are taken, if they be not
presently let go again, there ariseth such a fierce tempest . . .
that a man would thinke the verie heavens were falling, and
the vaulted roofe of the world running to ruine; insomuch that
the fishermen have much ado to escape with their lives: whereupon they confirmed it as a law amongst themselves that if any

chanced to hang such a fish upon his hook he should suddenly cut the line and let him go.'

In her long and romantic history through folklore, myth and legend, the mermaid is sometimes confused with other species of sea-folk – Mermen, Tritons, Nereides, Water-horses and the water spirits of the Indian and China seas, but in classic form she can never be mistaken for a fish for she is often beautiful, with long golden tresses, and is sometimes spied upon a rock, plying her traditional comb with one hand, while in the other she holds a mirror.

The image is known to the modern world, as it has been throughout the centuries, and although no one can reasonably accept the existence of such a charming, and unlikely creature – there are people who claim to have seen mermaids; sometimes at a range of only a few yards. In some instances the same mermaid has been reported by different people, in the same locality, over a period of weeks or months – and on occasion by more than one person at the same time!

No one can readily believe these extraordinary stories, but in reading through *Sea Enchantress*, there can be little doubt people have reported what they *think* they have seen with absolute conviction, and have been ready to swear to it. And if this is so there must be an explanation.

From a rational point of view it would seem to be the 'ocular illusion' denounced by Mr. Edmonston. Could these people, in fact, have imagined they saw a mermaid, the accepted form of which would exist in their subconscious? And if so, could several people experience the same hallucination at the same time – and why?

These are questions I asked myself when reading this book, and in pursuit of a reasoned answer referred to another book, which is equally interesting, though now difficult to obtain. It is called *Apparitions* by G. N. M. Tyrell. It first made an appearance in 1943 as a pamphlet, but was later revised and published as a book in 1953. Within it reference is made to the

'Census of Hallucinations' undertaken by the Society for Psychical Research, many years ago, and as the results of this census run contrary to expectation, I will attempt to summarize without becoming too involved in statistics.

Very briefly, therefore, these are the facts concerning the census.

In 1889 at the International Congress of Experimental Psychology, held in Paris, the fundamentals of the plan were studied and approved, and the task formally entrusted to Professor Henry Sidgwick. Five others were involved, including two women, and all were educated and competent investigators. As a result the work went ahead with thoroughness, and particular attention was paid to those features known to be of interest to psychologists.

The prime purpose of the census was to 'test for evidence of telepathy, by questioning a representative sample of the public', in a discreet and reasoned manner – 'intending to reveal what proportion of the population experiences sensory hallucinations during the hours of wakefulness, particularly of the externalized kind which constitutes an apparition'.

Altogether answers were obtained from a sample of 17,000 persons, from all walks of life, of different ages and nationalities. The material thus collected was analysed from various points of view – due consideration being given to its relationship to sex, age, nationality, and perhaps most important of all, health.

Results showed that 9·9 per cent of the 17,000 people questioned admitted to the experience of sensory hallucination, at some time or another – of the type described in the carefully prepared question form.

Even more remarkable perhaps, they also showed that 'collective percipience of telepathic hallucinations' was by no means rare – because out of the total of 1,087 visual hallucinations, 95 were *collectively* perceived: which is again roughly 9 per cent.

The fact that this work was undertaken some sixty odd years

ago in no way detracts from it, or the soundness of the methods employed, or the adequacy of the statistical sample and data – in fact Tyrell himself states: 'So far as I am aware, no detailed criticism of a reasonable kind has been made by any adverse critic of the census results up to date.'

But, the problem does not end here, because in trying to resolve whether or not these hallucinations contained evidence of telepathy, it was necessary to establish how many of them corresponded with external events – and whether these coincidences exceeded the number which might be expected statistically, on the basis of chance alone.

For example, if someone experienced an hallucination while fully awake in which he or she recognized a friend, within a few moments or hours of that friend's *death*, in another place; a coincidence would be provided.

The results showed that there were a number of apparent 'coincidences' of this description – but for the purpose of analysis it was decided that some latitude should be established, since the hallucination and the death sometimes occurred 'nearly but not quite at the same time'. Finally, a latitude of plus or minus twelve hours from the time of death was agreed upon.

Taking the average death rate over a ten year period for England and Wales (1881–90 rate of 19·15 per thousand) it was possible to establish that the odds against one person, taken at random, dying on any one day was about 1 in 19,000 – which is the same as 19·15 in 365,000; within a corpse or two.

But, when the results were analysed, and excluding those 'coincidences' which occurred before or after the twelve hour limit – no less than 30 death-coincidences occurred in 1,300 cases of hallucination; which is a proportion of 1 in 43 and *not* 1 in 19,000, the statistical chance average!

Which fact provides food for thought.

Again, as with the mermaid hallucinations (if that is what one can call them) there is no apparently acceptable explanation to which we can point – which is a polite way of saying that we are

still very ignorant about many things; despite our enlighten-
ment in the field of physical science; and in this regard we may
usefully refer to the words of Dr. Johnson, who had something
to say on the subject of apparitions . . .

'This is a question which, after five thousand years is still
undecided; a question whether in theology or philosophy, is
one of the most important that can come before the human
understanding.'

No. 3 – The Oddity at Orford Ness: On 18th January, 1962, I
received a letter from a Mrs. Mildred Nye, of Denmark Hill,
together with a sketch of what appears to be a very strange
creature; and with permission of the writer I venture to include
both; the letter reads:

My daughter and I have just finished reading your book, . . .
I myself have talked to a woman who lived on the edge of the
loch and had seen the Monster several times; once she saw two
small ones playing together!
You may be interested to hear of the peculiar fish that was
brought in at Orford Ness, Suffolk, a few years ago – I was
staying there and saw and handled it. The story is this:
Just off Orford Ness there is an island . . . and anyone wishing
to fish or shoot wildfowl there has to have a permit. One day
a fisherman went out in his boat, taking with him a man who
had a permit to shoot, and who had his gun with him. When
pulling in their fishing net they noticed a terrible commotion –
some large fish appeared to be entangled in it. To save the net
from destruction, and because the thing was too large for the
boat the fowler shot it, and they towed it on to the shore. Later,
I saw it on a motor-lorry – of the kind with no sides. The body
took up the length of the lorry and the tail hung down over the
end and trailed in the dust. I was told it measured 17 or 18 feet.
The tail was as long as the body; it was shaped like a cow's tail
and had a bunch of webbed fingers at the end that formed a fan

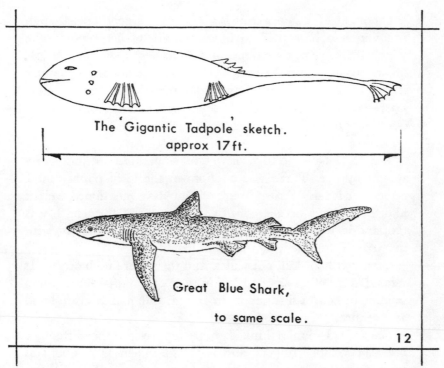

The 'Gigantic Tadpole' sketch.
approx 17 ft.

Great Blue Shark,
to same scale.

12

FIG. 12

shape, when I spread them out. It had four large flappers, two on each side, like hands, each finger larger than mine and webbed in-between. The fingers were boned, evidently, because I could not bend them. The eyes were small – and shut with two lids; top and bottom – and another across the corner.

. . . Three holes like inset pipes – big enough to take my walking-stick which I poked into them.

. . . A small frill of fins where the tail joined the body.

I was told that the Curator of the (local) Museum came out by car to see the thing and could not place it at all. I did not hear – indeed – could not find out what eventually happened to it . . .

P.S. The drawing is very poor, but I have tried to make the proportions right.

I thought Mrs. Nye's drawing was quite a good one, though peculiar, and it seemed to fit the details of her report. The sketch of the eye intrigued me, and as she described the multiple lid arrangement and the body features in such a sensible manner it was obvious she must have examined the carcase at close quarters – and this prompted me to write and ask some further questions: to which she replied . . .

Weight: I have no idea of weight, and could not judge any weight by size. There was a photo in the local paper and I remember it said '17 feet long'. It may have mentioned weight also, but I have no memory of it. About half the length was tail, and its body girth was more than I could encompass with my arms. I am 5 feet 8½ inches in height.

Colour: It had skin, not scales, and there were no blotches. It reminded me of an elephant's skin in colour and texture. It was smooth in contra-distinction to rough, but had a granulated appearance.

Flappers: I don't think I quite appreciate the difference between 'webbed fingers' and fins. The fingers were about as thick as my middle finger. They were stub-ended, not sharp like a fin, and the skin between was opaque. It looked like a thin edition of the body skin. I *think* there were five fingers (not quite sure) and the two outside ones were not quite as long as the others. They seemed to join a kind of wrist before entering the body.

Holes: The holes were on either side, set at a slightly forward angle (see Sketch). I should say they were gills. They were lined with the same kind of skin and went in a good way. I put my stick in.

Mouth: I cannot swear to teeth, but I have an impression there were some; long and pointed.

Eyes: Small and rather rounded; piggy eyes really. I do not remember the colour or what the pupil was like. But, I feel pretty certain about the eyelid, because I said to myself 'cats have three eyelids, but I didn't know that fish have'.

Condition: It was quite fresh, and had only been caught a few hours and was not at all discoloured nor decomposed – otherwise I should not have handled it! I was so interested that I spent about twenty minutes examining it. The two men who caught it were being treated in the village pub and there were only one or two other people inspecting it. By and large it was rather like a gigantic tadpole.

Armed with this information, I next wrote to the Museum in question – but was surprised to learn that a large animal washed ashore about the same time had been identified as a Blue shark: not by the Curator, but by one of his assistants. In reply I enclosed a copy of Mrs. Nye's letter, and requested that I might be put in touch with the person who saw the fish and identified it.

In response to this second missive I received a more detailed account – stating that the shark was some 11 feet in length; that it had been identified by a competent observer, and that the cause of death was oil which had clogged the gill slits. It had been washed ashore about 4 miles south of Orford Ness.

It was also suggested (and I feel quite rightly) that either the description I possessed was in error as to the length and the form of the creature, or it wasn't the same animal. If the latter was the case, then the Museum had not received any report of such a beast at that time.

Certainly the two descriptions are much at variance but, on re-examining the details I think it is (just) possible there may be another explanation which could help to solve the riddle, and vindicate both observers.

In the first instance it is hard to believe that a trained observer could have made such a bad mistake, because although the Blue shark is by nature an ocean-going fish, seldom found in waters below 65° F. it is a well-known species, and numbers of them are caught during the summer months off the extreme south coast of Cornwall. But these seldom exceed 200 lbs. in weight, and thus if the very much larger carcase at Orford Ness, some 130 miles to the northward was that of a Blue shark, it is possible it may have been dead for some time, and in a partly decomposed state.[15]

Looking at Plate 12 and Sketch 12 it can be seen that the spine of a shark continues right out to the tip of the tail fin, and also that the Blue shark, like others of its kind has a curious extension to the fin at its upper extremity, much like the rudder trim-tab on an old-fashioned biplane – and it is not difficult to imagine the 'cow's tail' as the spinal remains of the big tail fin, with this fan-like appendage at the end of it.

Furthermore, the 'piggy eyes', the 'granulated' skin, the suggestion of 'long and pointed' teeth are shark-like characteristics – and the finger bones could have been fin rays, stub ended by friction with the sand as the carcase rolled about.

Of course there are some obvious things about this explanation which do not fit Mrs. Nye's account, but it is the only one I can think of which does not invoke the 'coincidence' rule, so often applied in defeat – the coincident appearance of both a Blue shark *and* a gigantic-tadpole carcase – and in further defence of it I would add that in the case of certain sharks, including the Grey sharks *Carcharinidae*,[16] and the Blue shark *Prionace glauca*[17] a covering called a nictitating membrane can be moved across the eye to provide protection during attack – and this could have appeared as a third 'eyelid'.

Oddity No. 4: The account following was sent by Mr. Peter Costello, of Dublin. It is from page 100 of *The London Magazine* of 1743, under the heading 'A Letter from Cambridge': Tuesday, February 1st:

[15] Surprisingly enough, dead bodies of sea animals can appear quite 'fresh' until they have been out of water for a while, due perhaps to the putrifying parts and fluids being washed away, or absorbed by scavengers while still in the water. I have noticed this with both seals and fish, though it is a matter of degree: perhaps one should say 'relatively fresh'.

[16] Ref: p. 206, *About Sharks and Shark Attack* by Dr. D. H. Davies (1964), Routledge and Kegan Paul Ltd. London.

[17] Ref: Letter to me from British Museum (Natural History) Dept. of Zoology. PJW/BJ dated 29th April, 1965.

'A few days since an amphibious monster was brought hither, which has drawn the attention of the most curious of this University, who are unable to assign a proper name to it; some of our gentlemen call it a sea-lioness:

'It was taken the 6th of last month at Fordike Wash in Lincolnshire, asleep on the sands: It was supposed to have followed a large shoal of herrings, and having overgorged itself, fell asleep, and was discovered by some fishermen, who immediately got some proper weapons and several bulldogs, by which means they took it.

'It killed one of the best dogs in the county, and wounded four or five others; but lost one of its eyes in the engagement. It is bearded like a tyger, weighs 500 lbs., the fore feet are like a bear's, the hind like a fan, two feet wide when extended; its tail is like a neat's tongue; It is seven feet and a half long, and nine feet round. It is now alive and well, and made a present to the University, and as the sight of it is free, great numbers of people flock to see it.'

It seems likely this creature was a bull sea lion rather than a 'sea lioness', because a mature bull does possess a handsome ruff of fur round its neck, which might, at a pinch, be described as a beard. Furthermore it is a powerful beast, with ferocious jaws, and could give a good account of itself. Outwardly it bears small resemblance to the sleek and immature females found in zoos, or balancing beach-balls at the circus. There is a fine specimen to be seen at the Royal Scottish Museum at Edinburgh, which has an interesting and varied collection of seals, and well repays a visit. But if a seal provides the explanation in this oddity case, the next, (sent by Mr. Patrick Bury, also of Dublin), is not so easily resolved:

The *Evening Herald*, 1st August, 1963: 'Monster Seen in Irish Lake. . . . A Monster, 8 to 10 feet long with two protruding tusks and a hairy head scared the wits out of three youths who were returning from a fishing trip on Lough Major, Co. Monaghan. The youths, G. Reilly (18), Talbot Duffy (17), and

Paul Pentland (12) said they saw the "Monster" splashing up
and down in the lake like a sea lion. Although frightened, they
watched in amazement for a few minutes, but decided to make
for home quickly when one of them threw a stone in its direction,
and it made towards them at great speed . . .' Badly frightened,
the boys ran across a field, but were overtaken by the terrier
dog, which had at first stayed behind to bark at the "thing"
but which shot past them with its tail between its legs, gaining
an easy first in the race for home.

'Questioned later, it was suggested the Monster might have
been a large otter, but Talbot Duffy denied this flatly, stating
that he had shot plenty of otters. Returning the next day, the
boys found that the dozen or so large bream left on the bank
the night before had disappeared, only a few bones remaining:
and later another local man, Paddy Brady confirmed the boys'
description, having also seen the creature surface; and it is now
considered to be responsible for the disappearance of pike from
the lines set by anglers, because on occasion only the heads are
found, attached to the baited hooks.'

Here again a seal would seem to fit the picture, but the question arises – how did it get into Lough Major, which is some 36
miles from the sea, and does not drain into any major river?

Oddity No. 5: 'The Egg That Makes 30 Omlettes' runs the
heading to a short column in the *Sunday Express*, London, 6th
May, 1962, describing a gigantic fossil egg found in Australia.
It reads . . . 'Perth: Australia's 1,000,000-year-old egg is
exciting world scientific interest. It is 11 inches long, and 8½
inches wide. The egg was found thirty-two years ago by a
ten-year-old boy. Now a farmer, he showed it to a naturalist,
who gave it to the Perth Museum.

'Experts there say the bird that laid the egg must have been
over 10 feet tall and weighed 800 lbs. . . .'

Reference to a fossilized bird's egg, however unusual or
monumental in size must appear out of place in this chapter,

because there is no clue to suggest its parent had anything to do with the water. But I have introduced it because it is probable there were giant aquatic birds in prehistoric times – and to quote from the letter of an authority, it even seems possible that an unknown species exists today.

On 20th February, 1962, Ivan Sanderson, F.L.S., F.R.G.S., F.Z.S., wrote from New York in connection with the L.N. affair and aquatic egg-layers in general. He said:

'Coming to birds, we have Hesperonis which was quite big, had a long neck and probably feather-type covering like a penguin, which looks absolutely slick when wet.

'From the 3-toed, 18-inch long tracks I looked into on the coast of Florida in 1948, I *know* there is some enormous penguin-like bird that can waddle out on land; and probably when it wants to lay an egg – *an* egg I say. You don't know about the Giant-Three-Toes do you? I'll have to send you some files. Anyhow their foot tracks have been photographed at the bottom of the north Atlantic by the Woods Hole Oceanographic Inst. . . . They came in two types: a typical Ornithopod dinosaur with scales and a long tail (vide: South Africa) – and with two front flippers and huge back feet, short legs, and no tail (vide: Queensland; Nantucket; and our Florida bit).

'I am prepared to affirm . . . and so are some zoologists from Christchurch, N.Z., who chipped a fossil skeleton of a seven foot penguin out of a cave roof . . . that the latter type are not only birds, but penguins because of the unique arrangement and proportions of the claws and toes . . .'

True to his word, Sanderson later sent a copy of his report on the Florida foot-prints; which runs to some forty pages of typescript. It is one of the most interesting documents I have read.

Sponsored by W.N.B.C. in New York, and the *Herald Tribune*, the investigation was entirely thorough, and details were sent at the time to the American Museum of Natural History.

Some very brief notes concerning this extraordinary affair are included under Appendix Note D at the back of this book.

Oddity No. 6: Australia's Moha Moha has for long held a place in the annals, and one suspects, the hearts of monster hunters; because of its apparently absurd appearance – and yet if the details of Miss Lovell's eyewitness account are considered, the 'monster turtle fish' she describes seems less a part of the realm of fantasy.

Two original accounts are available, the first appearing in *Land and Water*, 3rd January, 1891 is from a contemporary letter by Miss Lovell, and the second her very much expanded version appearing in the *Great Barrier reef of Australia* by W. Savil-Kent, F.L.S., F.Z.S. – and treated by him in a mildly facetious manner, despite the confirmation of an affidavit signed by the First and Third Keepers at Sandy Cape Lighthouse, a wife and two daughters, and another white man – not to mention 'Robert the black boy, who set his mark against it': each of whom admitted that 'We, the undersigned saw the Moha-Moha (as described by Miss Lovell) making for the shore of Sandy Cape[18] on 8th June, 1890.'

But if he treats the matter with professional reserve it is understandable, because if Miss Lovell's account is both truthful and accurate then Australia must be credited as the visiting place of an unknown marine animal as technically improbable as the Duck-billed Platypus. Excerpts from her long and oddly worded report to Savile-Kent read as follows:

Walking along the beach in very calm weather, Miss Lovell first noticed the head and neck of some strange creature unfamiliar to her . . . 'I went to the edge of the water and saw a huge animal, lying at full length,[19] which was not at all disturbed by my close proximity to it, enabling me to observe the glossy skin of the head and neck, smooth and shiny as satin. Its great mouth was open all the time it was out of water.

'In about a quarter of an hour or so it put its head and neck slowly into the sea, closing its jaws as it did so. I then saw what a

[18] Sandy Cape is at the extreme northern tip of Fraser or Great Sandy Island, about 170 miles north of Brisbane.

[19] Her overall estimate of length was 30 feet.

long neck it had, as it moved round in a half circle, and also perceived the head and neck were moving under a carapace. When the head was pointing out to sea it rose up, putting a long wedge-shaped fish-like tail out of water over the dry shore, parallel to myself, and not more than five feet from me, not touching the sand but elevated. I could have stood under "the flukes of its tail".

'The only part of the body that had marks like joints (like in size and shape to a common brick) was also on dry shore, but *resting* on the sand: the great dome-shaped carapace, dull slate-grey, was standing quite 5 feet high, and so hid its long neck and head from my view, which before it rose I could see as a long shadow on the water. The carapace was smooth and without marks of any sort. The fish-like part of the tail was as glossy and shiny as the head and neck, but of a beautiful silver grey shading to white, with either markings or large scales, each bordered with a ridge of white, but if scales, not like those of a fish in position, as the fish's scales lie horizontally, while the Moha's, if scales, lie perpendicularly, each the size of a man's thumbnail. It had a thick fleshy fin near the end, about 3 feet from the flukes, and, like them, chocolate-brown. The flukes were semi-transparent; I could see the sun shining through them, showing all the bones very forked. One of the girls asked me if a shark had bitten a piece out of the tail, and the other wanted to know if I thought it was an alligator! The fish-like part was quite 12 feet long . . .'

When on shore the animal was motionless, but Miss Lovell goes on to describe how it suddenly gave a twist to its tail, and slid into the water, disappeared, and then reappeared some distance out . . . 'I seemed only to have taken one breath when I saw its tail out of water about the place where the steamer anchors, sending a quantity of fish into the air. Then I saw it give a twist of its tail and it disappeared altogether . . .

'As I was so close to it for at least half an hour, I was able to study its shape and colouring . . . The parts I did not see were the legs. I stooped down and tried, but in vain, to see them, though the Moha was standing in only a foot of water, but the Black[20] described them as being like an alligator . . .'

Accepting this as an honest account of the Moha, and Miss Lovell's courage, or foolishness in approaching it quite so closely the one question I would ask myself is – could she have been mistaken about a 'carapace'? Could this possibly have been a *rigidly distended* part of the body – because the description of it puts me in mind of the dome-shaped back of the L.N.M., which (despite objections from the critics) was photographed at close range by flashlight in May of 1960 by a Mr. Peter O'Connor? (Vide: Plates 3 and 10 in *Loch Ness Monster*).

Oddity No. 7: Australia supports another famous tradition for water monsters, in the *Bunyip*, a more or less fanciful marsh and river dweller which features in aboriginal legend – persisting through to modern times . . .

Brisbane Sunday Truth, 9th May, 1965. 'Hunt for the Bunyip' – 'Shooting parties of residents of Mirramac Plains (inland from the Gold Coast) this week are determined to crack the eighty-year-old mystery – is there a Bunyip in the area? And there's nothing funny about it because there is definitely SOMETHING out there which roars and barks, and is terrifying children . . . the locals are going all out to find it and so rid the area of years of fear and superstition.

'Sane strong men reported the weird goings-on last week. Gilston dairy farmer Mr. T. Hinde, said he had heard a strange "barking type of roar" in the Nerang River near his property. On several mornings he had found the river churned up and muddy. The spot was about 8 feet deep, but the mud had been splashed well up on the bank. Mr. Billy Hill who lives about two miles away, also heard the same blood-curdling roars. Others in the area have seen the river swirling around abnormally, stirred up by some mysterious force.

[20] In her account Miss Lovell states the black boy had seen the Moha on the previous Monday, on shore – presumably with legs showing.

'Those who do not believe in the theory of the Bunyip (defined a swamp monster invisible to white people) say it is a large crocodile. There is conclusive evidence that crocodiles once inhabited the area, but none has been seen for decades. Old-timers, however, have no doubts – "Yes, it's the Bunyip again," they say. . . .'

The *Australian Encyclopaedia*[21] goes into the legend at some length, from which it appears that the name *Bunyip* was first 'applied by Aborigines from Victoria to an alleged water-dwelling Monster, the existence of which appears to have been widely credited' – and this later was used for water creatures reported in lakes, rivers and swamps in south-eastern Australia, and Tasmania too. Descriptions varied enormously. In 1847 a newspaper item referred to the Bunyip of Kine Pratie, described 'as having much resemblance to the human figure, but with frightful features, and feet turned backwards!' On the Hunter River it seems to have produced the earliest cowboy-noises on record – becoming known by the names 'Yaa-hoo' and 'Wowee, wowee' – but, in March of 1828 a surveyor called McBrian claimed to have seen a strange Monster 'an animal of prodigious length' in the Fish River, on the road to Bathurst: and that another was seen elsewhere in the same river.

Dr. Bernard Heuvelmans treats the matter seriously in book *On the Track of Unknown Animals*, giving the space of a chapter to it, and producing much useful information and a number of possible theories.

Perhaps the most plausible of these relates to the Diprotodon, a colossal wombat as large as a rhinocerous, thought to have frequented swamps and rivers, before being driven to extinction by drought following the last ice-age.

Between 500 and 1,000 skeletons were found in a fine state of preservation in 1953, in the dry north-west of southern Australia, by Professor Ruben Stirton from the University of California.

[21] Publisher: Angus and Robertson, Vol. 11, quoting Charles Barratt's *The Bunyip* (1946).

Preserved in soft clay, the herd was thought to have wandered on to the dried-up surface of a lake in search of water, only to break through the crust and perish.

Heuvelmans considers the remnant survival of the species, bearing in mind that even the more arid parts of Australia are not entirely without water and that the Diprotodon was similar in type not only to the tapir, but also the rhinocerous, which has learned to exist in very dry sun-scorched areas – but whether it will ultimately provide an answer to the riddle, no one can be certain.

'*Blob-oddities*', *8:* 'Boneless Sea Monster – Carcase Baffles Scientists' . . . runs the heading to a short column in the *Daily Telegraph*, 9th March, 1962.

'The body of a giant sea monster which has been washed up on the desolate West Tasmanian coast has baffled scientists. It is 20 feet long and 18 feet wide and has no defined head, eyes or other sense organs. It is believed the Monster was first seen on the beach two years ago but it was brought to the notice of scientists . . . only a few days ago.

'A party of scientists reported in Hobart that it had a frill and gill-like slits. They said the body was in an advanced stage of decomposition, but the flesh was extremely tough, like glass fibre and it had apparently been on the beach about twenty months. Its estimated live weight was about eight tons. The scientists believed the body was definitely not a mammal. Samples are being chemically analysed and more experts will probably be flown to the body soon . . .'

This was but one of several references to appear in the Press at the time, and from day to day I watched for new information, or the statement that the Tasmanian Monster was something really unusual – a new type of animal, of enormous size, with simply extraordinary features – but after a week or two the news came through that it was just an ancient decaying mass of blubber, thought to have been dumped by a whaling ship –

though how this final verdict fitted in with the previous description, is hard to understand.

A somewhat similar report of more recent origin comes from Auckland in New Zealand, described in Australia's *Townsville Bulletin*, 24th March, 1965 . . .

'Mystery Mass of Flesh and Hair – Auckland, N.Z. (A.A.P.) – Officials are puzzled over a huge, shapeless mass of flesh and hair which has appeared on the sand at Muriwai Beach here.

'The "thing" was first sighted a week ago by a Marine Department officer. Then the hairy blob of flesh was 30 feet long and 8 feet high. It is slowly being swallowed by the sand but more than 20 feet of it was still showing yesterday.

'Auckland University's zoology department head (Professor J. E. Morton) said: "You can rule out whales because of the hair, and you can rule out sea elephants and sea cows because of its size."

'The object has a tough quarter-inch thick hide. Under this is what appears to be a layer of fat, then solid meat. Hair four to six inches long covers its length. Cut from the hide and washed clean, the hair has a soft woolly texture.

'A senior forestry officer who tentatively prodded the mass of flesh said he had first thought the blob might be a dead whale. "But have you ever seen a whale in a fur coat?" he asked.'

A letter to the Department of Zoology at Auckland's University, produced a down-to-earth reply from Miss J. Robb, Senior Lecturer in Zoology, who had been given the job of getting at the facts. She commented . . .

'The reports of its hairiness were made by an enthusiastic newspaper reporter. . . . Certainly, the photographs he had taken seemed to show densely matted fibres, several inches long. When I examined some of these fibres myself, however, it was obvious that they were long strands of fibrous connective tissue – all that remained of the outermost few inches of blubber, the softer parts of the tissue having been either chewed or shredded by small fish, etc., or eroded away by the action of sand and water. While identification of the exact species (of whale) was not possible, it was most likely to have been a humpback. I am sorry to have nothing more exciting to report.'

In a way so was I, but this clear and, no doubt accurate assessment may in future help to solve the problem of 'hairy' carcases, which keep appearing in different places.

Oddity No. 9: From a translation of the article 'Are there still Big Unknown Animals on Earth?' by Dr. S. K. Klumov, Institute of Oceanology, Moscow; printed by the Soviet journal *Priroda* (Nature), in August 1962:

'... In 1951–56 I was working in the north-western Pacific, engaged in the study of the whales of the Far East. I visited the coastal whaling-stations in the Kurile Islands, went to sea aboard the whalers, took part in the hunts and met many of the whaling men, who are folk of great experience. And one day, as I was standing on board with some of them and we were watching a fairly big shark swim past the ship, showing its great fin, the harpooner Ivan Skripkin said to me: "You're a scientist, eh? Will you explain to me please what kind of beast it is that we have seen almost every year for several years running not far from the Komandorskie Islands?[22] The creature always appears at the very same place, and we always see it at the same time: usually in the first half of July. The area is not far from Komandor, say 30 miles or so south-east of there, in the Pacific. We run into it once or twice a year when we are whaling there. Of course its no whale. We know whales: you can tell a whale by its appearance, its colour, its dorsal fin, and by the way it blows.

"This thing doesn't blow, and it doesn't stick its head out of the water, but, like that shark there, it only shows the top part of its back. The back is enormous, very wide, and smooth, with no fins at all, and black in colour. It surfaces, does a roll, and plunges again. But it leaves a tremendous 'trough'. Only big sperm-whales leave as big a trough as that when they plunge.

[22] Off the Kamchatka Peninsular, approx. 55° N, 166° E.

160

We haven't once been able to get close enough to this thing to get a shot at it, but we'd love to have a go with the harpoon gun, just to find out what it is. But we never managed it. We've made lots of guesses and argued among ourselves as to what it is, but nobody's been able to come up with a sensible answer. Can it be some sort of fish? It's a good 10 metres (33 feet) long, if I'm not mistaken, and I don't think my eye deceives me. Now, how's that for a mystery?"

'I regret to say that I was not able to tell harpooner Ivan Skripin there and then what it was. Maybe a giant squid? Although we don't know of giant squids that are black, black is pretty common amongst deep-sea fish. But anyway, to this day I cannot find a precise answer to his question . . .'

Oddities 9, 10 and 11 : Number nine stems from a letter and newspaper report sent me by Mrs. Hope Smeeton of Crumlin, County Antrim, Ireland.

From the letter . . . 'On pages 169–70 of your book, you refer to tales of Monsters from various localities. When you were in Wales did you ever hear of the dreaded "Afanc", mentioned by George Borrow, and often quoted in Welsh folklore? This dragon-type Monster inhabited deep pools or lakes and in the past ages terrified the inhabitants of different localities, being finally dragged from their retreats both by Hugh Gadarn, a Cymric hero, and by King Arthur himself. These Afanc, of no known species, may perhaps belong to the genus of strange aquatic monsters referred to in Irish, Icelandic and African stories . . .'

From a newspaper report . . . *Daily Telegraph,* 1st March, 1934:

'Coastguard Meets Monster by Night – Eyes like saucers, two huge humps' : When fishermen told us a fortnight ago in Filey that they had seen a Monster of unclassified but awe-inspiring species, about three miles out to sea, we were sceptical. The fishermen, perhaps discouraged, said no more, and we concluded the Monster had gone off to the same retreat as its Loch Ness relative.

'Now, however, Mr. Wilkinson Herbert, a Filey coastguard, says he saw the thing on shore last night; a dark moonless night. He was walking along Filey Brig, a long low spur of rocks running out into the sea, when:

' "Suddenly I heard a growling like a dozen dogs ahead, walking nearer I switched on my torch, and was confronted by a huge neck, six yards ahead of me, rearing up 8 feet high!

' "The head was a startling sight – huge, tortoise eyes, like saucers, glaring at me, the creature's mouth was a foot wide[23] and its neck would be a yard round.[24]

' "The Monster appeared as startled as I was. Shining my torch along the ground, I saw a body about 30 feet long. I thought 'this is no place for me' and from a distance I threw stones at the creature. It moved away growling fiercely, and I saw the huge black body had two humps on it and four short legs with huge flappers on them. I could not see any tail. It moved quickly, rolling from side to side, and went into the sea. From the cliff top I looked down and saw two eyes like torchlights shining out to sea 300 yards away. It was the most gruesome and thrilling experience. I have seen big animals abroad, but nothing like this."

'Mr. Herbert's description tallies with those given by fishermen who reported seeing the Monster at sea.'

As this remarkable account is now nearly thirty years old, there seems little chance of following it up – but in compensation I am able to include one that is equally peculiar, and in some respects similar.

It comes from the *Scottish Daily Mail*, Saturday 3rd February, 1962:

'The Thing – A glowing Monster scares man on beach: A luminous "thing" from the sea, 30 feet to 40 feet long and leaving

[23] Cross-reference: Mr. Gavin's report of the 'Soay Beast', page 65.
[24] Or just over a foot in diameter.

a giant footprint. . . . That, says thirty-four-year-old Mr. Jack Hay is what he saw on the beach at Helensburg, the Clyde resort, just before midnight. He was out with his spaniel, Roy, when the dog "suddenly turned whimpering with fear, and cowered behind me".

'Then said Mr. Hay, "I saw the thing – about 40 yards away. I made out a massive bulk with a sort of luminous glow from the street-lamps on the esplanade. It did not move for about a minute, then seemed to bound and slithered into the water. I saw the thing swim out. It had a long body and neck, and a head about 3 feet long. I watched until it was well out in the water and had disappeared. There was a strong pungent smell in the air. I was really scared and Roy was cowering at my feet. We walked towards the spot and Roy started to sniff the ground. I shielded a match in my hand, and saw where the sand was scuffed – and there was a giant footprint. It looked like three huge pads, with a spur at the back. The thing was not a seal. I have been a sailor – but it was not like anything I have ever seen."

'Several householders in the area have heard strange noises, and roaring sounds from the beach at the east esplanade. Mrs. Moffat, of Sommerville Place said: "My pet dog is allergic to strange noises, and for the past two days he has been scared to go out of the house for some reason." '

A part of this account I find difficult to interpret is the reference '. . . I made out a massive bulk with a sort of luminous glow from the street-lamps on the esplanade . . .' Does Mr. Hay mean that it had a luminous glow of its own? or that the street-lamps created this impression? It is hard to say, but the question of luminosity conveniently leads to the next oddity report.

Letter dated 19th May, 1962, from Mrs. Trude Bryant of Bury St. Edmunds . . .

'Some years ago I was walking along the sea front at South-wold, with a friend: it was early evening, but the sun was still shining and the light good. We were both looking out to sea, and to our surprise we saw a moving object, between 20 and 30 feet in length – resembling a string of lights, travelling at a tremendous pace towards the pier.

'We were amazed, as we had never seen anything like this before; and I noticed a man and a woman beside us watching the same thing. The "lights" were presumably phosphorescence; slightly submerged, as I do not remember any ripples being visible. In a matter of seconds this object had headed towards a pier and out of sight.

'I could not estimate the speed of travel, but it moved very quickly . . .'

There seems to be some doubt as to whether these 'string of lights' actually broke surface, because in a previous letter Mrs. Bryant compared these objects to a drawing which appeared in *Loch Ness Monster*, showing the multi-hump body shape sometimes exhibited by our old chum in Loch Ness. Her exact words were . . .

'I am very struck with the drawing on page 22 (shape No. 6) . . . a few years ago, my friend and I were looking out to sea when we saw shape No. 6 travelling at a furious pace. There appeared to be lights on the humps . . .'

If these objects, which are typical of so many 'Great Sea Serpent' reports actually broke surface; could it be the low sun was reflecting off a wet skin surface, creating an impression of lights? Because although phosphorescence is common in the sea at night it is hard to imagine it being visible in the daytime.

In putting forward suggestions of this kind I do not mean to express doubts, but conditions of poor light, surprise, fright, or the momentary glimpse of something unfamiliar could cause an observer to draw a wrong conclusion.

On the other hand, it is the *observer* who is best able to judge the conclusions of others – in relation to something they have not actually seen.

The Ultimate Oddity : Frank Edwards, in his recent book *Stranger than Science*[25] refers to an extraordinary aquatic beast under the heading 'Captain Seabury's Serpent'; and as the preface states 'The author has carried out extensive research to establish the authenticity and accuracy of all these fascinating stories' – we should consider what he has to say about it.

The first two paragraphs read . . . 'Sea Serpents are customarily relegated to the realm of fantasy, but only by those who haven't examined the records of the good ship *Monongahela*, and her incredible catch.

'The *New Bedford Morning Mercury* first published the account in February of 1853, just about a year after it had happened . . .'

The record goes on to state that on the morning of 13th January, 1852, a lookout called the Captain's attention to an object in the water about half a mile distant. It appeared to be of enormous size, but its writhing movements indicated something was wrong with it. Thinking that it might be a harpooned whale in the last throes of death, Captain Seabury ordered three longboats away at once, taking his place in one of them.

Approaching the beast he drove his harpoon into it – but with disastrous results. A 'huge head 10 feet long' broke surface, and in seconds two of the boats were capsized. The creature sounded, taking a thousand feet of line – and as there was no means of raising it, the line was made fast. Captain Seabury then went aboard the *Rebecca Sims* which had pulled alongside, and talked to her skipper Captain Samuel Gavitt.

Next morning, the *Monongahela* began to take up the line around her capstan, but before half of it had been recovered, the beast's carcase floated up to the surface . . . 'It was a massive, monstrous thing, unlike anything any of those present had ever seen before. Longer than the *Monongahela* (which was more than a hundred feet from stem to stern) the Monster had a huge body about 50 feet in diameter. The long neck, some 10 feet thick, supported a head like that of a gigantic alligator . . .

[25] Publishers: Lyle Stewart, 1959: Pan Books, 1963.

165

containing ninety-four teeth in its jaws. The teeth were uniformly about 3 inches long and hooked backward like those of a
snake.

'The body of the creature was brownish-grey, with a light
stripe about 3 feet wide running its full length. There were no
fins and no legs, so it was assumed by those present the creature
propelled itself by means of a 15-foot tail, a knobby creation
like the back of a sturgeon.'

Subsequently an attempt was made to strip the carcase in the
manner of a whale, but to no effect. Cuts with flensing spades
showed it to be tough-skinned, without blubber.

The Captain then ordered the great head to be hacked off
and placed in a pickling vat. A drawing of the beast was made
and signed by all on board and together with his own report
it was passed to Captain Gavitt of the *Rebecca Sims*, homeward
bound for New Bedford.

Arriving safely this information was entered in the records –
which is a point of some importance, because it was not until
years later that the *Monongahela*'s name-board was found on the
shore of Umnak Island, in the remote Aleutians, indicating her
fate: and that of her crew, and the pickled Monster's head.

Odd though this story may appear, there seems to be a
quantity of substantiating evidence – though not all of it is in
agreement. For example in the 17th May, 1964, edition of the
New Bedford *Sunday Standard-Times*, Eileen Lardner writes
about the Sea Serpent, and in particular the *Monongahela*'s
catch, quoting from a letter written by Jason Seabury and sent
home 'by way of a passing ship months later . . .', in which some
precise measurements are included.

'As the creature was stripped of its outer, fatty layers, which
were melted down in try pots, the men made minute observations of it, under Captain Seabury's direction . . . "It was a
male creature 103 feet 7 inches long; 19 feet 1 inch about the
neck; 24 feet 6 inches about the shoulders; the circumference
about the largest part of the body, which appeared somewhat

distended, was 49 feet 11 inches. Its head was long and flat, with ridges. The bones of the lower jaw were separate and the tongue had its end shaped like the head of a heart.

' "The tail ran nearly to a point, on the end of which was a flat, firm cartilage. The back was black, turning to brown on the sides, then yellow, and on the centre of the belly a narrow white streak ran two thirds of its length.

' "The head," he said, "possessed ninety-four teeth, very sharp, all pointed backwards. The creature had two spout holes . . . and four swimming paws." '

These latter comments rescue the *Monongahela's* Monster from the ranks of the truly improbable, because a body of such vast dimensions would be almost impossible to control in the water without fins or limbs of some description. For example, although a whale uses its tail as a means of propulsion it has had to develop its forward limbs as control surfaces, in contrast to the rear, which have atrophied, disappearing entirely into the body.

But if the report is authentic, just what are we to make of it? – In short, has there ever been another creature remotely like the one described?

Looking a long way back to prehistoric times the answer would seem to be in the affirmative, because there were at least four huge marine animals with heads like alligators: and three of these were reptiles. A species of crocodile, which grew to 50 feet or so in length: the *Kronosaurus*, of the Lower Cretaceous period, which had a skull 10 feet long, and terrible jaws with pointed teeth – and the equally ferocious looking *Ichthyosaurus*. There was also a mammal called *Zeuglodon*, about 70 feet in length. This slender creature looked much like a sea serpent, but its fossilized bones from the oceans that once covered most of Alabama show its close relationship to modern whales.

But if the *Monongahela's* Monster owed its parentage to any one of these it must have evolved considerably during the sixty to a hundred million years since they existed: increasing in size

FIG. 13. 'Battle between sea monsters'.

and length, and developing the ability to swim at great depth, and breathe at the surface without being seen.

This of course is pure conjecture, but it should be borne in mind that adaptations in nature are continuous, and serve to meet a changing environment or habit pattern.

The marine iguana has developed toes and a flattened rudder-like tail for swimming in a relatively short period of time – and in the opposite sense, we humans have *almost* disposed of a tail, the rudiments of which remain as the coccyx, of which there is fortunately no longer any outward indication.

But it is equally true that in the majority of 'oddity' reports of unknown marine animals there is an almost total lack of supporting evidence – so the field of conjecture remains open – and imaginative as the battle between sea monsters shown in Fig. 13.

This intricate engraving comes from a book published in 1882, called *Moses and Geology*, and seems, in conclusion, to prototype both the *Monongahela's* beast, and the more infamous 'Great Sea Serpent'!

5

THOSE ENIGMATIC CARCASES

IN chapter nine of my previous book, four eyewitness reports and a sketch appear, of the 'Deepdale Monster' carcase – washed ashore on the lonely coast of Orkney main-island about Christmas-time in 1941.

Opinions varied as to what the creature was. Local men who examined it thought it was quite out of the ordinary, but the official view was different. Based on a series of photographs, and the opinion of voluntary experts the carcase was written off as a Basking shark, though by this time it had been on shore for over a month and was in a ruinous state of decomposition.

This view was, and still is, refuted by one witness, Mr. Bill Hutchison,[1] who saw it when comparatively fresh and almost complete – and as I knew that he was an experienced seaman and fisherman in Orkney waters, where Basking sharks are not uncommon I concluded he was very probably right.

Since then, however, I have been able to collect much additional information concerning the Deepdale mystery, and other apparently similar 'Monster' carcases washed ashore in Britain, in more recent times – and as this is all very interesting, and controversial, it provides grist for the monster-hunter's mill.

For convenience, and reasons of clarity the chapter is arranged under the following headings:

[1] Witness to the appearance of a 'Great Sea Serpent' in the Bay of Meil, in 1910, off Orkney main-island: referred to in 'Osborne Leviathan' analysis.

1. More of the Deepdale mystery.
2. The 'Girvan' Monster carcase.
3. The 'Barra' Monster – or desiccated carcase.
4. The Basking shark hypothesis explained.
5. A poet's lament for Monster-hunters.

MORE OF THE DEEPDALE MYSTERY:

Thanks to the untiring efforts of Mrs. Armain Hutchison in searching the back issues of the *Orcadian* newspaper, and the kind permission of its proprietor Mr. Robert F. Miller it is possible to fill in some of the gaps concerning this curious affair.

The first report of any significance comes from the pen of the late Mr. J. G. Marwick, former Provost of Stromness, and a competent naturalist. It appears in his column 'Nature Notes' of the *Orcadian*, 29th January, 1942 . . .

'On Tuesday night 20th January, Mr. P. Sutherland Graeme, of Graemeshall, Holm, rang me up to say that as he knew I was interested in natural history, it was only right I should know of the strange creature which had been washed ashore at (Deepdale) Holm. He proceeded to tell me where to find it, and enumerated many details (which really sounded unbelievable to me).

'It was with great expectation my brother and I proceeded last Thursday (22nd inst.) to see that strange and I might well say, unique creature.

'The scene at Holm is 2½ miles from St. Mary's village. We drew up at the rough hill track leading to the farm, and walked down to the beach three quarters of a mile distant . . . a cloud of gulls rose from the beach, so we knew the object of our journey was close at hand. We hurried over the rough stones . . . and there lay the – well I am at a loss to name it – the remains of some creature, the like of which we had only seen in the imaginative drawings of pre-historic denizens of the deep – call it a Monster if you like!

'The outstanding features to me, were its small head, long thin neck; massive hump; long sinuous back and tail parts. We made a fairly thorough examination of the carcase, commencing at the head.

'The lower jaw was missing; no teeth or the appearance of any in the upper jaw: skull being bare of skin was of gristle, very much resembling the gristly bones of a skate, but certainly not like the skull bones of any land animal; head rounded on top with very large eye sockets on either side; apparently its eyes had been large. Down the centre of the skull was a hole which I took to be for breathing purposes, and above this was a slight cavity in which apeared two tiny holes in its upper part. Head 18 inches from snout to back and 10–12 inches across . . .

'The neck from base of skull to where it joined the body was 3½ feet roughly and 6 inches broad. A small hump was visible along the back, less than a foot high; then came the large hump or dorsal fin, which was quite intact and one of the most prominent features. This hump was 2½ feet high – and on its upper edge were several thick hairs much worn and broken by rubbing on the beach; the hump was rounded on top and curved towards the head and tail of the animal – being 2 feet 6 inches wide at the base. Proceeding towards the tail were a whole series of small projections plainly visible for several feet along the back, but not at all in the nature of the large hump already mentioned. Then, 7½ feet from the centre of the large hump was a third hump, not quite so prominent as the smaller one in front, but a distinct hump nevertheless. From this to the tail were more of the small projections, but at the extreme end of the tail the flesh was all gone, leaving the backbone in sight, several sections of which were broken off and what had been the utmost end of the tail was a piece of gristle – as I saw it the total length of the creature was 25 feet. I should have stated the detached tail-piece fitted lengthwise to the backbone, not across it as in the case with the tail-flukes of a whale.

'Proceeding from the tail towards the head . . . on the side of the body was a projection, obviously the stump of what had been a tail flipper . . . passing the entrails, we came to the front flipper which was 3 feet 9 inches long and fully a foot broad, curving to a point. . . . This flipper was strongly attached to the shoulder of the creature, all of which was composed of the same gristly substance already mentioned. The shoulder appeared to be massive and strong and the front then curved up to the neck. . . . The body being devoid of skin through action of birds and weather was of yellowish-white colour, the white being mostly fat, or so it appeared. The only skin I saw was on the tail portion and was in the nature of a hard horny substance, yellowish-grey in colour. . . . The tail portion was not round, but more flat like as it lay on the stones, and the widest part of the body I estimated to have been 3 to 4 feet deep, apart from the large hump. . . . In giving an estimate of weight I ventured to suggest half a ton . . . but my brother doubled it easily . . .'

In full, Provost Marwick's article runs to considerable length, and indicates clearly enough that he thought the carcase was extraordinary – and of sufficient interest for him to make the journey a second time to glean further information; and it was on this trip that he spoke to a Mrs. Anderson whose husband had first found the carcase lying on the beach about 200 yards from their house – a week before Christmas.

'It was whole at that time, but stinking even then, and some parts were without skin, while the belly, which was large, resembling a cow ready to calf, was beginning to burst open. It was grey in colour, and it had two long things like whiskers sticking out from the sides of its head, one on each side. (I found out that these antennae were each five inches long, and part of one remains on the skull, which I now have.) – No steps were taken to inform anyone for she thought it was just a dead shark, or, as she expressed it, "A funny sort o' shark with a neck at both ends".'

The second visit showed the carcase to have been largely eaten away by the gulls, and in order to save something of value before it broke up completely, Marwick removed the skull at the second vertebra, and put it in a sack along with most of the front flipper. These items were later stowed in a tub, and sprinkled with salt to help preserve them.

In a subsequent article for the *Orcadian*, 5th February, 1942, he wrote; 'I judge it to be one of a species considered extinct many ages ago – a marine saurian in fact – or marine reptile. The very nearest I can come to it is the order of extinct reptiles called "Ichthopterygia", a family of marine reptiles which had a whale-like body, with skeleton like a (land) animal, limbs modified as paddles or flippers, and with biconcave vertebrae – which this creature had exactly, viz. sections concave on each side . . .'

'As newly discovered creatures are usually named after some outstanding feature in their anatomy or from the locality in which they were first found, I propose to name the one found at Deepdale Holm the *Scapasaurus*, which in my opinion fits it as well as any other.'

The reason for this curious name is that Deepdale is in the vicinity of Scapa Flow, the great wartime naval anchorage – and the fact that Provost Marwick gave a name to the animal at all demonstrates he was sure it was of an unknown species, because no person concerned with natural history, whether a professional or amateur, would do this without considerable thought.

But, whether justified or not the name seems to have caught on because on the 12th February, 1942, another letter appeared in the *Orcadian* describing a second apparently similar carcase, washed ashore on the uninhabited island of Hunda, a few miles distant. It was by a Mr. W. Campbell Brodie, of St. Margarets Hope, and reads . . .

'A Second Scapasaurus? . . . Less than a fortnight after the appearance on the beach at Deepdale, Holm, reports reached me that a similar creature had been washed ashore on the Hope of Hunda, also in the Scapa Flow area. Unfortunately several weeks had elapsed between the time of its first being observed and that of my setting out to investigate.

'However, on February 5th, along with James Macdonald and Andrew Laughton I made the journey across the island of Burray and thence to the island of Hunda.

'We were rather sceptical of the reported dimensions of the second Orkney "Monster" and we intended to verify these for ourselves; but on arrival at the very stony beach on the island a strange sight met our eyes. A huge elongated yellowish-coloured creature lay embedded in the sea-wrack, wedged firmly between the boulders.

'Closer inspection revealed that this was indeed no ordinary denizen of the deep, but truly a creature of "Monster" proportions. All that remained was the skull and vertebral column, together with several appendages or fins consisting of cartilaginous material.

'There were suggestions of a hump of a fatty nature, on the top of which was another cartilaginous fin, similar in structure to the larger fins lying beneath the vertebral column. The back of the latter was covered with greyish-black tough skin with a hairy appearance. From some parts we obtained hair of a coconut fibre nature, about four to six inches in length. The skull of the creature was composed of a gristly substance, definitely not bony and there was no evidence of teeth. On the anterior part were two antennae, four inches long, and laterally two large sockets which may have contained the eyes.

'On a raised part of the skull was a large cavity, possibly a blower hole, about midway along its dorsal surface. Immediately behind this were two smaller holes, all communicating with the mouth region.

'Of a mouth or lower jaw there was no sign although we found a cartilaginous part, somewhat like a horse saddle in shape. We could not discover the articulations for this part or any part of the skeleton.

'We proceeded to measure the carcase – the length was 28

feet approximately, there being 65 vertibrae making up the spinal column.[2]

'The head alone measured 2 feet long and 1 foot broad at its widest part. The appearance of the vertebrae was unusual, there being no spinous processes present. Each individual vertebra was bamboo-like in appearance and was joined to the preceding one with an elastic-like membrane. One of the large flipper parts measured 3 feet in length . . .

'We were so convinced that the creature was of a similar species to that found at Deepdale, Holm, that we hired a boat from Mr. John McBeath and removed the skeleton in sections to St. Margarets Hope, and now are exhibiting it locally in aid of the Red Cross.'

However extraordinary and exciting these two finds may have appeared to laymen, official opinion was in no way disturbed by them . . .

Report in the *Orcadian*, 5th February, 1942: 'More About the Monster – declared a Shark by South'

'On Saturday last, the Receiver of Wrecks, Kirkwall received a telegram in the following terms from the Natural History Museum, Kensington, London – "Many thanks for the photographs. Large body is that of a Basking shark. . . . No further interest. Writing you later."

'The telegram was in response to sixteen official photographs dispatched from Kirkwall on Friday by the Receiver of Wrecks. . . . The Royal Scottish Museum, Edinburgh authorities have also declared the carcase is that of a Basking shark. . . . However, in certain quarters locally, the view is entertained the carcase is *not* a Basking shark, and in this connection Provost Marwick yesterday telephoned us as follows:

' "Since writing my article, I have had a call from a gentleman who is a lecturer in biology at Durham University, on the research side of that study.

' "I showed him the head and other parts of the creature in

[2] Appendix Note E refers.

my possession. He was astounded, and confirmed my opinion that the creature was of a very ancient type, unknown at the present day, so far as he knew, and undoubtedly a sea reptile . . ." '

This last comment seems to put the 'cat back amongst the pigeons'; but on 19th February the *Orcadian* published yet another letter, which appears to greatly strengthen the official view . . .

'Further opinions on the two dead "Monsters" located recently, are to hand. These endorse earlier verdicts that the remains of the Holm carcase where those of a shark and confirm that the Hunda "Monster" was another shark.

'We publish below a letter to the *Orcadian* and the *Orkney Blast* by two members of the Royal Artillery whose civil qualifications entitle them to express expert opinion:

11th February 1942

'Sir,

'After examining the remains of the so-called Monster now at St. Margarets Hope, we think the following comments may be of interest to readers.

'The skeleton is entirely cartilaginous; the so-called "blow-hole" in the skull communicates directly with the cranial cavity and therefore cannot possibly be a whale type of blow-hole. The general make-up of the skull is typically Elasmobranch (sharks, skate, etc.) There is no indication of a true neck in the vertebral column; the first few vertebrae are comparatively small, but they increase progressively in size towards the centre of the body, from which point they decrease towards the tail. The articulation of the first few vertebrae does not differ from that of the rest of the vertebral column, consequently the so-called neck of the animal is no more mobile than any other part of the spine.

'The pectoral fin contains a large number of radials attached to the typically shark basal plates. The presence of a large number of radials is a non-reptilian characteristic; the number of radials in the fore limb of even the earlier prehistoric reptiles was, as far as is known, less than in this specimen.

'The so-called "hair" was examined and found to be very fine needle-like fin-rays formed of cartilage. The tail was incomplete, no indication of a "cow-like" tail was observed.

'The stomach was about $2\frac{1}{2}$ feet long and when split open longitudinally contained a spiral valve characteristic of sharks. The contents were not examined, these being badly lacerated.

'The absence of jaws and gill supports is of no great significance and may be explained by the fact that this part of the skeleton in sharks is only very loosely attached to the skull and vertebral column. No trace of the upper jaw was seen; in reptiles this is fixed firmly in the skull.

'We have little doubt that this specimen and the skull of another present at St. Margaret's Hope are the remains of sharks, probably Basking sharks.

(Signed) J. W. Jones, B.Sc., Ph.D.
W. Thorpe-Catton, M.Sc.'

Reading this clear statement the case for the St. Margaret's Hope 'Monster' almost ceases to exist – but, what of the Deepdale carcase just a few miles distant? What of the opinion of the lecturer in biology? And what actually became of the skull so carefully removed and preserved by Provost Marwick?

A letter from the (then) Keeper of Natural History, The Royal Scottish Museum, Edinburgh provides an answer . . .

'Dear Mr. Marwick,

'Thank you for your letter and for the parts of the "Monster" which arrived safely in Mr. Tod's charge. I have examined the material and am sorry not to be able to make it anything interesting. The remains are definitely those of a shark. I am having them preserved so that should any queries arise after a few years we shall be able to refer to them. I'm afraid you must have had rather a hard time with it and endured a good deal of smell. . . . The bristle was interesting, but when soaked out in warm water turned out to be like one of those long filaments on the fin you sent me. These, by the way, were the dernal rays of a fin.

Yours sincerely

(Signed) A. C. Stephen.'

These two letters leave little room for doubt as to the true identity of both carcases, because when experts examine physical remains they can be expected to come up with the right answers. But, despite this fact, I'm glad to say the defence remained undaunted . . .

Letter to the editor:⠀⠀⠀⠀⠀⠀⠀⠀⠀⠀⠀⠀17th February, 1942,
St. Margaret's Hope.

'. . . I have talked with probably 50 per cent of the fishermen at present engaged around Scapa Flow area, and still have to meet one who believes the "Monster" to have been either a shark or a whale. One trawler skipper compared it with a creature, long and slender in appearance and covered with long brownish hair, which, he stated, rose above the water and attacked the ship's mizzen sail. That Monster had a very long neck and a head resembling that of a cow. This happened near Hoy.

'Mr. David Wylie of Burray also tells me that a creature of similar appearance was seen in the Watersound between Burray and South Ronaldsay a little more than a year ago.

Yours, etc.

(Signed) W. Campbell Brodie.'

And finally:

Letter to the Editor:⠀⠀⠀⠀⠀⠀⠀⠀⠀⠀⠀⠀5th March, 1942,
Graemeshall, Holm.

'Sir,

'May one who is quite unversed in zoological lore venture to put one simple question to the experts who appear to maintain quite positively that the Deepdale "Monster" was, while it lived, a Basking shark?

'It is indisputable that – no less than five competent and in every respect credible witnesses noted two bristle-like

179

projections, one on each side of the upper lip of the animal, each 5½ inches or more in length and not less than ¼ inch diameter at the base, formed apparently of a substance resembling gristle. I have a sketch of the beast showing these projections and all five observers agree as to the correctness of the sketch.

'My question then is this: Is there any evidence that a Basking shark possesses these antennae?[3] Such pictures of him I possess do not show any corresponding features. If he does possess them, then I say no more. If he does not, are we to take it that he has in this case somehow assumed them after death by reason of the elements or during decomposition?

Yours, etc.

P. Sutherland Graeme.'

As Mr. Sutherland Graeme, C.B.E., first reported the Deepdale carcase, it is fitting that the case for the defence should rest with his challenging letter; to which there does not appear to have been any reply.

THE 'GIRVAN' MONSTER CARCASE

On Friday 21st August, 1953, the *Carrick Herald* published a photograph (see Sketch 14) showing the decomposed remains of a very large animal which had been washed ashore. Beneath it appeared a short descriptive account – under the heading: 'Was it a shark? Girvan Refuses Experts' Views on "Monster".

'Girvan woke up at the week-end to the discovery that it had had on its doorstep for over a week a "Monster", but as the days have passed those who have viewed the "thing" have become more confused and bewildered as scientists and experts have "blinded them with science" to confute the evidence of their own eyes.

'Washed ashore at the Dipple, near the works of the Alginate factory, the Monster answered to traditional conceptions – it was over 30 feet long; had a long neck of about 4 feet, surmounted by what seemed to be a smallish head as though of an

[3] Appendix Note F refers.

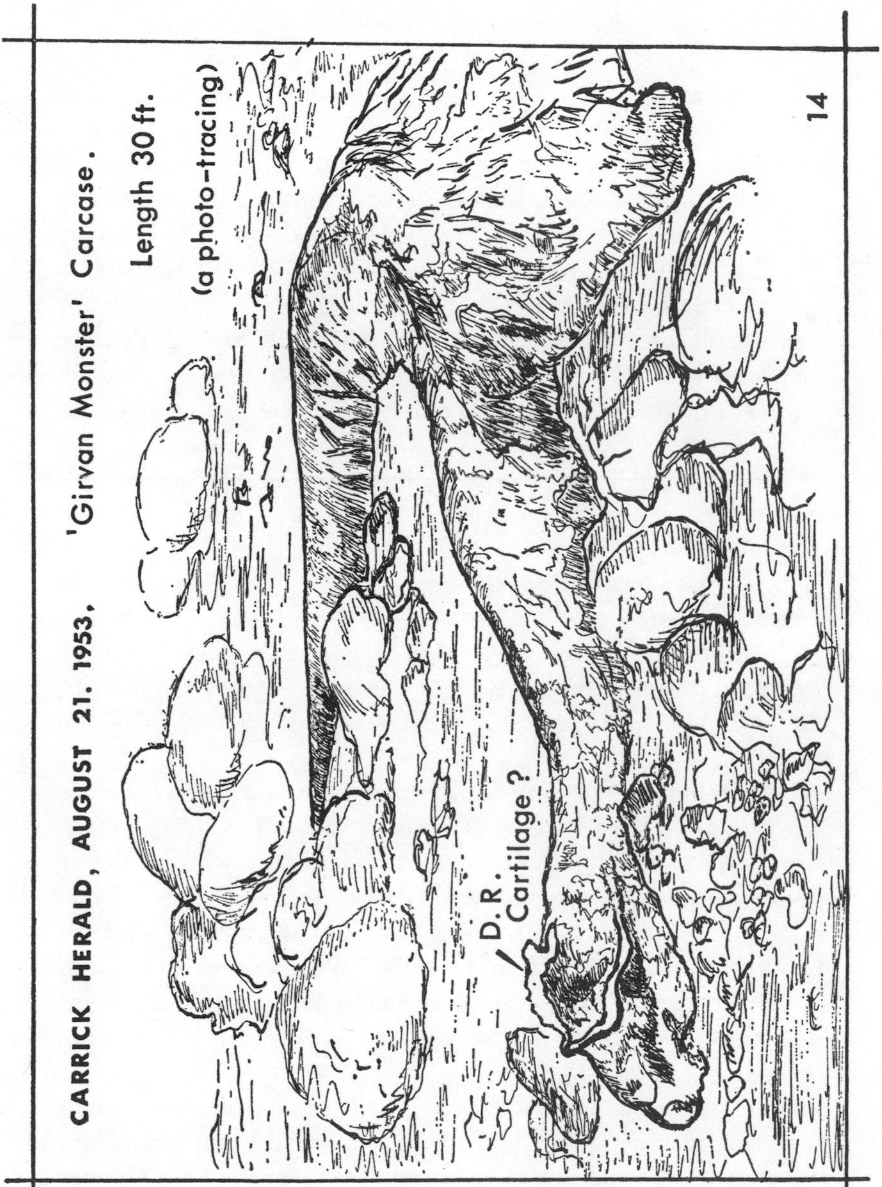

CARRICK HERALD, AUGUST 21. 1953. 'Girvan Monster' Carcase.

Length 30 ft.

(a photo-tracing)

D.R.
Cartilage ?

14

FIG. 14

animal like a horse or a cow; was covered in coarse grey hair; and had four short stumpy legs! What more could anyone want!

'As the unbelievers made the short trip to Girvan to scoff – and come away shaken – the staff at the factory complained that the Monster might be of great interest to all and sundry, but to them it was just "one big smell", and the firm which had maintained it was but a Basking shark, enlisted the aid of the Sanitary Inspector to gain permission to destroy it. Oil and petrol poured on the decomposing Monster was set alight, but merely charred the remains, and actually the tides were doing more to disintegrate the huge mass when the Marine Biology Department at Millport urged it was imperative close examination by experts be made before there was any further destruction. Experts who had studied pictures shared the express belief of Mr. A. R. Waterson, O.B.E., B.Sc., of the Marine Biology department of the Royal Scottish Museum – "nothing I have seen alters my opinion that it is a Basking shark" – and Mr. J. B. Cowey, lecturer in zoology at Glasgow University confirmed his view.

'But local fishermen in Girvan and district claim they are expert in distinguishing a Basking shark as any professor, "and that wis nae shark" sums up their reactions after viewing the remains.

'More than that! A number of them have claimed that before this finding of the Monster, that they have seen a strange creature in the seas off Ailsa Craig, and off Turnberry Point. Six or seven weeks ago, well-known Girvan fisherman the *Geisha* skipper William Sloan reports sighting the Monster on a return trip from Ailsa Craig, when a number of passengers saw it also. Ridiculed at the time – he is a well-known leg puller – he is now convinced that what he saw and the dead creature were one and the same.

'But skipper Carson and his crew had even a closer view when they saw it rearing its "long neck and small head out of the water, it was staring at us out of great round eyes," said Skipper Carson, "and I took a shot at it and it disappeared."

'A serious-minded student, whose "balance" is vouched for by a former Provost of Girvan, claimed to have seen the thing "foaming through the water at great speed" but said little about his discovery because of its unnatural appearance . . .'

THE 'BARRA' MONSTER – or desiccated carcase.

In July of 1961 I came to hear of an apparently exciting find on the shores of Barra, the last small island at the south end of the remote Outer Hebrides chain, off the west coast of Scotland.

I was at first interested by this report, which referred to a long-necked carcase, and made hasty arrangements to fly there in a private plane, hoping to see the thing before it was destroyed by the sea or putrifaction.

Before leaving, however, I received a copy of the Scottish *Daily Express*, of 18th July, publishing a photograph (see Plate 11) and a short column explaining that a Glasgow University Zoologist, Mr. Peter Usherwood, had flown out to examine the creature. His verdict was straightforward: it was the desiccated remains of a male Beaked whale – the apparent long neck being formed by the backbone, from which most of the surrounding flesh had fallen away.

As he was quite obviously right I cancelled the trip – though with some regret. I had been looking forward to the scenic delights which are a part of coastal flying – and perhaps the thought of returning with a part of the 'Monster' as material evidence: with which to confound the sceptics!

THE BASKING SHARK HYPOTHESIS EXPLAINED

The picture of the Barra carcase is important for two reasons. In the first place it proves that after decomposition a backbone can end up looking very much like a long neck – and secondly that the head of a whale of this type remains almost intact, despite the decomposition. But, a whale is a mammal, and a Basking shark a fish, with a completely different type of

183

breathing apparatus, and it is this difference which appears to provide an answer to the very natural question 'how can a Basking shark possibly be confused with the type of carcases found at Deepdale and at Girvan?' – because as is generally known these huge fish present a very shark-like appearance, with a large fish's tail at one end; a tubby cigar-like body and a blunt proboscis at the other. By no stretch of the imagination can such a shape be compared with or modified to fit the 'Monster' picture: and if this is so just what *are* the experts talking about?

In defence of their hypothesis, it is necessary to refer to a letter which appeared in the *Orcadian* on 26th of February, 1942, written by the late Commander R. T. Gould . . .

'Many thanks for the valuable information about your local sea monster. . . . I have notes on several such cases whose family likeness, both in gross and in detail, is very striking. One and all they relate in the finding, in a decomposed condition, of the body of a Basking shark (*Certorhinus Maximus*).

'The Basking shark seems to have been designed by Providence for the express purpose of looking, when dead and decomposed, as much like a sea serpent as possible, and as little as possible like his normal living self.

'He has practically no bony structure except a long tubular backbone, running from the base of his small skull right away to the tip of the upper lobe of his tail. The backbone is composed of separate vertebrae which are cupped, or socketed, so as to fit closely, and held together by a covering of gristle. He also has a pair of cartilaginous branchia, or gill-frames, held together round his backbone by the sternum (which is your horse-collar) and, apart from this he consists entirely of flesh and soft cartilage.

'When decomposed then, the only structure which he possesses is his skull and backbone (the gill-frames come away from the body) his sternum and such flesh as may be adhering around these.

'The net result is to give the impression of a creature with a very long, thin neck, a spindle-shaped body and a long thin tail – something on the lines of the fossil Plesiosaurus, and as

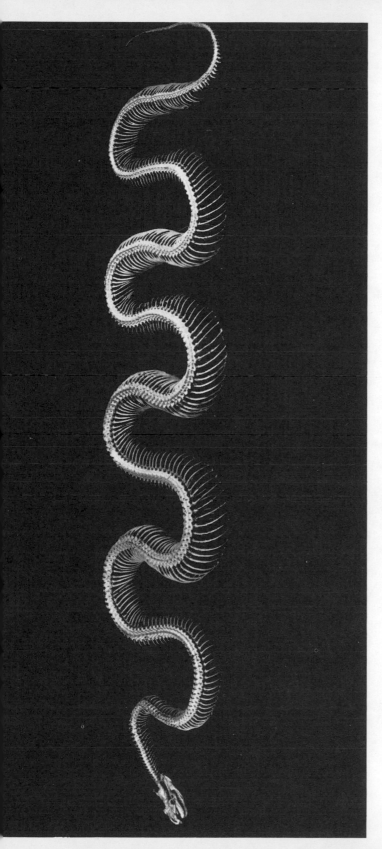

16   This photograph of a 23 ft. skeleton of a Reticulate Python, clearly indicates that the ribs are greatest at the 4th convolution of the body. This snake has an accepted maximum length of 33 ft. and shares honours for size with the Anaconda of South America, as the world's largest known species.

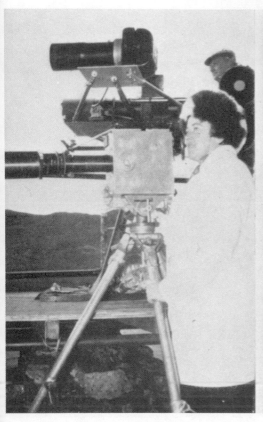 

17 LEFT Ro McPherson and Dick Hobbs close up on the big-rig and Newman camera. October hunt 1964.

18 RIGHT Exactly the position from which I shot the 1960 Monster film—some 300 ft. up on the south shore overlooking Foyers Bay.

These contrasting pictures show the massive long-range photo equipment at the main expedition site, and the lightweight, mobile rig I would recommend for private monster-hunters. A Bolex 16 mm. reflex and 6 inch lens is not difficult to hire or operate, and a car seat quite easily removed.

unlike as possible from the aspect – which the Basking shark presents when living. It is then natural enough that when such carcases are found, partly decomposed by people whose knowledge of marine biology is slight, that they should not be recognized for what they really are.

'The classic case is that of the famous 'Animal of Stronsa' washed ashore at Stronsay in September 1809 . . .

'It was never examined by any person of education and the evidence relating to it, although given on oath, is that of the local fishermen and crofters. Summarized the gist of their depositions is as follows: Length about 55 feet; Maximum girth about 12 feet. Neck slender and about 15 feet long. Tail the same. Head small, not exceeding a foot in length and 6 inches in width. From the shoulders a bristly mane extended nearly to the end of the tail. Skin smooth and grey. Organs of motion – three pairs of fins, one of which may have been a caudal fin. The skull and the sternum and some of the vertebrae were preserved and are illustrated in the *Memoirs of the Wernerian Society* (Vol. 1), Edinburgh 1911.

'The skull has now been lost, but I examined the vertibrae[4] in Edinburgh in 1933, and they are undoubtedly those of a Basking shark: it must, however, have been a huge specimen, for the vertibrae are something like 6 inches in diameter. I see no reason to believe that the reported length of the body (55 feet) was at all exaggerated. . . . A similar but smaller carcase turned up in the New River Inlet, Florida in the spring of 1885 but was subsequently washed away in a storm before any portion of it had been secured. Then there was the Pra Sands (Cornwall) of 1928 and the Querqueville (Cherbourg) carcase of 1934. . . . Later in 1934 one turned up somewhere in British Columbia and even the Director of the local Marine Biological Station failed to identify it for what it was. . . . Of the numerous known reports of strange carcases thrown ashore in the last 150 years, I have come across only one in which a Basking shark had not provided the *corpus vile*. That one is the Santa Cruz carcase of

[4] Appendix Note G refers.

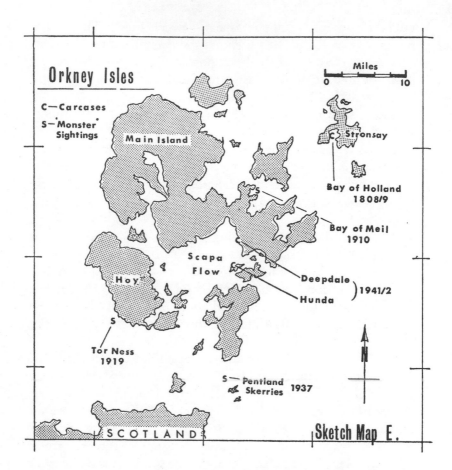

Orkney Isles

C—Carcases
S—'Monster' Sightings

Main Island

Miles
0   10

Stronsay

Bay of Holland
1808/9

Bay of Meil
1910

Scapa
Flow

Deepdale
Hunda
} 1941/2

Hoy

S

Tor Ness
1919

N

S — Pentland
Skerries 1937

SCOTLAND

Sketch Map E.

1925 . . . a specimen of Baird's Beaked whale (*Berardinus bairdii*). The skull is now in Berkeley College, California.'

So wrote Commander Gould – and if one cares to examine the anatomy of the Basking shark, there is much to be said for his theory; as Plate No. 12 will show – but on looking back over this controversial evidence, with its variations of opinion and conviction, it is difficult to arrive at any set conclusion. On the one hand we must accept the logic of Commander Gould, and respect the knowledge of the experts. We have to admit the probability that these carcases were those of Basking sharks –

and yet there were the anomalies – the fact that the 'Animal of Stronsa' was some 15 feet longer than the largest Basking shark on record – the large difference in the vertebral count between the Hunda skeleton and the one hanging in the British Museum – the 5-inch 'antennae' – the three fatty humps, and so on. I do not intend to argue the matter, because enough has been said, but before turning to the next chapter it might be useful to consider the Orkney Island group, an outline of which appears in Sketch Map E.

On this map I have shown where these incidents occurred, including the Bay of Meil sighting in 1910 (Hutchison's 'Sea Serpent'), and also the Island of Hoy sighting in 1919, details of which were published by Gould in the *Case for the Sea Serpent*; from which Mr. Mackintosh Bell's eyewitness account is well worth considering:

'In 1919, after demobilization, I went to Brims Walls, Orkneys, to spend a month's holiday by taking my place as one of the crew in a cod-line fishing boat, belonging to fishermen friends. . . . The very first day I was there, I think it was about 5th August, I went afloat with a crew of four at about 9.30 a.m. for the purpose of first lifting lobster creels, and then for cod fishing.

'On making our way to the creels, which had been set in a line between Brims Ness and Tor Ness, my friends said, "we wonder if we will see that sea monster which we often see; and perhaps you will be able to tell us what it is".

'We got the creels; hauled some, and were moving slowly with the motor, when my friends said very quietly, "There he is."

'I looked, and sure enough about 25–30 yards from the boat a long neck as thick as an elephant's foreleg, all rough-looking like an elephant's hide, was sticking up. On top of this was a head which was much smaller in proportion, but of the same colour. The head was like that of a dog, coming sharp to the nose. The eye was black and small, and the whiskers were black.

The neck, I should say, stuck about 5 – 6 feet, possibly more, out of the water.

'The animal was very shy, and kept pushing its head up and then pulling it down, but never quite going out of sight. . . . It disappeared, and as was its custom swam close alongside the boat about 10 feet down. We all saw it plainly, my friends remarking that they had seen it many times before – just about the same place. It was a common occurrence, so they said. As to its body, seen below the water it was dark brown, getting slightly lighter as it got to the outer edge, then at the edge it appeared to be almost grey. It had two paddles or fins on its sides and two at its stern. My friends thought it would weigh 2 or 3 tons, some thinking 4 to 6. Not only my friends, but others, lobster fishing, got many chanches of seeing it . . .'

Subsequently Mr. Mackintosh Bell supplied two rough sketches, and estimates of size. . . . Body and neck together about 18–20 feet long; circumference of body 10–11 feet and about 4–5 feet across the back; head about 6 inches by 4 inches 'very like a black retriever'.

Gould perhaps felt this strange creature may have been an unidentified species of long-necked seal. For one thing it had a small eye, and whiskers, and there was no report of a tail; and its shy behaviour and dog-like head sounded like a seal – and I would be inclined to agree, but for the 'neck as thick as an elephant's foreleg, all rough-looking like an elephant's hide' – because the short furry hide of a seal looks glistening and sleek when wet: but as the history of the Orkney Island Monsters is sufficiently complicated already, the matter is better left to rest.

A POET'S LAMENT – for Monster-Hunters

On 13th February, 1942 a poem appeared in the *Manchester Guardian Weekly*, by one 'Lucio' – a person of quite unusual wit:

THOSE ENIGMATIC CARCASES

FAR TOO FISHEY

Yet again the doubting Thomas
takes our precious Monster from us
and proceeds once more to bomb us
    With disclosures stern and stark,
Lo! our portent meteoric
doped with dismal paregoric
sinks from Monster prehistoric
    To a common Basking shark.

With our portent oceanic
it was ever thus, in panic
came the learned ones tyrannic
    With their formular of doubt;
Then as fast as they are able
they dismiss the peoples fable,
and with "Basking shark" as label
    Leave the Monster down and out.

When we thought we had before us
an undoubted something-saurus,
from the days when all was porous
    In the world's well-watered dish
These confounded men of science
setting fancy at defiance
go and put their cold reliance
    On an unembellished fish.

But the Monster fan, unbeaten
calls for something more to sweeten
yarns so mouldy and moth-eaten,
    And he takes a stouter stand
On some long delayed survival
from days distant and archival
when the lizards had no rival
    In their lordship of the land.

We need something more terrific
than these learned lads specific;
I defy their scientific
   And uncompromising quiz.
Their pretensions need unmasking,
here's a question for the asking –
How could any shark go basking
   With the weather what it is?

6

REFLECTIONS ON THE WATER

THE light was failing. I stood amongst the rocks, surrounded by a scatter of equipment. Cameras, lenses, tripods, sound recording apparatus, batteries, bedding, cooking pots, food and clothing – lit by the glimmer of a fading electric torch. It was late August of 1964. The eighth expedition.

Dizzy with fatigue, I stepped forward to the water and drank of its purity – its cool, faintly mineral flavour lingering a moment; utterly refreshing.

Stripping off my shirt, I sensed a prickle of raindrops before splashing the water into my face, and over my body, cleansing the sweat of exertion – the expression of effort in lifting this pile of equipment a hundred and fifty feet above the water, then down through a slither of lichens and undergrowth, beneath the trunk of a fallen tree; down again to the lake-shore edge, to this hidden place, from which to continue the watch.

It was after ten o'clock. Arriving with the sun already low in the west, obscured by a barrage of mountain tops it had taken a shuttle of journeys to and from this place to loosen the muscular cramps from days of motoring; the blood pounding in my ears. But here I would stay for a week, in almost perfect seclusion.

I rolled myself in a blanket, and lay down on the shingle to sleep, in peace. The only sound the faintest rustle of a breeze and of ripples on the shore, in whispered harmony.

Rising with the dawn I set to work to prepare the hide – the

191

ambush; a peculiarly technical business with so much equipment to attend to.

First the camouflage, allowing only a gun-slit aperture for camera traverse – and next the bubble-level adjustment of a tripod, shoulder high with the superlative Arriflex sixteen-millimetre on top of it: the attachment of lens and powered film magazine, with four hundred feet of colour negative stock.

Connecting the batteries I checked the motor drive, and carefully shaped a loop of film round the guidance rollers, engaging the transport claw before shutting the gate with a snap. I tripped the micro-switch, and reset it, then gingerly touched the firing lever watching the fluttering transfer of film, and take-up on the spool. Pressing it again to make sure, I clicked the light-excluding plate into position and locked it – before running to adjust the speed, watching the indicator needle settle at twenty-four frames per second.

Stooping to the sound-recorder, with its coil of cables, I tested the battery circuit and set the gain and power switches. Checking for levels I played back, hearing an unfamiliar voice, no longer modified by the bones of my skull – then turned to unpack the secondary cameras.

With technical settings made I took the final step in preparation; and by far the most important. I set to work to train in the use of this equipment. A remoreseless sequence training, printing in the memory a pattern of reactions, so that when the emergency arose, excitement would not obliterate my senses.

In recent times, technical strides in optical science have put the monster-hunter in a commanding position. The big, ultra-flexible zoom lens now enables him to approach an object of up to a mile or more in distance, and stay within frame and focus of it down to a matter of yards. It is the perfect weapon, this variable piece of optical artillery; the view through which on a reflex camera is a constant source of entertainment – but it forms only a part of a range of equipment, the controlled use of which will, I believe, ultimately defeat the sceptics.

Over the years, I have had chance to develop a specification,

19 The author standing by the long-range optical artillery—
Castle Urquhart Battlement Site. The rotating Moy-head carries
two F.24 still cameras, with 20 inch lenses, and a 36 inch lens
attached to a 35 mm. ciné camera and 1,000 foot film spool. Power
driven, the rig is sighted through a telescope, and operated by a
single switch. Photographic range is enormous.

20 The southern shore of Loch Ness is a place of great natural
beauty, and tranquillity, where one can watch for days, in solitude.

and the means of meeting it – and *training* in the use of this very special equipment is paramount. Every move must be planned, every contingency considered, every situation rehearsed, until the operator acts instinctively, with icy efficiency. Thus it is that even the solitary watcher has plenty to occupy his mind and physical capacity.

On this particular expedition, bad light, due to rain and mist and thundercloud, posed something of a problem, in contrast to the year before when I had watched through sunshine – and a bout of pneumonia – but it was enjoyable; and I no longer suffered the weather, having learned to protect myself from it, whiling the hours away in thought, and the routine of observation.

The southern shore of Loch Ness is an utterly peaceful place, and as the hours and days slip by one becomes suspended, as it were, in time, and away from the clatter of life the mind, which is much like a pool of water, becomes free of surface interference – and it is possible, sometimes, to peer down into it, and trace in the outlines of thought the shape of things which lie unsuspected. Truths; the simple facts of which defy the complication our society sets about them, in its hasty drive to rationalize – and denounce the unexplained in terms of fraudulence; when in truth it is our state of human ignorance which lies at the root of the matter.

Standing, watching, waiting, the gentle rain falling in patterns across the water – or hissing in storm-cloud fury through the branches above I pondered many things, the contrary nature of which was often surprising – a conclusion of opposites; and as the venture drew to a close, for the first time there was no stunning sense of failure, or physical exhaustion which had in the past caused me to notice a curious metallic taste in my mouth – the reaction of some organ of the body – the 'bitter taste' of defeat, perhaps.

The sun came out, and with the welcome loan of a rowing boat I loaded up the equipment, and paddled slowly back, looking down through the clear but peat-stained water, the colour of rich brown tea; down at the rocks and boulders shelving off rapidly into mysterious, shadowy depths . . .

Later in the year, in October I spent two weeks with the main expedition which had been in position at Castle Urquhart, since early in the summer.

Sponsored by the Bureau, with backing from the *Observer*, and ATV, and David James as leader, it obtained its strength from the voluntary effort of a great many people, who kept watch from a platform mounted high up on the ramparts.

At first there had been two sites – a second opposite on the southern shore; but as the weeks went by costs rose, and it was decided that if the hunt was to be extended one of them had to close. Manpower became a problem too, and bad weather dogged the expedition.

But despite these handicaps, and a continuing failure to film the beast, which kept appearing with maddening consistency in different parts of the loch,[1] morale remained high.

Arriving during the first week in the month, I assumed the post of Group-commander with some hesitation. After years of solitary effort I wondered how I would fit in with the other members, and had doubts about the equipment: but as things turned out I needn't have worried about it.

The crew was made up of a scientific photographer and his wife, a bank manager, and a cheerful American – the wife of a U.S. government man residing in Britain: together the best of company, and in a short while we had an efficient team manning the lofty platform with its ultra long-range equipment. (Plates 17 and 19.)

We had field telephone and visual links with a pair of secondary camera sites, disposed to cover each other and extend the arcs to include the whole of Urquhart Bay – and by working a

[1] The beast was actually seen on more than one occasion by expedition members, in one case from a boat at night, at a range of just a few yards (causing the solitary oarsman to row as never before!) A list of reported sightings for 1964, and early 65, appears under Appendix Note H.

series of watches arranged a periodic change of scenery. The search required an almost continuous tour of duty, from daybreak to dusk, but with so much at stake no one complained about it, knowing that a last minute success would save the expedition from a crippling financial loss, and vindicate those who had watched so patiently before us.

But, as the Gods decreed, the venture went down to defeat; and as the final seconds ticked away we saluted the Monster fittingly, in a local barley brew – the fiery liquid joining our hands in comradeship, and the desire to meet again the following year, and see the thing through if we could.

Later we said good-bye to Wing Commander and Mrs. Cary – Basil and Freddie, of boundless hospitality, on whose property the expedition camped throughout the summer. Retired, the Carys live in a house some 200 feet up on the southern shore of Urquhart Bay, and as Freddie has spent much of her life at Loch Ness her knowledge of wind and water, and the Monster, is quite exceptional. In all she has seen it on four or five occasions, and as her testimony, and advice relates to the area of water overlooked by the expedition it is important to take note of it – as recorded for me in a letter dated 28th November, 1964 . . .

'. . . I have written an account. . . . It may not be brief enough, but bits of it might be of use. It is very wet and cold now, certainly not "Nessie Weather"!'

The account in full reads:

'The first time I saw the Loch Ness Monster must have been about 1920 when I was a child. I was out in a boat with my brother fishing, about a ¼ mile east of Temple Pier. The water was quite rough on that occasion, and my brother was rowing. Suddenly a huge black hump appeared out towards the middle of the loch. It was just like the bottom of an upturned boat and must have been over 20 feet long and about 4 feet above the water at the highest point of the hump. I am a pretty good judge of size because I know so well the look of a 14-foot fishing boat. I was very frightened, and asked my brother to go back into Urquhart Bay.

'The next time I saw Nessie was in July 1954. By that time we were living in a cottage on the loch-side near Urquhart Castle. About two o'clock in the afternoon I was in the field beside the loch which was flat calm. I saw a huge black object crossing from the far side towards the Castle. It was travelling at great speed and making a terrific wash, and as it came nearer I saw a salmon leaping out of its way. It turned west and disappeared beyond the Castle.

'A fortnight later, four of us had another marvellous view of the Monster. The loch was like a mirror. My son Major W. H. Davidson, and I were in the field about 11 a.m., the great black hump suddenly appeared just off the Castle point right below us, it caused a great commotion in the water as it surfaced, and it stayed still for some minutes. We stopped an A.A. man on his motor-bicycle who was passing, and he watched with us. My married daughter Mrs. D. S. Lucas was also watching it from the window of her bedroom upstairs. After a time the creature moved off into Urquhart Bay. When it was about half-way across it turned and came back towards us, still on the surface, and making a great wash. It then turned east and went right up the loch towards Brachla, and after a time we lost sight of it. We must have been watching it for about twenty minutes.

'The next time was August in 1960. I was in the field looking down at the loch. I suddenly saw a terrific commotion in the water quite close to me, which must have been made by some huge creature – then about a ½ mile farther east I saw a great black hump crossing the loch from north to south . . . which suggests there must be more than one creature in the loch.

'In August 1963 my youngest daughter saw Nessie only about 15 yards from shore. She called to me to come and see it. By the time I got there the black hump was disappearing, and then we both saw a great V-shaped wash in the calm water as it made off towards the middle of the loch.

'Every time I have seen Nessie, apart from the first occasion when it was rough, it has been very warm sunny weather, and Loch Ness has been flat calm. Apart from my own sightings, almost all the sightings by other people that I have heard of, have been under the same conditions. I think it is a complete waste of time to look for the Monster when it is cold, and the loch is rough, but if the expedition continues to watch during the summer – it can only be a matter of time before they get a decent picture of Nessie.'

Looking back over the last five years, I wonder how many times I have said that to myself – 'it can only be a matter of time'?

Optimism is deep rooted in the nature of man, but in itself it is not a complete justification. There must reasonably be something more, some inward compulsion to drive on towards a goal in the belief that there is a worth-while purpose in attaining it.

In the case of the Monster there has never been any doubt in my mind about the need to 'discover' it, which is self-evident, but in attempting this it has been necessary to measure the action taken against other things, to honestly justify it.

The cost has been great – at a private level seemingly impossible to meet in time and money, and yet, in meeting it, by some strange alchemy I am the richer for it, and my family no less independent.

And so too in the contrary nature of thought the Monster justifies itself in terms of opposites; because I do not believe it is in itself important. Dramatic, extraordinary, exciting, a zoological wonder perhaps – but not important, in the sense that it is only an animal – like an elephant, or for that matter, a cow, which is equally marvellous: and in due time people will come to recognize this fact.

But, in the way it relates to our scientific society, over the last thirty years, it is of *enormous* importance, because it reflects a pattern of behaviour which, for all its sophistication and twentieth-century knowledge is no different to that demonstrated over the last three hundred years, and more.

197

In short, in the case of embarrassing unexplained phenomena, science just 'doesn't want to know' – and safeguards its traditions and petrified establishments, by simply ignoring the facts: and for this reason it is imperative that voluntary work continues at Loch Ness.

We stand, I believe, on new frontiers of discovery which will test the credulence and courage of man, and his ability to adapt in thought will depend on his mental flexibility – on his state of *dynamic open-mindedness*, which can best be described in terms of the modern photographic lens, of variable focal length. The zoom lens, which can, in a trice, open out to take in all the picture, or close down to examine a part of it in smallest detail.

We must have this type of mental outlook, and at Loch Ness we have such a rare opportunity to demonstrate the need for it.

Thus I would say that in the time that lies ahead, we must man the battlements again, and face the enemy. The cold wind; the weather; the erosion of disappointment; the doubt and prejudice so deeply entrenched, for in doing this we defend a principle – a Standard if you like, and a handsome one at that. Untarnished Cloth-of-Gold, which flutters boldly in the breeze!

It is the Truth.

7

BRINGING 'MONSTERDOM' UP TO DATE

IN the years that have passed since Freddie Cary made her predictive comment in 1964 so much has happened at Loch Ness it is only possible to summarise events—and in connection with the study and pursuit of information generally I can present some recent reports which quite literally bring 'monsterdom up to date.'

Perhaps one of the most interesting stems from a letter written to me in 1966 by a Mrs. Lilian Lowe of Harborne, Birmingham, England.

'Dear Sir,
Having just read your book *Loch Ness Monster* we thought you might be interested in our experience. It took place on June 21st, 1965 at about 9 p.m. (summertime).

'Three of us, my husband, my cousin and myself were standing on the end of Mingany Pier, Kilchoan, Ardnamurchan, looking out to sea, which was mirror-like with not a ripple on the surface. My husband was looking through binoculars, (Taylor Hobson ex-army x 6), at the old ruined Mingany Castle.

'I saw what I thought to be a seal appear above the water, about 100 yards offshore. Then, another hump appeared, directly behind it and a few feet away. As it moved I came to the conclusion that the two humps belonged to one object. I said "What's that?"

199

My husband immediately sighted the creature but was silent. He said afterwards he was too amazed to speak. He could see a huge shape about 40 feet long beneath the water, and after a few moments said "a submarine I think." He then noticed what seemed to be legs or flippers paddling at the side of the body, creating a turbulence beneath the water. My cousin and I could only see the two humps moving steadily along and waited for a decision as to the identity of the creature, but all my husband could say was that he had never seen anything like it in his life. The two humps were very solid and dark and shiny, and the skin seemed to be like hide.

'I was anxious to see it through binoculars . . . but just as I had it in view the creature submerged.

'It seemed to be similar to the Monster described in your book. In fact although we had not read 'Loch Ness Monster' then, we agreed it was a monster we had seen, but said "no one will ever believe us." Indeed, when we spoke of it in the Hotel, the remark was "A bit off its beat wasn't it? I expect it was a Basking shark."

'I must state that my husband has exceptionally keen eyesight and has seen Basking sharks off the Cornish coast and is convinced the creature was something he had never before encountered. The two humps were nothing like fins, being much more solid, like the conning tower of a submarine: which was the reason for his first remark. I'm sorry it was not in Loch Ness we saw it—but thought you might be interested.'

Mrs. Lilian Lowe need not have apologised for the location of her monster, because unless she and her husband were mistaken the report provides another X—or 'Marine Visitor' mark—for the 'Scottish N.W. Highland Monster Map' on page 59. After some further correspondence she commented . . . 'The sensation of being stunned at first sight of the monster is exactly what we experienced. My husband said he also felt alarmed when he saw the size, and what appeared to be the legs, and that if the creature had changed direction and headed for the shore, we should have got in the car, which was just behind us, and started the engine ready to *move*. We should also think twice about going for sea trips in a small rowing boat, like the one in which we were taken to the Island of Hunda in 1963.'

In 1967 I received another interesting letter from a resident of Birmingham—a Mr. P. Sharman, who described an experience on a part of the Welsh coast which I knew very well indeed, having spent some of my boyhood at a place a few miles to the northward.

'Dear Sir,

I have just read the book 'More than a Legend' about the Loch Ness Monster, and your book 'The Leviathans.' Throughout both books there are many descriptions of monsters resembling the Plesiosaur. They remind me of a creature I saw when on holiday in late August, 1963. In a rocky cove, near New Quay, Cardigan Bay, Wales, I noticed an animal greatly disturbing a colony of seals. The creature drawn was slowly moving its four paddles to and fro as if in readiness to make a sudden move. At one end of it there appeared to be a long neck and a small head poised above the water as if to strike out suddenly. The seals around it were making off as though the fear of death was upon them. This led me to suspect the creature was making ready to kill a seal. After I had watched the thing for a few minutes I realised there was a remote possibility that I was looking down upon a floundering Basking shark. This seemed more and more probable, so I left the scene.

'Later, during that week I was exploring another

201

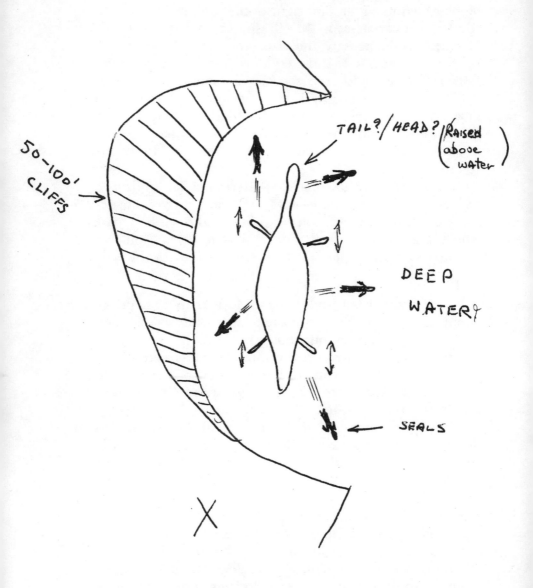

15   Mr. Sharman's sketch.

cove about half a mile from the spot where I saw
the strange animal. Here I saw the carcase of a seal
with a huge chunk bitten off from its neck and shoulders. This practically cut the body in two and I could
not help wondering what creature could have made
such a horrible wound. Of course it could be that I
saw a Basking shark half in and half out of the water
and mistook the tail for the head and neck of a Plesiosaur type creature. But I saw no dorsal fin; and are
Basking sharks aggressive to seals? The creature, comparing it with seals, must have been 30-40 feet long,
and was a brownish black colour. I was looking down
at it from about 100 feet at an angle of about 50
degrees. It must have been about 8 feet wide. Please,
could you give me your views on my statement?'

I wrote back to Mr. Sharman to say that in all the
years I had known the Cardiganshire coast I had never
seen a Basking shark in that vicinity—though seals were
common enough. Dangerous sharks were not seen
either, though a harmless species known as a Tope
was sometimes caught from boats in deep water. One
could not however rule out a Killer whale, but these
animals have huge dorsal fins and most distinct pie-
bald markings which he could hardly have missed from
his vantage point. Nor do they have long necks and
small heads! Altogether his account so astonished me
I may have seemed doubtful about it in my letter to
him, because he replied . . . 'Thank you very much
for your letter. I suppose you must receive letters
from spoofers, but I can assure you I am not one. It
is perfectly O.K. to publish my account and sketch . . .
I can be more exact about the position where I saw
the creature. It was the first cove south of Cwmtudu
. . . etc. etc.'

From this second letter I gained the impression that
Mr. Sharman really did know about the coastline at

New Quay, which is a tiny, beautiful Welsh-coast village nestling in amongst a series of coves along the shoreline. It bears no resemblance to its more popular namesake resort in Cornwall, called Newquay, which is much bigger, and seething with tourists in the summer.

During the next half-decade at Loch Ness—between 1965 and 1970—a great deal of importance happened, and as each 'monsterhunting' season opened, hopes remained high, and efforts were redoubled.

In 1965 I made two more private expeditions and one for the Loch Ness Phenomena Investigation Bureau, which had closed the Urquhart Castle battlements site and moved to Achnahannet, a field overlooking vast stretches of water some two miles to the west. There was a small wooden camera platform and one dingy caravan-trailer in support. I spent a week there in torrential rain, with a team made up mostly of Americans who stood up to the ordeal with commendable good humour. It was a poor year for sightings, and with one exception (see Appendix note I) these were of little interest. The physical strain of these adventures was beginning to tell on me, and in September of that year, working alone on the southern shore, I suffered another attack of illness, and came close to losing my life in a tiny car-top boat which I had brought in to ferry my equipment. This forced me to the conclusion that I must continue working privately, with no more than two expeditions a year, or alternatively do just one stint as a Group Commander for the LNPIB. I decided on the former plan—because it was obvious the Bureau's activities were gaining in strength and self-sufficiency, and that my efforts from the south shore would be complementary. For some reason, it remained almost deserted by monster-hunters.

But if 1965 was a bad year (only 9 sightings of

'tolerable authenticity' were logged by the LNPIB), in other respects it proved to be a turning point. An American professor teaching at the University of Chicago visited the Ness, met David James, and was invited to become a Director. As a biochemist of standing, his acceptance was encouraging for the Bureau, and it was not long before Roy Mackal made his dynamic presence felt by raising funds and creating serious interest in the United States.

In that year also, a short sequence on 35mm film showing twin wakes on the surface of Loch Ness was submitted to the R.A.F. for photo analysis, and the results were so encouraging David James invited me to submit my original 1960 sequence too. This I was glad to agree to, knowing the R.A.F. was expert and unbiased.

Early in 1966, the Joint Air Reconnaissance Intelligence Centre 'Photographic Interpretation Report No. 66/1' was sent to the LNPIB, with a request that its contents should not be published immediately—but the press had in some way found out about it. The resulting announcements and mistakes, made it necessary to publish the report in full. This was done, and the 'JARIC' report, as it came to be known, was printed as a Crown Copyright pamphlet, with an introduction by David James.

The result was encouraging, for within the 2,000 word technical analysis based on precise measurement of the original filmed image, conclusions had been drawn which were of technical interest and which had a profound significance.

The object photographed was NOT a surface vessel and had a speed of some 10 mph. No estimate of length could be made due to the distance and angle of photography, but 'it is doubtful if a non-planing hull of under 16 feet could achieve this speed.'

205

The height of the object when filmed above water (*i.e.,* before it submerged to move just below the surface) was about 3 feet. In para. 15 the report went on to comment . . . 'One can presumably rule out the idea that it is any sort of submarine vessel for various reasons, which leaves the conclusion it probably is an animate object.' And in para. 17 . . . 'If animate, the surface shape of the object will not be angular. As expected, the apex of the triangle has a rounded shape. The slope of the sides of the triangle suggest that there will be some increase in width below the waterline and, even if slight, means the width of the object is at least 6 feet. Even if the object is relatively flat bellied, the normal body "rounding" in nature would suggest that there is at least 2 feet under water, from which it may be deduced that a cross section through the object would be NOT LESS than 6 feet wide and 5 feet high . . .''

This would be roughtly equivalent to the cross section through the body of an elephant!

I was not surprised by the report—and I was pleased by its conservative nature. I had measured the boat sent out afterwards in length and beam, as a check on scale . . . and the 'JARIC' report estimated its length as 13.3 feet, from the measurements made in the film. I knew it to be 14 feet, in fact.

For the first time the question 'Where is your scientific evidence?' could be answered. As a result, despite the continuing harassment of ctitics, the Monster began to assume an aura of respectability. From the date of publication of the report, serious interest in the phenomenon began to increase, and more and more private individuals with a scientific training became directly involved with the research. After six years of negligible progress this was encouraging, and I was grateful to the LNPIB for suggesting the analysis and to the R.A.F.'s long range photo experts for doing such a splendid piece of work, which was in itself a vindication.

During 1966 and 1967 I made four more private 'marooning' expeditions to a small island at the Foyers River promontory, a low lying triangle of alluvial silt, with a crescent shingle beach and a growth of natural scrub. From this idyllic spot I missed seeing the Monster on two occasions, which was reported close to me from a ship in transit through the loch and an LNPIB rowing boat; and in consequence I retreated back to higher ground, from which I could hardly miss a sighting. In 1967, too, I was fortunate to win a scientific award from Kodak, in Britain, for a report on the subject of my long-range photographic work at Loch Ness. Worth some £1,200 (about $3,000) it placed in my hands equipment which previously I could only hire for short periods at a crippling cost.

In 1966 the LNPIB continued operations, employing infrared filmstock for the first time, to penetrate the mist, which had in the past ruined sequences of film.

But in spite of some 29 accredited sightings, no new film was exposed—and it was not until the following year that a new 35mm film sequence was obtained on black and white filmstock, showing a big V wake developing on calm water, with nothing clearly visible causing it. Shot at considerable range a sense of scale was established by a local pleasure boat, well known on the Ness, appearing conveniently in frame, at which point in time the wake died out at the apex, giving the impression that the object causing it had dived.

In 1967, too, due to the perseverance of Professor Roy Mackal in the U.S.A., Field Enterprises Educational Corporation of Chicago made a large research grant to the Bureau of some $20,000, and this hand-some donation was supplemented by a further £1,000 put up by the Highlands and Islands Development Board, in Scotland. With this type of sponsorship the LNPIB made extensive plans for 1968, increasing its camera sites to five vehicle-top telescope cameras, which were driven into positions of advantage and manned by expeditioners. Between 1965 and 1966 visitors to the small LNPIB exhibition at Achnahannet had increased in number from a trickle to a flood—from 1,000 to over 25,000—and thereafter the numbers kept increasing.

In 1968 the LNI, or Loch Ness Investigation was established as the operating arm of the parent body, or 'Bureau,' as it was now almost universally referred to. Membership was becoming truly international; and with the dawning of scientific respectability, a new at-tempt to locate the beast on sonar was made in August, by a team from the University of Birmingham, in Britain. Professor D. Gordon Tucker and Hugh Braith-waite, a senior research associate, tried out a new type of digital sonar, with interesting results. A narrow fixed-beam of sound was pulsed across the loch, and the echo response displayed on sonarscopes, which were photographed every 10 seconds, over a two-week period.

Three targets, designated A, B, and C appeared to be of significance—the first rose from the bottom of Urquhart Bay 600 feet down, at a velocity of 100 feet per minute. It had a horizontal velocity of some 7 m.p.h., almost moved out of the beam before descend-ing again to the bottom. It then rose at 120 feet per minute. Object B could have been a shoal of fish swim-ming at constant depth, so was not considered to be of any special interest. Object C appeared on three frames only, and thus would have been within the beam for some 30 seconds. Its behaviour was startling, with 'a horizontal velocity component along the range axis of the order of 7.5 m/s or 15 knots while diving at 2.4 m/s or 450 feet per minute. It appears to have a length of several metres.'

Cryptic comments such as these mean little to the layman, but to those familiar with fish behaviour and swim bladder tolerance to pressure change, such velocities rule out fish, as does the 'length of several metres.' The largest animal in Loch Ness, other than a stag swimming on the surface, would perhaps be a 40 pound salmon some 4 feet in length.

Birmingham's own comments were reserved, and they made no claims they could not substantiate . . . 'Since the objects A and C are clearly comprised of animals, is it possible they could be fish? The high rate of ascent and descent makes it seem very unlikely, and fishery biologists we have consulted cannot suggest what fish they might be. It is a temptation to suppose they must be the fabulous Loch Ness monsters, now observed for the first time in their underwater activities! The present data, while leaving this a possibility, are quite inadequate to decide the matter. A great deal of further investigation with more refined equipment—which is not at present available—is needed before definite conclusions can be drawn.'

In the 1968 Annual Report of the Loch Ness Investigation the following paragraph appears . . . 'Their results as published in the *New Scientist* of December 19th, 1968, are reproduced as an appendix to this Report. They were rapidly attacked by *Nature* (Dec. 28th, 1968) and by the *Times*, and by a letter from Dr. Maurice Burton in the *Daily Telegraph*, on the grounds that the sonar equipment had been tested by the Fisheries Laboratory at Lowestoft, when it had been found to be "prone to ambiguities." What the source of this information was is far from clear as the equipment had never left the hands of Birmingham University. There the matter rests at present.'

In this report some 14 sightings were accepted out of the usual collection of sighting reports, representing perhaps a third of the whole—LNI being scrupulously careful in accepting only those which had corroboration or significant detail. Coincidentally, it was noted that only 3,717 salmon had been counted over a dam at the mouth of the River Beauly (close to the River Ness exit) as opposed to 12,749 the year before. It was apparent therefore that the dread game-fish virus had taken hold of the fish-stock which, with commercial fishing, had dwindled alarmingly. As monster-researchers had long believed salmon to be a primary item of diet for their elusive quarry, these figures raised the inevitable question 'Could the Beasties continue to survive?'

In September of 1968, I gave up the insurance business which had paid the bills since abandoning my profession as an aero-engineer in 1961—the better to hunt the Monster—and became a full time participant. During the previous years I had managed to put in many expeditions, but it was becoming obvious that the search required full time concentration if it was ever to succeed. It was a chilling move to make, but justifiable, and when I made a training cruise in the 8 metre catamaran CIZARA, off the western Scottish coast in June, I decided to charter her for a surface-photography boat on Loch Ness. I travelled up to Fort William to join her at the entrance to the Caledonian ship canal, and with my family aboard, and the owner, motored the craft through the forty miles of lochs and waterways, of entrancing natural beauty, into the Ness. Here we hoisted sail and travelled the length and breadth of the lake, taking three days in the process.

CIZARA was a fine craft, and we were sleeping seven on board. The family and Mr. Smith, the owner, then departed leaving me to 'loner' the huge and almost deserted expanse of water, over the next two-week period.

By the end of this time I knew more about the environment and the thrills and fears of an almost hermit-like existence. The fantastic beauty of the Ness, with its looking-glass surface and mists at dawn and equally its ferocious moods and blasts of wind which threatened to drive CIZARA to destruction on the rocks, combined to entrance me and constrict my bowels with anxiety. On two occasions during the course of this splendid and erratic expedition, when we had all been living aboard, we had seen water disturbances which were inexplicable, and once when driving along the north shore road shortly after sunset Mr. Smith, my wife, and all four children had seen a large humped object moving through the water just offshore, creating a wash. I stopped the car, jumped out, and ran back to where the trees no longer obscured the view, at the sighting place—only to find that the object had disappeared.

CIZARA proved to me that it was feasible to work from the water providing one accepted the risks and had the full time use of big zoom-lens equipment. The Kodak award had made this possible.

Again, in 1969, I was able to work from the water, though for a very much longer period—for 82 days and nights, living and drifting endlessly aboard a tiny 16 foot cabin cruiser, which I had named WATER HORSE. I became a water animal myself and was accepted as such by the local wildlife, because I moved silently with the hull camouflaged and with outriggers mounting underwater hydraulic stabilisers, of a unique design. Without them I could not have withstood the instability, but their action made a platform of the cockpit from which I could shoot photography as well

211

as from the deck of CIZARA, which weighed nearly ten times as much and had double hulls.

During this season, Urquhart Bay became the focal point for submarines, sonar, film companies, and the press, involving a multitude of people and a mass of equipment. For once the peace and loneliness which I had come to accept as inevitable when working from the southern shore or alone in CIZARA was destroyed, but was replaced by human warmth, humour, activity, and the most bizarre experiments. Field Enterprises of Chicago had put up money for a tiny one-man sub to work with the LNI and had accepted my offer to help out as surface liaison boat. Dan Taylor, a Texan of much submariner's experience shipped over VIPER-FISH by freighter, a bright yellow, two-ton fibreglass boat, with a diving potential of several hundred feet. For a period of several months we worked together.

Ashore, at Temple Pier in Urquhart Bay, a giant five-ton animated model monster was in the process of being constructed for a film, 'The Private Life of Sherlock Holmes'; and with Urquhart Castle leased for filming, too, the whole bay became alive with boats and film crews, the model monster, and a second submarine named PISCES, a sophisticated deep water submersible painted a brilliant orange.

Later, another boat, JESSIE ELLEN, moved into the bay, a handsome, bluff motor vessel designed and run by her owner and skipper. She helped with the model monster and the sonar crews for Independent Television News, which was preparing blanket national coverage of the 'Great Monster Hunt.' Independent of all these operations, another sonar workboat, RANGITEA, moved in to fit out with a type of mobile sonar rig—a Honeywell Scanner 11—brought over from the U.S.A. by Robert E. Love, Jr., sponsored by Field Enterprise, working through the LNI.

PISCES was soon diving regularly to the bottom of the loch and producing some interesting observations. The topography in the Urquhart Bay area was not a flat plain of silt, but potholed and fissured. She spotted two deep pits on sonar, one just south of the Castle, 970 feet in depth, thus increasing the official maximum depth by more than 200 feet. Most fishlife disappeared below 30 feet, but a white eel was seen at 820 feet, and a small white flatfish burrowing along through the silt at 350 feet. In the main reaches of the loch valleys were discovered, some extending for hundreds of yards; and in the craters currents were experienced, on one occasion whirling the submarine round in a counter clockwise direction. A deep sonar target.was picked up just off the bottom in 470 feet of water. PISCES homed on it, but it rapidly disappeared off the screen when approached within 400 feet. Distinct thermal layers were encountered between 60 and 40 feet, which interfered with both sonar and underwater telephone systems, but incredibly normal surface-radio contact could be maintained underwater down to 90 feet, and on one occasion to 120 feet—in itself a phenomenon—thought by some to be explained by the suspension of mica in the loch water.

Altogether PISCES made 47 dives and spent some 250 hours underwater; and her jovial crew of experts became a part of the shore community at Temple Pier, which had grown up so suddenly. During the course of her underwater explorations two other events occurred, which had nothing to do with the research. Ancient weapons were spotted in the silt of Urquhart Bay, probably dumped there after the battle of Culloden near Inverness, when the 'bonnie Prince Charlie' uprising of 1745 came to its disastrous conclusion; and a little offshore, the bones of an old wooden ship were found, sunk in about 100 feet of pitch black water.

VIPERFISH, too, had her moments of excitement. In Fr. J. A. Carruth's annually updated booklet 'Loch Ness and its Monster,' reference is made to one in particular: 'Mr. Dan Taylor the former United States Navy submariner talked about the one occasion when he may have been near to encountering a creature in Loch Ness. "I was about 130 feet down when I suddenly found that the bottom had been stirred up. I thought at first it must have been my own prop wash and I stayed there for a few minutes. Then I found I was facing up the slope, not down. An ordinary fish could not have turned a two-ton submarine right round . . . Something might have been sitting there and left in a hurry when it heard me coming. Unfortunately I did not have my forward search sonar going at the time." '

To add to the 1969 entertainment on Urquhart Bay, trials with the giant model monster began with buoyancy problems, developed with the first animation tests— when the great contraption was towed through the loch by an underwater cable drawn by a powered winch ashore—and ended in catastrophy, when it sank in a storm. Fortunately I had 'shot' it the day before from high up on the mountainside with a 300 mm lens, securing a unique sequence of film with the model moving its head and jaws in a most realistic manner, as it surged through the water. It had weighed 5 tons and had cost a small fortune of money. Subsequent film had to be shot in tanks.

The International Television News sonar venture introduced a powerful 'pinging' device, which must have scared underwater creatures off for miles in each direction; but later in the year when Bob Love in RANGI-TEA had the loch to himself and doggedly plodded up and down the length of it, he scored several hits. One sonar contact lasted 2 minutes 19 seconds, with some very large object which traced a looping path ahead of the boat before moving out of scan.

This was the second major sonar result in two years, and it was to produce further generous support from Field Enterprises in Chicago, for continuing work in 1970.

The long summer of 1969 was remembered for the colour and variety of experiments and the interest shown by the press, TV, and film-makers too; in addition to the 'Sherlock Holmes' model-monster epic, another colour film was shot by Walt Disney Productions, over a two-week period. Ken Peterson, the producer, and an expert Scots camera crew exposed several thousand feet of 35 mm film. This included interviews with witnesses, the LNI operations, submarine activity, the beautiful scenics of the loch, and the work by independents, such as myself in WATER HORSE. Ken, predictably, was a man of imagination and artistic talent, who had worked on animation with Walt Disney himself, in the early days.

By the season's end, however, in late September, with the departure of all but a few, Urquhart Bay had again become a tranquil place. I had been on the water for over three months and had lost some weight. It was growing colder; and my feet, in contact with the glass hull of the boat, had to be 'defrosted' in hot water every two or three hours. It was time to stop.

For ten years I had hunted the Beast—in this time only once seeing it on the surface: the occasion of the 1960 film. To be sure, in CIZARA and in WATER HORSE I had been close to inexplicable disturbances, on no less than seven occasions, and twice I had 'missed' sightings at relatively close range due to mere circumstance; but the fact remained that one man working hard with good equipment for an extended period could *not* be sure of renewed success—the odds were so great, the loch surface so huge, one had to

215

accept the reality of this fact. It was no good pretending otherwise. I might see the Monster in the next ten
minutes, or perhaps not for another ten years.

I decided, in consequence, that outside of hunting
occasionally for fun—like an annual fishing holiday—
the only sensible alternative was to become involved in
the communal activities which would, eventually, beat
the odds. In short, to help with the type of activity
fostered by the Loch Ness Investigation Bureau.

It was not a decision I particularly enjoyed making,
because I was a 'loner' by choice. It was so much
simpler and so much more efficient to work alone, and
there was a certain spiritual quality about it. Working
from the south shore, with its peace and tranquility,
and from the surface, too, with its dangers and excitement, I could always escape from people and the tourist
traffic of the north-shore road, which in the summer
months was continuous. And yet I had to admit that
I had enjoyed the human company, the warmth, and
the high spirits which flowed in Urquhart Bay during
the unforgettable summer of 1969.

In September I pulled little WATER HORSE out
of Loch Ness, and with the brown algae adhering to
her hull, trundled the long way home, sleeping one
last night in her en route. Curiously, I only noticed
the movement of the boat once I came ashore—I seemed
to lurch about, my body mechanism instinctively attempting to balance out the movement which it had
come to accept as normal, which no longer existed. It
made me feel distinctly seasick.

In October I was invited to run the field and surface
photographic operations for the LNI in 1970. It took
me some time to decide, because of the inevitable com-
plications and the months I would have to be away
from my long suffering family. But they had come to
accept these activities as a part of life.

I accepted. There was much to be said for the LNI, although in 1969 it had almost been swamped by volunteers, most of whom were young people. I felt that if I had any contribution to make, it must be in trying to get the crews operating as truly effective cameramen and the difficult long-range photography simplified to a point where results were adequately clear.

I spent the winter months writing letters, visiting people, and giving talks and lectures in preparation. The potential of air photography had always appealed to me so I paid a visit to a man of considerable talent —a true innovator, who designed, built, and flew his own tiny one-man autogyros—Wing Commander K. H. Wallis, C.Eng., A.F.R.Ae.S. Retired from the R.A.F., he had since concentrated on the design and development of these astonishing machines.

As a result of a visit to his home and construction centre in Norfolk, among the farming flatlands of East Anglia, and a demonstration of the autogyro in high wind conditions, we made arrangements for Ken Wallis to fly for the LNI in 1970. The object would be to patrol the loch at several thousand feet, then spiral in on a target with engine throttled back, shooting photography through frame mounted 'gun' cameras and a fast shuttered Nikon F.

In early spring I travelled up to Loch Ness by train to inspect the LNI basecamp at Achnahannet. Battered by winter storms, the old green-painted trailers presented a dismal sight, huddled together and deserted. There was deep snow on the mountains, and the loch lay icy calm and remote in the frozen stillness. I scouted round for new camera sites, climbing the dizzy forestry roads overlooking the water, a thousand feet below; then returned home.

On May 23rd I came back to face the odds, the

217

problems, the weather, a multitude of different people, and the ogre of finance, over a five-month period as Surface Photography Director for the Loch Ness Investigation. From the comparative sanctuary of the years spent one-man monster-hunting I had stepped into the very centre of a vortex of activity and would work in cooperation with Bob Love, who was returning as Underwater Research Director for the LNI, sponsored again by Field Enterprises.

By mid-summer I had become accustomed to the kaleidoscope of human relationships; the changing crews; the new reports of monster sightings which focussed at Achnahannet; the visitations from the press and TV, and a dozen other variations, which served to make each day different from the last. It was exhausting. I rose each morning with the light and helped with the setting up of cameras and crews down the line of outstations, returning for breakfast before continuing the job of running the investigation—sometimes right through to midnight. There were no days off. There was no time for them; though once every six weeks or so I caught the sleeper down to London and spent a day or two with my family, who would shortly be travelling up to stay at Achnahannet, during their summer vacation. My eldest son was now a young professional soldier in the Royal Armoured Corps, and my youngest, Angus, who had been born on the day following the TV showing of my film, in 1960, was now an active ten-year old.

It seemed hardly credible that I could have been hunting the 'Beastie' ever since.

With the arrival of Ken Wallis and his tiny autogyro, towed behind an equally diminutive Min-Cooper 'S,' operations had an almost Wellsian air about them. Ken was tall, had a twinkle in his eye, and a sweeping grey moustache. He walked with the long strides of one used to pacing out take-off distances, upon the minimums of which his very life depended. Not everyone realised that an autogyro was different from a helicopter, and would ask impossible feats of it. With its simple rotating wing and ultralight structure the 'gyro could lift off within a hundred yards of spin-up, but it needed a flat surface to run along and an unobstructed line of flight. Given this, it would climb away like a gadfly, the sun shining on the two discs of its rotor and four-bladed prop.

The 'Wallis 116,' with a smaller Maculloch engine, held world speed and altitude records for the type, and Ken had been awarded the famous Seagrave Trophy for his contribution to aeronautics. The machine we were using was the more powerful 117, which he had Christened the 'Watchful.' Photographically it was a success; and although no monster surfacings were recorded from it, we proved that using a small autogyro, air photography was both practical and definitive.

The summer operations in 1970 were so complex I decided to present them in a chart for the public to view, in the LNI's exhibition trailer. At one end of this the autogyro appeared, neatly boxed as an experiment. Next to it I placed the long-range photographic teams representing more than a hundred individual cameramen who would have to be trained and supported, at the five main camera stations. My own boat WATER HORSE was scheduled to go back on the loch but with a more powerful engine, enabling me to move rapidly from one place to another, and out of weather difficulties. Basecamp operations were in the centre, with a line drawn vertically representing the water surface. To the right of this Bob Love's underwater team and experiments were laid out, and on the right of this again more experiments scheduled by the Academy of Applied Science team from Massachusetts, who were new to us.

One of the basecamp projects included a harbour building operation—a task involving off-duty crews who had to raft in boulders and dump them in a line underwater. In time these 'wetsuit slaves' became so expert at bombing rocks into position that the harbour walls began to assume shape, building up neatly from the bottom in eight feet of water.

To help with the harbour project a beach-combing operation was started, using FUSSY HEN, the clinker workboat; and this brought in heavy timber, old oil drums, and other finds, of varying degrees of usefulness. It was a popular diversion.

Between the land and water based experiments, Birmingham University again set up transducers in an attempt to repeat their success of 1968, working from a scaffolding pier the LNI had constructed in Urquhart Bay. Later, too, in August, Bob Love returned with his electronic gadgetry and a crew of specialists. During the winter months I had persuaded several experienced monsterhunters from Britain to join forces with him, and before long Temple Pier in Urquhart Bay was the scene of much activity, with workshops and trailers and boats crowding the scene.

RANGITEA, the sonar boat, moved in; and KELPIE, a powerful fibreglass cabin cruiser, skippered by Ivor Newby, hooked up in the bay ready for four months of operations, servicing the underwater experiments.

At the Achnahannet basecamp, the P.R. exhibition trailer became jammed with tourists, of all nationalities; and from out of this enormous flow of people—30 to 40,000, perhaps during the course of the summer—I learned of another extraordinary 'sea serpent' story.

A man came in one day and asked to be introduced. Apparently he had been aboard H.M.S. GALATEA during the war as a Chief Petty Officer. It was November of 1940. The ship had been mined shortly before, and Mr. Ratcliffe, my informant, was badly shocked by the explosion. Whether this could have affected his judgement it was hard to say, but at sea once more GALATEA, a light cruiser, encountered an immense sea animal. A huge and ugly head, with a curious mane-like appendage draping down its neck, extended upright from the sea, on a long neck-like protrusion. Behind, at intervals, enormous looping coils broke surface. Mr. Ratcliffe's dimensions seemed quite incredible, and I could not accept them. However, I had no doubt about his sincerity. As a check on his powers of estimating distance (and therefore scale), I suggested Mr. Ratcliffe tell me how far he though it was across the loch. He said 'about 500 yards,' with an air of confidence. It was more than 2,000 yards in fact.

He told me that an order came down from the bridge of GALATEA for target practice with the forr'd 0.5 inch machine gun battery. This opened fire; and Mr. Ratcliffe, who was on deck, watched the tracer arc and saw the creature's head jerk and shiver, as the bullets struck. GALATEA was in action almost daily at the time, in the North Sea and the English Channel, which was alive with enemy aircraft. No doubt every opportunity at target practice was justified, with men's lives at stake, but when the creature disappeared from view the rumour quickly went round that the ship was doomed, for a certainty. The 'Beast' was not real at all, but a manifestation of death; and to open fire on it was tantamount to suicide!

In due course H.M.S. GALATEA was sunk, like so many other proud ships of the Royal Navy, but it was not until December of 1941 that she rolled over to a torpedo, off Alexandria, in the Mediterranean.

I later found this out from the Imperial War Museum; because Mr. Ratcliffe very sensibly suggested that as all gun firing practices were logged, I might find some mention of the 'monster' target recorded in the GALATEA's log. The museum knew of no references to the incident and did not know if the log had survived; they referred me to another department. So there I let the matter rest.

Another diversion during the summer was a short seven-day expedition to Loch Morar, near the western Highland seaboard. I went there with four of my family, intending to enjoy it as a holiday—a working holiday, with Ken Wallis and the autogyro, and WATER HORSE, both of which had not previously been used for monsterhunting away from the Ness.

Morar had long carried a Water Kelpie tradition, similar in detail to that at Loch Ness; and sightings had previously been reported. I knew of only one man who had tried his luck there in recent years, but in 1969 something occurred which tended to make us take the sightings seriously. A collision was reported between a small local motorboat, with two men on board, and a very large unknown water animal. Various accounts of this were published, and in 1970 the first 'Loch Morar Survey' team was formed, intent on making an ecological study of the environment and a thorough search for evidence.

Arriving at this remote and beautiful lake we found the LMS crews manning three lonely camera stations, two of which could only be supplied by water.

We had arranged to stay at a croft-house, some distance down the only access road, which petered out a mile or two beyond. The lady who ran it was sister to one of the men in the boat, who had previously discounted the monster. She told us that after the event he had changed his mind about it. The experience had shaken both men, and they no longer doubted the

presence of a colossal unknown creature living the lake—
'Morag,' to give it a local nickname.

During the week at Loch Morar we enjoyed ourselves
and worked hard in the process. We flew the 'gyro
out of a convenient farmer's field without incident
except for a near collision with a golden eagle near the
mountain tops; and for the first time I piloted WATER
HORSE at full power, with the new engine. The result
was gratifying. The small craft, which had carried me
sedately about the year before at half a dozen knots,
was designed for speed; and when I opened the throttle,
it skimmed away across the glassy reaches of water
trailing a shimmering cascade. Hydroplaning was new
to me, and I delighted in it. It added another dimension to my work—the power to move quickly, and out
of danger should the wind whip up. I had learned the
need for this and had no desire to be sunk or to drown
in the icy, crystal water. Unlike the Ness, Loch Morar
had no peat discolouring it. It also had areas of shallow
water and in places shingle beaches.

There was no sign of 'Morag,' but sightings had
been reported; and on one occasion the LMS camera
crew (consisting of one man marooned on a high rocky
promontory) missed a surfacing by only a few minutes.
He was down the cliff, collecting water for the camp-
site.

Back at the Ness, in September, a cheerful group of
enthusiasts arrived from the United States under the
flag of the 'Black & White Scotch Expedition,' working
with an infra-red night camera. Under the leadership
of Jack Ullrich, a widely travelled expeditioner and
rare-animal collector, they based themselves with Bob
Love's encampment at Temple Pier, in Urquhart Bay,
under the auspicies of the LNI. A comprehensive
'Press Book' announced their purpose and intention,
but in the event some difficulty was experienced with

their infra-red equipment. During their stay, however, they made contact with some interesting witnesses, through the LNI, and recorded interviews. They also joined with Bob Love's team of divers who were working on the potentially interesting wreck, found the year before on sonar in Urquhart Bay. A marine archeologist from the Fort Bouisand Underwater Centre in the south of England travelled up to study it; and when measurements and photos were taken, the possibility arose that the craft was a 'Zulu,' a unique type of bluff-hulled sailing vessel constructed about the time of the Zulu wars, a hundred years ago.

Back from Loch Morar WATER HORSE was slipped into Inchnacardoch Bay and then moved up at speed to the small harbour we had constructed at Achnahannet. The trip took thirty-five minutes, travelling at thirty knots. With the ten-horse engine in 1969 it had taken two and a half hours in rough water, which had nearly capsized the boat.

On August 30th, while out drifting at the mouth of Urquhart Bay late one afternoon, I spotted a tall, fat 'telegraph pole' sticking up from the water, perhaps half a mile distant. I shouted 'look at that' to my eldest son and Murray Stuart, another experienced monsterhunter, who were standing in the cockpit, as I dived into the cabin for my binoculars. It was choppy at the time, and equipment was safely cushioned on the seats. I heard both comment excitedly . . . 'My God, look at it *go.*'

In a matter of seconds the object had streaked across the water, disappearing behind a promontory near Urquhart Castle. It was such a brief experience—and there had been no time to focus cameras—but it had been entirely real. Starting the motor, we plunged through the choppy water but found no evidence of anything on the surface. Discussing the sighting, we concluded it must have been the head and neck of one of the larger animals. It must have stood ten feet at least out of the water. My son's eyesight was exceptional, and Murray sketched the object he had seen which he declared thickened near the water, curving slightly at an angle when moving fast. My own view was momentary; and since I did not see the movement or the curvature, I believed the neck was moving away from us when first sighted. Then it must have turned to the right just as I went into the cabin.

In ten years it was only my second physical sighting, but again, it was no figment of the imagination. Three of us stood witness to the fact.

* * *

On June 17th, 1970 I had seen a letter from a 'Dr. Robert H. Rines, President of the Academy of Applied Science, Belmont, Mass.' to David James enquiring about 'details of any food bait or other attractants that you may know of, which you have tried in the past . . . ' The letter went on to say that experiments were being planned using sexual as well as food attractants, also 'recorded sounds of the various types of underwater creatures possibly relevant to the loch, which could be used in coordination with the various sonar and sound listening posts. . . .'

The Academy of Applied Science team of five did not arrive at Loch Ness until well into September, and only three took part in the actual baiting and sonar experiments. They were unobtrusive but active, and quickly set up the Klein Associates high definition, side-scan sonar in Urquhart Bay.

Dr. Martin Klein, the designer, attended the chart recorder housed in an old shed near Temple Pier, where Bob Love's equipment was based; and the transducer, or sound-pulse generator, more generally known as the 'fish,' was first rigidly attached to an old pier piling about three feet from the bottom and ten feet from the surface. Only one of the side-scanning beams was monitored, and this scanned outwards into the waters of the bay.

One of the special attractant buoys was placed in front of the sonar as it was operating, and the equipment recorded this operation quite clearly. During these early tests boat and diver activity on the sunken wreck nearby caused some interference, but these movements were monitored to provide a yardstick against which to measure other types of echo.

They were not long in coming—at 6 p.m. some small echoes were recorded suggesting fish, and then, at 6:10 p.m., three distinct echoes showed objects moving through the beam.

Perhaps they were not from fish but from three sections of a single larger moving object. At 6:46 p.m. and 6:55 p.m. similar traces appeared on the chart at distances of 365 feet and 380 feet, respectively.

A subsequent test with a diver directly in the sound beam produced a strong echo of a different character.

Excited by these mysterious echo patterns, Bob Rines and Marty Klein continued operations the following day but experienced so much boat noise and interference that they decided to remove themselves and their equipment to the unfrequented deep-water areas of the loch. I was able to help them, because I had WATER HORSE moored down at Fort Augustus, under the lee of the Abbey's harbour wall, where I had tied up overnight in the catamaran CIZARA. It was a private place and somewhat inaccessible, but one could load heavy equipment directly into a boat.

Because I had been of the opinion that sonars were the cause of much disturbance, I had avoided them whenever possible in WATER HORSE, but by now I had met the Academy people and liked their cheerfully dynamic approach to problems. Besides, the MK-300 side-scan sonar developed by Klein Associates had such a high frequency sound pulse and such a short one (0.1 of a millisecond), it would prove inaudible to animals. Or so I was assured.

I offered the boat and myself to skipper it, and promised to take two crew members and the sonar to places which might prove rewarding, along the precipitous and deserted southwestern wall of the loch—the great towering cliffs, which plunged almost vertically down to the bed of the loch. It was here that Torquil MacLeod had watched the monster partly out of water on February 27th of 1960, and had measured it optically, through graticulated lenses. Here, too, repeated sightings over the years made me wonder whether a 'territorial' claim was laid by one of the creatures under water. I knew this was characteristic of many aquatic animals, the big males in particular; and Torquil had calculated his 'beastie' to be at least 45 to 55 feet in visible length—the hinder parts remaining in the water! This indicated to me a big specimen: a bull perhaps. Curiously, in times gone by, the term 'Water Bulls' was common. Indeed, in Gaelic legend, 'Water Bulls are always to be found at Foyers'—the place at which I had shot my film of one in 1960.

On the first day out from Fort Augustus we lowered the sonar onto the bottom, attached to a metal frame, but without apparent result, and, subsequently, for the next two days we towed the 'fish' in the more conventional mobile mode, trailing it behind the boat at two knots or so directly off the shore. It appeared remarkably stable and moved beneath the surface emitting sharp periodic clicks, until it was lost to view in the dark-brownish water. We lowered perhaps 250 feet of cable; and as the device responded to the echoes, the large double-sided electronic chart-recorder traced

227

exotic sepia patterns, showing the bottom, sidewall, and surface echoes—and echoes returning from objects moving in the water space between.

I watched fascinated: standing for hours at the wheel, as WATER HORSE gently nosed along the sidewalls. By some remarkable good fortune the loch was tranquil and windless, after weeks and months of rain, wind, and truly wretched weather. This helped to eliminate spurious surface echo clutter from wave peaks; and as the chart unfolded, we traced the sheer walls and the bottom hundreds of feet below. Fish came up clearly as pencil dots, the smallest presumably trout and the larger ones, salmon, ranging up into the 30 pound scale.

At two places we recorded very large blips. One was precisely in the 700 foot trench we found directly below the patch of scree on the mountainside for which I was heading the boat—the very place where I had suspected that such a blip might exist. These blips were many many times the size of the nearest fish trace and appeared to be quite clearly in the water-column. I watched Marty Klein's face as they came up on the chart. He was only feet away from me, sitting in the cabin surrounded by batteries and equipment. As a layman I had no real understanding of the significance of marks on the chart, though as an engineer I knew about sonar principles. He showed little if any outward surprise, but as an expert in electronics and sonar design his entire mental effort was concentrated on the machine; and the readout caused, if anything, a sharpening of this very evident mental focus. These were dramatic moments, heightened by the towering backdrop of rocks and the looking-glass lake, devoid of surface boat activity for all but short periods of the day. We worked long hours, well into the evening, then returned next day to repeat the searching, finding more large blips on the sonar and some extensive schools of deep-water fish. These we concluded were the 'arctic char' referred to in the early sixties by the small expedition fielded by students from Oxford and Cambridge in which fish finders were employed systematically for the first time. As a possible item in the food chain, they could prove to be important.

Working again late into the evening, we brought in various essences, hormones, and fish-luring substances concentrated and freeze-dried for the Academy of Applied Science by research laboratories in the United States: among them the Food and Chemical Research Laboratories in Seattle, the Harvard Medical School, the Natrick (Massachusetts) Laboratories of the Army, and International Flavors and Fragrances (IFF)—perhaps one of the most sophisticated substance analysts to be found anywhere today.

Together these concoctions were used in varying quantities and places, and were supplemented by 'chumming' with salmon oils into which Bob Rines showered pebbles. These were then dumped overboard from the 'Moo-scow' dinghy in an attempt to lay vertical streamers of scent which would attract the Monster to the surface. Unfortunately none of these experiments appeared to produce results, so in almost total darkness we set off for Fort Augustus once more, putting the crew ashore at the old canal pierhead, where cars and camera vehicles were waiting. There were three aboard the WATER HORSE and one towing behind in the dinghy, smothered in salmon oil. One new member of the party was Mr. Isaac Blonder, President of the Blonder-Tongue Laboratories, in New Jersey. He had brought a kit of hydrophones through which he had both listened to underwater noises and played back various recordings of sounds made by eels, salmon, and dolphins, but again without apparent results.

21   Bob Rines, Martin Klein, and Tim Dinsdale with the
side-scan sonar 'Fish' aboard WATER HORSE.

One curious incident, however, had both intrigued and frightened us. We were lowering the hydrophone overboard in the immediate vicinity of the 700 foot trench where the big blip had been recorded. After paying out only a couple of hundred feet of wire, the hydrophone appeared to strike some underwater object and bounce along it before continuing its descent. This produced some loud rasping noises through the speaker on the boat which made us jump. There seemed no rational explanation for this, other than a submerged log drifting deep beneath the surface; or alternatively the Monster which we had recorded on sonar coming up to investigate. It was a real experience, and in a small 16 foot overloaded boat a disturbing one.

Due to other commitments, Marty Klein and Ike Blonder had to leave shortly after this event, the former to make arrangements for sea tests with his sonar 'fish' off the Norwegian coast—but before his departure we trailed the device up-loch mapping contours on the way. The weather had degenerated, and with a choppy surface there was some interference from wave-top echoes on the chart, and this made me appreciate our good fortune when the windless glassy water had stretched as far as the eye could see, giving perfect results.

On September 28th, Bob Rines, President of the Academy of Applied Science, drafted a preliminary report, 'Sonar Contacts, Sept. 21st-24th, 1970 at Loch Ness.' It was in two sections: the first referring to the contacts in Urquhart Bay with the sonar fixed, and the second to the towing operations at the southwest end of Loch Ness.

It was a reserved but interesting statement which together with his own scientific verbal presentation formed the basis for a national press conference in London a few days later.

Unfortunately, there was little scientific coverage at the conference, and the news came out with the usual scattering of errors and minor dramatisations, though some reports were serious. These events, however, proved to me once more the vital need for close-up movie photography, which no one could dispute. Sonar and sound recordings underwater—however valid and scientifically exciting—would never prove the 'Beastie' to the public—and without their acceptance the mystery would remain. It was a disappointment. We had worked hard to get these results.

With the departure of our American friends from the Academy the LNI continued its photographic watch right through the 23rd of October, but with dwindling crews and the persistently awful weather. Bob Love's 'Brigade' down at Urquhart Bay continued stoically through the icy mists of autumn, working experiments underwater.

The night before I was due to leave the base camp at Achnahannet—the scene of such wonderful teamwork, human activity, and ingenuity, and such an enormous voluntary effort—the first of the equinoctual gales came roaring down the Loch, gusting to over 100 miles per hour. It was at night, lit by pale green moonlight; the great Loch below showing its majestic splendour in a herring-bone pattern of coursing wave tops, perhaps eight to ten feet tall and moving at unbelievable speed. It was the infamous wind-driven wave form that had drowned so many people in the past, swamping their fishing boats when it caught them unawares.

In 1968 I had spent such a night in the catamaran CIZARA, behind the jetty wall at St. Benedicts Abbey, and had listened to the scream of the wind in her rigging, thanking God I wasn't out in it. Again the year following on precisely the same date, the 21st

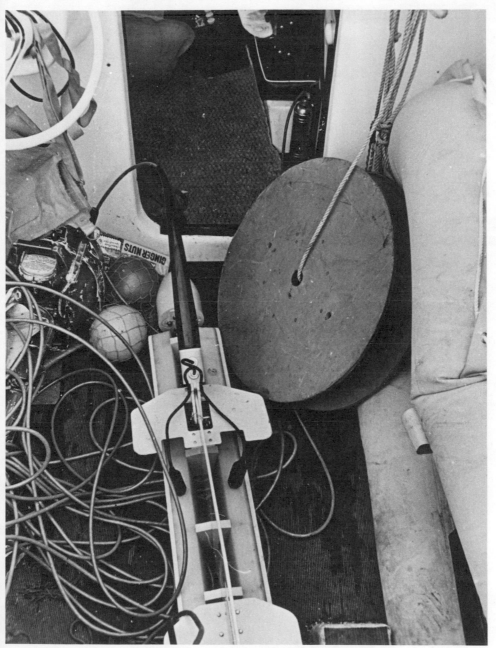

22 Cockpit of WATER HORSE showing side-scan sonar
equipment.

of September, I had slipped into Inchnacardoch Bay in little WATER HORSE just ahead of the mounting gale and the waves. It had been a night of such wind velocity; the serenity at dawn, with the Loch once more in tranquil mood seemed ethereal—unreal by contrast.

And now the wind had come again, but a month delayed. We drove back from Drumnadrochit late in the evening. Rounding Strone point, with the ancient castle ruin below, we met the full force of it. Branches were down, and the base camp at Achnahannet a shambles. It looked as though a bomb had hit the place. The fearful blasts blew one trailer onto its side, smashing it; and as I stepped towards my own house-trailer, it came to meet me, broadside on. It was full of equipment, and I was afraid it would begin to trundle down the mountainside towards the loch 200 feet below. Fortunately the framework underneath jammed on a pair of metal ramps, which saved it.

I left the next day, convinced that in 1971, if the LNI was to continue operations, it must stop work before the equinox or risk the loss of life and equipment. Wind force of such a magnitude was a real hazard.

I spent the winter months once more preparing for the coming year's activities, having accepted David James' invitation to continue in office in 1971. But as the months went by, it became apparent that finance would be a problem. Field Enterprises Educational Corporation of Chicago, for so long the principal sponsor, decided not to continue underwater work in 1971. No one could blame the company or its directors for their decision. The hunt had continued for such a long period, and they had already been more than generous. It meant, however, that Bob Love would probably not return in 1971, leaving me to run both the above surface photography, and the underwater operations—a truly daunting prospect.

234

In April of 1971 I visited the Academy of Applied Science in Massachusetts and under the direction of Bob Rines spent nearly three weeks travelling about, lecturing, appearing on TV and speaking on radio, in New York, Boston, Washington, and in the New England states. I found America to be the powerhouse of human activity I had imagined it to be—and the hospitality unlimited. And, as a result of a private talk given at the Academy in Belmont, Professor Harold Edgerton at M.I.T.—a pioneer in the field of underwater strobe-light movie photography—promised to prepare a special camera and intensely powerful stroboscopic flash for use in Loch Ness, and Loch Morar.

This was an unexpected breakthrough, because with such equipment the Academy team could shoot clear time-lapse movies underwater. I had seen some of Professor Edgerton's films taken in the sea, of starfish and sand-dollars apparently all rushing about, due to the time-lapse effect. The clarity and colour were astonishing.

Later, when visiting the Blonder-Tongue Laboratories in New Jersey, I talked to the President (Mr. Isaac S. Blonder), who showed me the hydrophone and sound-recording playback equipment he was devising for use in Loch Ness in 1971. Ike was full of the same enthusiasm he had shown the previous year, and I recognised the ingenuity of his scheme—to monitor underwater sounds and, while recording them, play back incoming noises momentarily after they were received. In effect, this would make an underwater animal 'talk back' to itself and, it was hoped, would cause it to become inquisitive and seek the source of the emission. The technique had been tried out with birds, with noticeable effect. It was exciting to learn, too, that when listening with hydrophones in the vicinity of the great trench we had found in September the year before, off the precipitous southwest shoreline, pulse-like emissions had

235

23 Klein Associates side-scan sonar in mobile mode.

been recorded; and analysis showed double 5 milli-second bursts in the 4 to 8 kilohertz range. Whether this could be an animal sonar no one could be certain, but the fact remained that when photographed on a cathode ray tube, the regular physical shape of the pulse was clearly evident.

Another unexpected and interesting by-product of the sonar work in this region with the Klein side-scan was the discovery of distinct ridges and undercuts in the sidewalls of the trench—the first positive evidence of the 'underwater caverns' which had for so long featured in the local lore at Loch Ness, for which there had been no real proof at all. Upon visiting Martin Klein at his own compact design and manufacturing centre at Salem, New Hampshire, I found him to be excited about this discovery, the representation of which on the chart was as clear to the eyes of an expert as it was meaningless to the layman. He explained to me the nature of the trace and spent more time showing me his collection of photos of peculiar looking under-water research craft and deep-diving submarines, in some of which he had worked at great depths. He was absorbed by the water environment—the last real un-explored frontier on our planet. His work and no less his attitude towards it and life in general intrigued me. Marty was no ordinary inventor.

During the course of my visit I had so much to do and so many places to go, at such velocity, I began to lose track of where I was, leaving details entirely in the competent hands of my host Bob Rines. When the *New York Times* called to arrange an interview and asked where precisely I was staying, I could only tell them 'at the moment in New Jersey.' This was literally true. I knew the name of my temporary host but not that of his house or even the locality; and as I would be moving on to somewhere else almost immediately, it mattered little.

As an escape from this whirlwind of activity, Bob Rines motored me out to Cape Cod one sunny weekend, to Provincetown and other delightful places. During this short period of time we relaxed and enjoyed ourselves and visited a man who had worked previously with the Coast Guard as a crew member on a motor lifeboat out of Chatham. Bob had heard about Joe Patrick and his peculiar 'sea serpent' experience before. We visited him at his seaside store in Provincetown, famous for its collection of original wood carvings of whales and other maritime relics and curiosities.

Joe Patrick invited us inside his home at the back of the store. Shelves lined the walls, with beautiful painted wood carvings of ducks as ornaments, his own painstaking handiwork. Models of sailing ships held my attention. Provincetown has a long history of whaling and the sea; and just a little further up the coast at Gloucester the 'New England Sea Serpent' first swam into the news in the early nineteenth century. R. T. Gould and others had written about it.

Joe told us about his experience in a manner we found convincing, and backed this up with an excellent sketch. His verbatim account reads . . .

'The run was from Stage Harbour, out of Chatham to Nantucket. At a point between Handerkerchief Light Ship and Cape Pogue—three or four times I observed this thing, never getting a clear view of it—always a choppy area—always on the way over—never on the way back.'

'This thing looked like a head, I would say 36 inches out of the water, and I would think 30 feet long. I could see three humps; never seen the tail end. Looked like it seemed to have a sort of blackish colored neck and head. It looked something like a cow, but without cow ears. It had an eye where an eye should be: blackish green in color. The humps on his back I

238

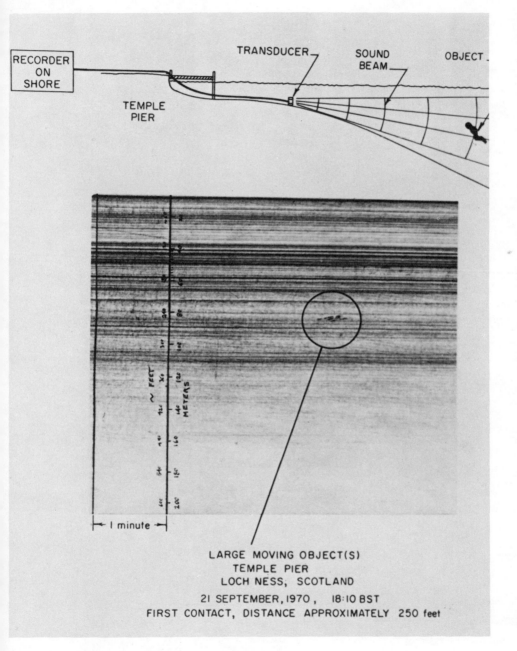

RECORDER ON SHORE · TEMPLE PIER · TRANSDUCER · SOUND BEAM · OBJECT

← 1 minute →

LARGE MOVING OBJECT(S)
TEMPLE PIER
LOCH NESS, SCOTLAND
21 SEPTEMBER, 1970, 18:10 BST
FIRST CONTACT, DISTANCE APPROXIMATELY 250 feet

24   First sonar contact.

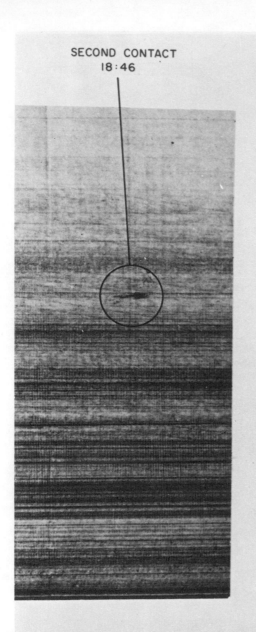
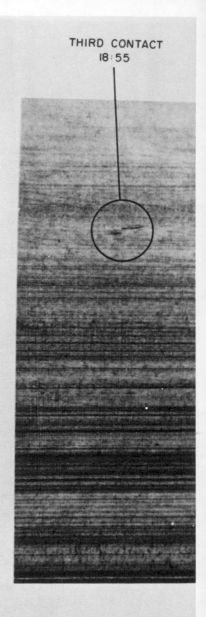

SECOND CONTACT
18:46

THIRD CONTACT
18:55

LARGE MOVING OBJECT(S)
TEMPLE PIER
LOCH NESS, SCOTLAND
21 SEPTEMBER, 1970

25 Second and third contacts.

would say had about six indentations. I saw about three humps, greenish in colour. Maybe it was a big snake.

'It was in 1939 or 1940, a Coast Guard motor lifeboat, with a motor helmsman and two other crew members, out of Stage Harbor.

'About two years ago, a fellow heard about this thing and approached me on the subject. He told me what he had seen, then I told him about my experience. He told me at this time that he became calmed, and he got some very close shots (camera) of what he had seen; and every time he took a shot the creature turned his head. He gave me his name, but right now I can't think of it . . .'

In fairness to Joe Patrick, every effort was made that evening to corroborate his story by calling local people and past crew members—but without positive results. With the passage of years, memories fade, people die, and past events seem unimportant. The only contact made with a member of the crew established he would have been below decks in the engine room at the time of the encounter—assuming he had actually been aboard at the time. No trace of the lone photographer resulted.

But throughout these enquiries Joe Patrick made no attempt to embellish his story and apologised for the lack of success, in a manner which could leave no doubt as to his sincerity. Both Bob Rines and I left convinced of it.

Perhaps the best supporting evidence for the existence of a 'New England Sea Serpent' can be found in the meticulous writings of R. T. Gould back in the 1930's. On page 158 of his classic original work *The Loch Ness Monster and Others* he records . . . 'Anyone who refers to Dr. Oudemans' book on the so called ''sea serpent'' or my own, will find many similar cases. In at least

Drawn

April 24–1971

I. T. Patrick.

16 Mr. Patrick's sketch.

two of these the analogy (to the Loch Ness Monster presumably: T.D.) is extraordinarily complete. They are the "New England sea-serpent" (1817-1819) and the creature seen in Loch Hourn (1872) . . . the early appearances of the New England creature were made in Gloucester harbour, Massachusetts. . . . The witnesses —who numbered twelve—made sworn depositions before a Gloucester magistrate (The Hon. Lonson Nash J.P.), and these were collected and examined by an *ad hoc* committee appointed by the Linnean Society of Boston (John Davis, Jacob Bigelow and Francis C. Gray). The testimony is in striking general agreement, and—taken in conjunction with the fact that most of the witnesses were seamen or fishermen, and all of them coast-dwellers—eliminates the supposition that any well known creature was seen. The 'Monster' which was often observed at very close range, was usually seen as a line of uniform humps. . . . In the Loch Hourn case—which is much more recent, and occurred in Scottish waters—the chief witnesses were a party of six (including two clergymen) who saw the creature on two consecutive days, and on five or six separate occasions, at distances which were often less than 200 yards. It appeared as a line of humps (the head and neck were occasionally visible as well) . . .'

A day or two before returning to Britain I visited the imaginative aquarium at Boston and spent a few entrancing hours there looking at the underwater life. I was given a copy of *aquasphere,* the journal of the New England Aquarium.

Inside was an article about a sea monster washed up at Scituate, Massachusetts, on November 15th, 1970. Weighing 15 to 20 tons, it had the usual cartilaginous skeleton, two big fins, and what appeared to be a small head and long neck.

A great many curious people went to see it, and Bob

Rines from the Academy of Applied Science was wel-
comed as an authority. The New England Aquarium
arranged for the carcase to be examied and for pieces
of it to be returned for analysis. In due course the
skull, or chrondocranium, was compared with that from
a Basking shark at the Woods Hole Oceanographic Insti-
tution, and when these proved identical, the mystery was
solved. The 'Scituate Monster' was the remains of a fish.

I read the article in *aquasphere* on the flight back to
Britain from New York. It was hard to realise that
within one week I would be back at Loch Ness searching for another monster: a real one. My visit to the
United States had been enjoyable, and at the last
moment a major lecture-tour agency had called offering
to book a future tour across the country. It was encouraging, and with the experience gained a rather
pleasing prospect.

I had taken off from Kennedy Airport late in the
evening, and about mid-way across the Atlantic Ocean,
the sun rose in a blaze of light, inconsiderately at 2
a.m. New York time. I realised there was little chance
of sleep before touching down at London. I had been
watching the movie and had forgotten the five hour
readjustment.

The familiar shores of Britain were soon beneath and
minutes later the maze of runways marking Europe's
largest airport. We landed in glorious sunshine and the
green of an English spring, and within an hour or two
I was back at my home in Reading.

※   ※   ※

The events and developments at Loch Ness and Loch
Morar in 1971 were so numerous and extraordinary
that it is not possible to do more than comment on
them briefly in this last chapter of the book. In due
course a full account will appear in a new book called
Project Water Horse, in which I hope to record some-

thing of the human story and details of the more bizarre experiments conducted over some fourteen years of fieldwork.

Shortly after starting work again at Loch Ness, a man came into the exhibition and volunteered the following information: In June of 1969 he and two other divers had dived in the close vicinity of the precipitous southwest wall. Using aqualungs, they descended to about 40 feet before swimming out and returning to the surface. Their experience en route was of such interest, in view of the Academy of Applied Science sonar report of 1970, that I asked our informant, Mr. J. K. Anderson, of Stirling, Scotland, to record details in a letter to me. On May 21st he did, from which this extract is taken . . .

'We crossed the loch in a rubber dinghy from Invermoriston, . . . on entering the water we found visibility about 20-25 feet but this decreased as we descended owing to the peat sediment causing light refraction. At a depth of about 25 feet we encountered a large boulder. We climbed round and over this—still going down. Almost immediately underneath it we saw a cut-back or over-hang approximately 5-6 feet wide. Owing to bad visibility we had no idea how far this extended in either direction. We bypassed this and at a depth of about 35-40 feet saw another similar geological formation. To perhaps make my point clear, I am enclosing a sketch with this letter indicating roughly the formation of the type which we saw.

'At this time on our dive we saw there was no further point in going any deeper owing to the decreasing visibility, and rather than follow the side of the loch back to the surface for fear of being trapped by an overhang, we swam due west into the loch, still submerged at approximately 35 feet. At a point where we were well clear of the shelf we surfaced and swam back to the dinghy.

245

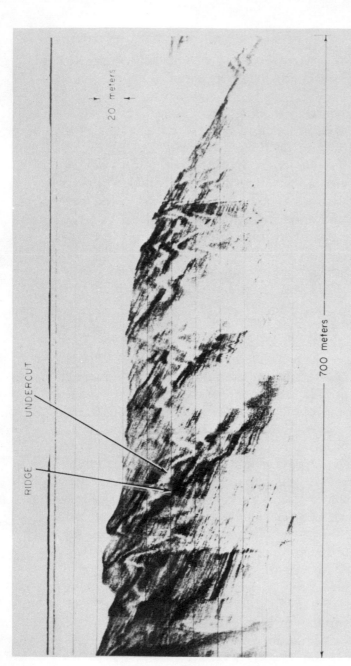

RIDGE

UNDERCUT

20 meters

700 meters

KLEIN ASSOCIATES, INC.
UNDERSEA SEARCH AND SURVEY
SALEM · NEW HAMPSHIRE · U.S.A.
SIDE SCAN SONAR
MODEL MK-300

M. KLEIN
R RINES
T DINSDALE

SLOPE TOPOGRAPHY
LOCH NESS, SCOTLAND

26 · Underwater caverns.

'This was not mentioned at the time because we had seen similar rock formations in Loch Ard in West Perthshire, and to us this was not of any significance. 'I trust this information will be of some value to you.'
Yours etc.
J. K. Anderson'

The precise value of Mr. Anderson's information lies in the corroboration it provides for Dr. Martin Klein's side-scan sonar results, which indicated these cutbacks on chart paper, and equally the validity of his technical interpretations. Both the location of the dive and the side-scan work was in the same area, although the people involved were entirely independent of each other.

During the early weeks of the hunt in 1971 a large number of Americans volunteered to work for the LNI, and among them was a young man from New England. It was his first visit, and by pure coincidence he told me of an event which reminded me of the Scituate affair. In late August of 1970 while racing in an 'eighteen foot sailboat, with a good sized keel,' he had collided with a Basking shark. This had occurred in the vicinity of the 'Middle Ground'—an upthrust ridge roughly in mid-channel between Martha's Vineyard Island and the Elizabeth Islands.

Three distinct 'thumps' were heard, then about 25 feet astern a two-foot brown fin surfaced momentarily. As this location is not far from the much decomposed carcase found at Scituate, in November of the same year, one cannot help but guess at the 'thumps' being the cause of it. Sharks, with their cartilaginous frame, are peculiarly susceptible to internal dislocation. The head-on attacks by dolphins can kill sharks—a fact which has been made evident on film.

The young American, to whom I shall refer as Dave,

247

volunteered some other remarks which were a contribution to the Loch Ness Investigation—beyond the hard work and good humour which characterised his daily efforts. It was a simple paragraph of words.

The year before I had instituted a small tradition at the LNI which came to be known as the 'Personality Book.' In it all the expeditioners entered brief details about themselves upon arrival—age, training, nationality, interests, and experience—then on departure they were free to complete half a page of comment—to say whatever they wanted to. As might be expected most comment was lightheared; some of it brilliant; some of it more serious. Whatever people wrote, others were free to read it.

'Dave' wrote the following . . .

'(If I may deviate from the humorous norm) Someone recently asked me why we hunt these creatures. It is easy to answer, but difficult to explain. We believe in them—not only the individuals themselves but what they in the large sense represent. They are a not-so-impossible dream and an enigma almost answered. On this world bound by technological complexities they are a return to nature, and a subtle reminder to man that he is not a master of all creation. It is a quixotic search for truth in a scornful world—a tedious search which someday must have it's end. And when we do place the final piece of the puzzle in position perhaps men will stop momentarily to gaze at inscrutible nature, and wonder about the deeper natural truths . . .'

These words characterised the search so perfectly that it was difficlut to believe they were written down by the youngest member of the team, a boy of seventeen, who incidentally recorded the fastest time 'on target' with the head-quarters long range camera, on which I trained all the cameramen. From the watch office several yards away, he raced down to the complex

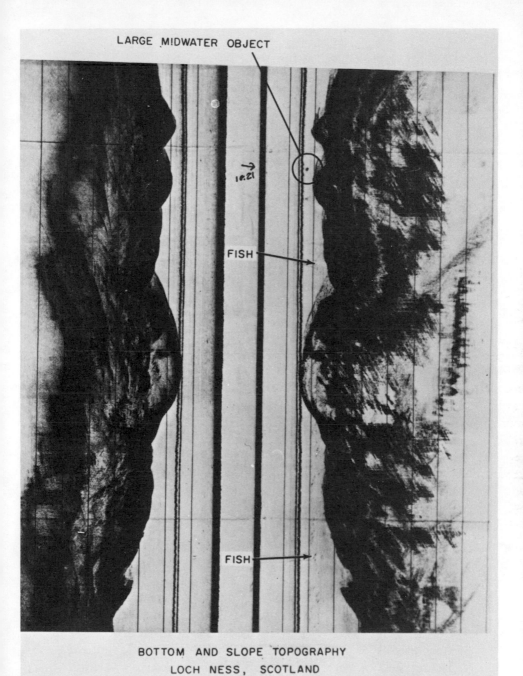

LARGE MIDWATER OBJECT

FISH

FISH

BOTTOM AND SLOPE TOPOGRAPHY
LOCH NESS, SCOTLAND

27 Large mid-water object.

camera mounting and swinging it around pinpointed his target through the reflector sight, in seven seconds. Normally it would have taken twice as long.

This incredible performance proved to me again that in every group of human beings there are those who by their skills and personality stand out, who are exceptionally able.

During the mid-May to mid-September operations at Loch Ness, kaleidoscopic patterns of events developed much as they had done the year before—with teams, individuals, and sets of equipment, complete with experts appearing briefly, only to be replaced by others.

By now I had become used to this never ending process and curiously addicted to it. Variety and uncertainty combine to intrigue, and as I had learned not to become disheartened by failure or too excited by success, the hunt progressed.

It soon became apparent that sightings were more numerous than usual, due, it was thought, to the fine weather and exceptionally warm spring. Witnesses would appear at Achnahannet, sometimes within minutes of their experience, hands trembling slightly from excitement. We recorded them spontaneously, and before long a bank of verbal information began to accumulate. It would have been possible to invent some of these stories but not the manner in which they were told— the inflexions in the voice and the individual modes of expression could never have been faked.

On two occasions camera crews had near-misses, when for one reason or another they moved station only to find the move had cost them a dramatic piece of film. By now we had almost come to accept these near-misses as inevitable. The long history of events at Loch Ness was crammed with such incidents, which affected groups and individuals alike. Some of the older local people attributed this to supernatural influence: shades of the 'Water Kelpie'—the dreaded Loch Ness 'hoodoo,' known by some of the Americans simply as 'The Hex.' A number of the people at the LNI secretly believed in it, because they found the continuing near-misses impossible to explain away on the basis of chance—or mischance.

Certainly, I had had my share of them, and before the year was out would experience two more; but I never doubted we would ultimately succeed. The great size of Loch Ness, the difficulties of light and shade, mist, and rough water, and the physical reaction to excitement made filming difficult. The year before a young LNI cameraman had shot film from high up on the northern shore, which had been ruined by the sunglaze. The photographer, whose iris had contracted to compensate visually, could see a hump ploughing through the water, but in the film one could barely see the wake. He was shooting into the light, through a mile or so of atmosphere.

With the arrival of Bob Rines, in June, with the strobe-light movie camera, we concentrated on proving tests underwater.

Loch Ness did not present a problem, for we had only to take the equipment out in a boat and put it overside; but in order to simulate the crystal waters of Loch Morar we had to find an alternative. All the nearby lochs and lochans (small mountain lakes) were stained brown with peat water. The answer lay in using the swimming pool at Inverness, some twenty miles away.

This was arranged through the authorities, who cooperated; but they insisted work should be completed by nine o'clock in the morning! At this time of the year the LNI was operational at 5:30 a.m., however, so this did not present a problem. A small team of volunteers carried out the tests, under the direction of Bob Rines. The twin tubes of the strobe-light and camera assembly were floated about, flashing periodically. Coloured underwater targets were photographed at different ranges.

As a result, work in Loch Ness proceeded. Many thousands of 16 mm frames were exposed during the season, and some curious results were obtained, though none of these shots positively identified the Monster.

We were fortunate to get results because, when the equipment was left out overnight, for the first time unattended, there was no sign of it in the morning.

This grave misfortune lead us to believe that local salmon poachers had cut the buoys adrift, allowing the attachment rope to sink to the bottom without trace. Alternatively they had towed them out into deep water to do the same. Traditionally, they resented intrusion.

There was just the possibility the Monster had become entangled in the cordage and had swum away with the equipment.

With the help of two professional scuba divers from Inverness, we searched the area, hoping to pinpoint the flashing beacon underwater, before the batteries ran out, but without result. In the fearful inky blackness, they groped about amongst decaying tree trunks and found nothing. It was a relief to get them safely back on board. They did establish however that the camera cradle had been sitting on the edge of a precipice, which we did not know existed so close to the shoreline.

Later we were to find the depth to be nearly two hundred feet and the precipice almost verticle.

Attempts to snag the cordage underwater, trailing a large grappling device, failed also, in spite of many hours spent criss-crossing Urquhart Bay. During this ordeal Bob Rines behaved with stoicism. The equipment was unique, and virtually irreplaceable. I felt that perhaps like others before him he would find the unexpected misfortune too much to bear and would

28 'The MacNab Photo' was taken in 1955 with a hand held
camera and 6 inch telephoto lens. It provides a clear reference to
scale. Urquhart Castle tower, on Loch Ness stands 64 feet.
Mr. P. A. MacNab, a bank manager, described the object as
being alive, and moving at 8-12 knots, he said . . . "I snapped
just as the creature was sounding." There are no rocks at this
locality, and the depth is considerable.

abandon the hunt. But he did not. He had already made up his mind to return to the United States to search out a replacement or alternative devices. I liked him the more for it.

Later, by some incredible piece of luck, the work boat FUSSY HEN returning from the grappling operations passed three marker buoys floating in the middle of the loch. It almost ran them down. At the end of the long line attached was the strobe-light and camera, still functioning. Why the buoys had not been seen before was hard to understand, but when the pictures were developed it was clear the camera had remained underwater for the whole period of time—travelling more than two miles contrary to normal drift, which is from west to east down the main reaches of the loch. Had the camera been pulled up for examination by poachers, the bottom of the boat or even their faces would have been photographed. But there were no such pictures. Just clear frames of water and in a few a trailing coil of what could have been the sisal attachment rope or possibly a vortex of cavitation bubbles. It was all very puzzling and a little mysterious, and no one was able to do more than guess at a solution.

With the temporary departure of the Academy people, my attention was distracted by other problems, among them the launching of NARWHAL, a massive ship's lifeboat which we had been renovating. She was from the BRITANNIC, originally, an old Cunarder of some 25,000 tons. Oddly enough the first voyage I had made to New York in 1952 had been in her sister ship, which had been bombed and sunk in the Red Sea, then salvaged after the Second World War. Much of my early life had been spent on or near ships and boats, and they fascinated me.

NARWHAL had been adapted for sailing with a heavy keel extension and a bowsprit, but after serving

254

the Fort Augustus Abbey School sailing club of the west coast and then in Loch Ness, she had been replaced by a 30 foot sailing cutter, and had been pulled ashore. Badly in need of repair, the LNI took over and laboriously put her to rights. We launched the boat one sunny afternoon using levers and rollers and muscle power. It was a herculean task, but with the help of a tow from the cutter, propelled by oars and the husky young Scots from the sailing club, we got her into the water.

After a period in Inchnacardoch Bay, I towed her the 18 miles to Urquhart Bay with little WATER HORSE. It was like towing a barge with a cork, but calm water and my 40 m.p. motor made it possible. We dropped anchor safely.

Next day we put a mooring down, a big concrete block with a ring and chain attached, which was floated out with buoys, then dumped into position. A reliable and competent Scot who had served the LNI in previous years worked as underwater-man in a wet-suit and mask. When the job was done and the main party went ashore, he decided to go out for a swim.

The swim caused him a most unpleasant nervous shock.

He saw something very large, cylindrical, about six feet in diameter, moving through the water slowly from right to left. There were no fins or visible protuberances, but the object extended out of view on either side of his facemask. He surfaced and raced back to shore, witnessed by my own son Simon, working with the LNI on leave from the Army. Later Simon told me the swimmer's progress had been quite dramatic!

The effect of this experience on the Scot, 'Brock' Badger, was real. He had difficulty in sleeping that night; and the day following he felt unwell. Normally

I knew him to be a robust and cheerful character. Because he made no attempt to volunteer information or exaggerate when I questioned him, I found his account all the more impressive. Within a few days the news had leaked out, and we had a visit from the press. To avoid a garbled account being published, we called a press conference, and the story was duly reported with good sense and reasonable accuracy. One paper in particular, the *Press and Journal,* put it on the front page, which is where it rightfully belonged, in my opinion.

29   The very famous 'Surgeon's Photograph' was taken in 1934 at Loch Ness, with a quarter plate camera and small telephoto lens. The shape it portrays is similar to the shape of the object I saw in Foyers Bay, on 6th September 1971—which was alive, muscular, and mobile. In both cases the object was at a range of 200 yards. T.D.

A little before this event, when NARWHAL was lying further down the loch at Inchnacardoch Bay, I had taken a week's leave, a busman's holiday, to work at Loch Morar for the survey team who were actively engaged on their second year of research work. I trailed WATER HORSE over, through the marvellous scenery, and with difficulty launched her. There were no facilities for launching boats at Morar. Again, it was a test of patience and muscle power, but I gained the help of the young men from the LMS basecamp, an incredibly ancient and dilapidated corrugated shed: the Village Hall, of about a century before. It was a place of character, and inside, quite roomy. It was full of scientific gear, a jumble of sleeping bags, tripods, and tousle-haired university students of both sexes. A swallows' nest with young in it was carefully avoided. No one wanted to disturb these tiny creatures or the aerobatic flutterings of the parents. Both birds flew in and out of an open window, feeding the gaping youngsters to a chorus of cheeps. I was intrigued by them, and no less the view of microscopic monsters from the loch, collected as a plankton sample. These amazing little creatures, which came in a wide variety of shapes and sizes, were being typed by a young biologist. The Morar Survey of 1971 was an extension of the work done the year before, scientifically, with photographic observation in support. There were three photographic sites—'Bracora,' 'Swordalnds' and 'Meoble'— lonely outposts commanding an immense view of the water surface. The latter pair were on opposite side of the loch, beyond Brinacory Island, and could only be supplied by water. They covered a part of Morar which was almost totally deserted.

On the way, at 20 knots, we missed a jagged tooth of rock by inches. I saw it in the wake a foot below

Mr. Isaac Blonder from the Academy and his eldest son had travelled up with us in convoy, bringing an array of hydrophone and electronic equipment, which we quickly ventured out to test. Unfortunately Mr. Blonder fell overboard when boarding the dinghy, but being of a sporting disposition he was not deterred by the paralysing chill of Morar water. The day following we spent many hours tracing the jagged bottom contours with an echo-recorder, helping the LMS team who were taking core-samples, and netting plankton.

The weather was fine, and tests with the stereo-hydrophone equipment produced sensitive results but no unexpected noises. We could hear outboard motor noises at great distances.

Encouraged by these early results, the next day we moved down loch and tried again, but Demons in the water came aboard and ruined the attempt. Every piece of equipment seemed to be giving trouble. There was nothing I could do but make space in the over-crowded boat, so I went overside into the dinghy and dozed contentedly; a Bolex camera resting on my stomach.

It was a hot, windy summer's day; and without a drogue to bring it bow-on to the waves, the small craft broached and rolled unmercifully. On board I listened to the endless muted conversation—the technical jargon of electronics, largely incomprehensible, persistent, and apparently without result. The failures multiplied.

By now the elder Blonder, the inimitable 'Ike,' succumbed to nausea. He had admitted to motion-sickness but resolutely refused to give in to it. But enough was enough, and I set course for home.

On the way, at 20 knots, we missed a jagged tooth of rock by inches. I saw it in the wake a foot below the surface—the invisible fangs of Loch Morar waiting to tear the bottom out of a boat. It had not been our day at all. I had no wish to drown in those icy crystal waters or sink into the abyss—over a thousand feet deep in places.

The next day we continued working, well into the afternoon but without technical success. The Blonders pulled out and returned to Loch Ness to join other members of their family who were on holiday. I was sorry—we had done our best, but there was not very much to show for it.

I looked forward to the arrival of Bob Rines, with the stroboscopic flash and camera. He was due on the 16th of July but was delayed until the 20th. I spent the interval virtually living on the surface of the loch, in WATER HORSE, and making sorties out to the distant end in company with the Morar Survey people. I ate with them each evening, sitting bunched together round a makeshift table. The were an engaging group: educated and articulate, and among them I felt at ease despite an age difference of twenty years or so. Our work and objective eliminated the barrier of time. We dressed commonly in the roughest clothing and returned each evening to the warmth and human company of the ancient headquarters shed to recuperate. Work on Loch Morar could be tough and isolated, but there was a pioneering atmosphere about it which reminded me of the early days at the Ness.

After the evening meal I would return to WATER HORSE and nose quietly in among the islands at the western end of the loch. These small rocky outcrops were densely wooded and matted with undergrowth. There was something primeval about them, and as the majority were untouched by man they bore a natural growth similar to the Old Caledonian Forest, which at one time covered the Highlands.

'Morag' had often been reported near the islands, and I would anchor at night in one of the numerous coves and inlets, ready to use my cameras at first light.

Loch Morar was steeped in legend. It was said a phantom dog would howl on moonlit nights from one of the islands. I did not know which one, and made no particular enquiry. Watching for the Monster at night could be an eerie business, and I had no wish to be howled at by phantoms.

On still mornings on this majestically beautiful lake there was no sound. At dawn the silence was complete; but when the sun rose, the hum of insects would grow steadily in volume: a low pitched vibrant thrumming of sound from a million tiny wingbeats. I had never heard anything like it, even in the tropics. It made one think of some enormous flight of hornets, and fearing that I might be too close to a hornet's nest, I would pull anchor and drift into deeper water. I did not get stung nor see insects in great numbers beyond the usual clouds of midges, which were soundless in flight. Perhaps it was that in the stillness of the morning the rocks and boulders served to amplify the sound.

With the arrival of Bob Rines and the special underwater camera, it was put to work at once shooting-in to the south of the island group.

The weather at Loch Morar could be very unreliable, and rainfall on the west coast of the Highlands is high. There is a great deal of mist, and knowing the discomforts of boatwork in such conditions, I persuaded Bob Rines to purchase a set of oilskins from Mallaig nearby: a small picturesque herring-fisher port. Events were to prove the need for them.

In the afternoon of the 21st of July I brought WATER HORSE to the small wooden jetty used by the LMS and loaded up. Bob and I intended moving right down the loch past Brinacory Island, to spend a night on the water with the strobe-light camera. The weather was deteriorating, but since we both had to leave on the 22nd at the latest, we could not afford to wait.

I steered a course through the rocks and shoals between the islands, then ran bow-on into the swell that was building up in the main reaches of the loch. The sunset was glorious, and we buffetted eastwards into the gathering darkness. I did not care much for it. Experience told me that two grown men and a boatload of equipment were better off in harbour in such conditions.

Our object was simple enough—to get the camera down in the vicinity of the patrol-line followed by Morag at a certain place, which had been noted from shore. It was almost dark by the time we got near to it, and the weather worsening: a black night, with wind and water combining to make the prospects dangerous.

Incredibly, we performed the tasks. Working as a two-man team, we managed to get the camera down, in exactly the right locality. We could see it blazing periodically in 30 feet of water. Anchoring in deep water, we swung under the lee of a rocky promontory and by careful juggling stowed enough equipment for us to lie down in the cabin.

Next day the sun shone, and we reloaded the camera with colour stock, leaving it suspended from a sling of floats and ropes, free to photograph downwards at a shallow angle, perhaps 20 feet from the bottom.

At one o'clock we hauled the rig and set off homewards, pleased with the results. Time alone would prove if Morag had patrolled by in the hours of darkness to be photographed, but we had shown that even in the worst conditions it was possible to remain effective and get results.

I put my dynamic, cheerful friend ashore with his equipment, whereupon he drove back with it to Loch

Ness to work with Isaac Blonder for a day or two before returning to the United States.

I returned myself on the 23rd, sorry at leaving Morar
and the people of the LMS: so full of character and
scientific knowledge. During the week at Morar I had
worked endlessly. The weather had been kind, and I
was burnt brown by the sun.

Through August and September the hunt continued.
My family travelled up and lived with the expedition for
several weeks. It was good to have them participating in
the work and entertainment, too. Our crews were international, talented, and amusing—and most were sorry
when the time came for others to take their place.

During this period there was another unexpected
diversion in the form of electronic experiments underwater. A Swiss scientist visited the LNI and brought
with him a device designed to influence mammals. We
tried it out but with no visible results. He left intent
on further study.

The LNI was not averse to such experiments, providing no harm came to creatures underwater and
providing, too, they were intelligently based.

By now the season's end was approaching, and with
a lull in reported sightings it seemed unlikely we would
obtain any significant photography. It was disappoint-
ing, but there were other compensations. I had found
a magnificent site for future operations at a place
called "Fasagh' on the north shore several miles to the
west of Achnahannet, which was again threatened with
closure, due to problems of access and other legal re-
strictions.

Arrangements made by the Board of the LNIB in
association with Glenmoriston Estates, the Landmark
company, and the Highlands and Islands Development
Board promised well for both the future 'P.R.' activity
and equally the research, based at Fasagh. But in-

evitably the project needed careful thought. Assuming progress was made with it, however, Achnahannet would probably remain as base for at least another year. In 1972 the LNI would be entering its tenth consecutive year of fieldwork. For me, it would result in a 20th expedition, having started research privately in 1960.

In the years between I had watched the growth of public interest and the expansion of voluntary scientific work, which was in itself an accomplishment—a justification for all the trust and sweat we had put into it.

Perhaps in 1972 our luck would change with photography, the one most effective weapon. We certainly needed luck because on the 6th September 1971 I sighted the Monster's head and neck close-up on the water surface, but was unable to take pictures. It took me completely by surprise.

Under motor power in WATER HORSE I was moving through rough water near Foyers, about mid-afternoon. Noise from the hydro works there was considerable, and the weather stormy—quite the wrong conditions for observation. Standing at the wheel I glanced to starboard and instantly recognised a shape I had seen so often in a photograph—the famous 'Surgeon's Photograph' of 1934—but it was alive and muscular! Incredulous, I stood for a moment without moving. All I could do was stare. Then I saw the neck-like object whip back underwater, only to reappear briefly, then go down in a boil of white foam. There was a battery of five cameras within inches of my right hand, but I made no move towards them.

The surprise of the encounter immobilised me and so upset my balance I ran the boat onto the shingle of Foyer's Point. Angrily, I cursed my own stupidity and shook off the paralysis. I put on my life jacket and dropped anchor, then switched on the tape recorder to capture details of the experience, before I forgot them.

The day following I checked distances and the size of waterbirds. There had been seagulls floating close to the head and neck, and my estimate of range could not have been mistaken. It was 200 yards away—perhaps a little more—and the neck extended four feet or so vertically. There was no freshwater animal in Britain which looked like it—that was absolutely certain. It had the 'Surgeon's Photograph' shape precisely, but was a little more thick set, and the head, or extremity, was curiously rounded. I had not seen a recognisable head, but the object could not have been a tail because of its behaviour and the direction of movement. To have been a tail it would have been going backwards!

No, I had seen the foremost parts of the Beast, and the experience proved to me that at close quarters it would be necessary to train a camera like a sub-machine gun—to shoot instantly and directionally. It was possible to do this, and the technique would obviate the need to obscure one's vision. It would be almost impossible at close quarters not to stare, and stare, with both eyes open. This explained why excited witnesses from shore had failed to take photographs. They could not bring themselves to interrupt vision. We had several witnesses arrive at Achnahannet who had actually been holding cameras at the time of a sighting.

The tape I had recorded proved to be convincing, and it was broadcast nationally on 'New Worlds,' a BBC scientific programme, and was reported in the press. The *Guardian* covered it, and as this newspaper in Britain has a reputation equivalent to that of the London *Times,* I felt we had made some progress.

＊＊＊＊＊＊

By mid-September the last crew had departed, leaving an emptiness behind. For months the camp at

Achnahannet had been alive with sound, laughter, and the stimulating currents of excitement. All operations stemmed from there, and more than 50,000 visitors had passed through in the information centre. Suddenly, it was quiet.

I retreated south for a week to see my family, then returned to help wind up the investigation and to attend a meeting at the Fasagh site.

Much depended on the outcome of the meeting. I showed a group of county architects and planners and local councillors over the splendid eight-acre site, with its rocks and trees and towering scenery; and they were suitably impressed.

On the 9th of October I towed out my trailer, leaving it at Fort Augustus, then came back to move WATER HORSE down loch. It was rough, the journey taking hours, my reserve of engine power being useless in such conditions. I felt I could not leave without a few days of private monsterhunting. It was in my blood.

Bob Rines had recently returned and was conducting echo-sounder tests in Urquhart Bay. We had been out together mapping bottom contours; now with NARWHAL available he could use her as a platform.

Scouting the wastes of unfrequented water near Fort Augustus, I recaptured something of the peace and loneliness which I had found in the catamaran CIZARA in 1968, but I slept ashore and watched for long hours with equipment set up on the tripod.

On the 13th of October a lady was introduced to me, a Miss Turner, secretary at the Abbey nearby. She had seen something in the loch near Invermoriston which attracted her attention. I taped her account . . .

'Just before I came into Invermoriston I saw a lot of people looking at the loch, and I saw a distinct line, or cut, right through the water which was like glass—running for about a quarter of a mile—and then whatever it was turned round, and there really was a *terrific* turbulence. I saw no head and no object, but something caused that—and there were no boats anywhere . . .'

Miss Turner was quiet and sincere, and was obviously impressed by this experience. She had not believed in the Monster previously. I made a point of asking her if she though the turbulence was heading in the Fort Augustus direction, but she said that it appeared to have reversed course, to go the other way.

With the fine calm weather which had settled over the area I knew there was a better-than-average chance of a sighting, and I watched religiously that afternoon and throughout the next day, setting up my equiment at a point overlooking the western end of the loch. I had intended taking the boat out in the morning to get the sun behind me, but it had been very cold at night and WATER HORSE was sheathed in frost, like sugar icing. Tendrils of mist swirled over the water, and by the time the sun had burned it off, it was ten o'clock. I left the boat moored where it was.

The water surface to the south was lost to view. I could not penetrate the sunglaze, which was dazzling. In consequence I had to write-off the Borlum Bay area for photography until the sun rose higher. Shortly after 11 a.m. I saw a tall monk stride down the jetty wall towards the Abby boathouse. He pointed and said something to a companion. I could just hear him indicating 'movement.' I called across, but he could not hear me; and as the sun was blinding, I could see nothing in that direction. I watched and waited, then drifted the boat that afternoon. The weather broke up, and the next day I pulled WATER HORSE out and trailed her back to Achnahannet for winter storage.

Stopping at the camp, I found that a short time after Miss Turner's sighting on the 13th, the Monster had been watched on the surface by several people, close to Invermoriston—among them, a police inspector and a sergeant. Both had completed sighting forms and had made tape recordings for the LNI.

On the 14th a monk from the Abbey at Fort Augustus and his friend had seen a huge head and neck emerge from the centre of a disturbance—in Borlum Bay.

I was staggered by this latter piece of news, realising that my failure to use the boat the day before had cost the opportunity to film an adult head and neck, at close range, and with the sun behind me.

Leaving the Great Loch, I drove southwards on the 16th of October, demoralised. After 12 years of pursuit it was hard not to become despondent. Would we ever succeed? Could we ever beat the cursed hoodoo? These were the questions that wandered through my head, and yet within I knew we could. I had no one to blame for not using the boat. There was nothing supernatural about that.

In due course I recovered morale, and realising the importance of these two sightings, I obtained an account of both. The first from the LNI sighting report forms, and the second from Fr. Gregory Brusey directly.

*   *   *

Police Inspector Henry Henderson, of 208 Old Edinburgh Road, Inverness, recorded that he and Sergeant George W. Mackenzie saw a large object travelling west to east in a straight line, about half was across Loch Ness at a point half a mile east of the Altsigh Youth Hostel. He estimated length overall as 25-30 feet and speed at 10-15 m.p.h. It was yisible from '14:15 hours to 14:17 hours.'

'. . . The first thing noticed was a wave pattern coming towards the shore below us. The water was flat calm and a "V" shaped wave pattern was coming in from about the centre of the loch. The first wave would have been about two feet high. Following the

17   Tracing of Police Inspector Henderson's sketch made in the Loch Ness Investigation's Standard Sighting Report Form, dated 13th October 1971.

wave outwards I saw two large black coloured "humps" about 10-12 feet behind the point where the "V" parted. I would say there would be at least six to eight feet between the humps . . . the impression was quite definite: they were connected below the surface. The objects were visible for two minutes at which time they appeared to go lower and lower in the water, and gradually disappeared. The significant point in this was that the water then returned to flat calm condition . . . the objects gave the impression of two large seals or dolphins sporting, but this was only an initial impression—as time went on it became obvious that the two objects were part of one large animate object, seen travelling over a distance of about half a mile.'

On October 19th, 1971 Fr. Gregory replied in the following words to the note I had left behind at Fort Augustus Abby requesting his account . . .

'On Thursday morning October 14th, I took a friend, Mr. Roger Pugh, the organist and choirmaster of St. James, Spanish Place, London, down to the loch-side to admire the view. It was a bright sunny day, and the loch surface was calm, and untroubled by any boats. Standing on the stone jetty near the boathouse we looked towards Borlum Bay, when suddenly there was a terrific commotion in the waters of the bay. In the midst of this disturbance we saw quite distinctly the neck of the beast standing out of the water to what we calculated later to be a height of about 10 feet. It swam towards us at a slight angle, and after about 20 seconds slowly disappeared, the neck immersing at a slight angle. We were at a distance of about 300 yards. . . .

(signed) Roger Pugh
Gregory Brusey'

THE ABBEY
Fort Augustus
Inverness-Shire.

18   Tracing of Fr. Gregory's sketch of live object moving through the water at Loch Ness 14th October 1971—Range 300 yards. Height above surface 10 feet.

This account had a special significance, outside of the circumstance which prevented photography. It supported the estimate we had made the year before, when three of us in WATER HORSE on Urquhart Bay reported a telegraph pole-like object moving through the water, protruding at least ten feet above the surface. This figure was probably thought to be an exaggeration at the time by the majority of people who had not seen the object. They were too polite to say so, but their very lack of comment made this apparent. It was understandable, too, but we were unable to reduce the figure to make it acceptable.

More importantly, Fr. Gregory's clear and obviously factual account enabled me to regain composure—'to stop momentarily to gaze at inscrutable nature, and wonder about the deeper natural truths . . .'

After so many years of endeavour in defence of the Truth concerning this amazing phenomenon at Loch Ness and Loch Morar too, time no longer mattered very much.

What still mattered was our common objective—the proof, the protection and study of these great unknown animals; and the manner in which we set about achieving it.

APPENDICES A—J

A

Prof. William Buckland, D.D., F.R.S., lived from 1784–1856' and was principally responsible for establishing a readership in geology at Oxford in 1818; but perhaps his most important contribution lay in his ability to present palaeontology and the past history of the earth in vivid terms. In 1956 J. M. Edmonds of the dept. of Geology and Mineralogy at Oxford commented – 'In the "Bridgewater Treatise" and in his lectures, fossils were no longer treated as markings on stones or even as the dead remains of unknown animals; they became the key to the understanding of the sequence of past inhabitants of the earth. An impression of a footprint on a slab of rock could disclose the size, attitude and even the shape of an animal; a tooth show how a creature lived; coprolites reveal the shape of intestines and the undigested fragments of the food . . .'

In 1845 he was appointed Dean of Westminster, but continued lecturing, but it was not until 1850 that his hopes were realized and the 'natural sciences' included among the subjects in which undergraduates might be examined for a degree; an early but significant step forward, in our search for knowledge.

B

In the analysis I did in 1959, based on 100 eyewitness reports, a specific reference to colour appeared in twenty-eight cases. Of these 39 per cent described the animal as 'dark', 29 per cent as grey, 25 per cent as brown, and 7 per cent as blotched. The preponderance of 'dark' reports could be accounted for by the effect of silhouette, or of distance or poor light. For example, on 2nd September, 1961, a Miss M. Watchorn of West Bridgford, Nottingham, wrote to me as follows . . . 'In May '58 I was opposite Urquhart Castle on the beach. There is a ruined cottage on the land side of the road at that spot. The sky was clear blue, bright sun; time, early afternoon. Something approached from the west, it was about the size of a tin can but did not bob up and down, nor did it sway as a branch would have done. It moved quite steadily in a straight line parallel with the shore, not far out and was *not* affected by the movement of the water – this means it had considerable underwater anchorage – far more than a boat.

'As it came towards me it looked very dark – not blue-black but brown-black. As it passed me, the sun shone on its reverse side and that was red-brown. The two colours were quite different. I realized that, in shadow, the object deceived as to its colour, it was actually reddish-brown. I had no binoculars so can only say that what I saw, by its movement, could have been the Beast's head. My opinion is that the Beast's colour is, in fact, reddish-brown and that this is shown up only by direct sunlight; that, in shadow or in dull conditions, the colour appears dark . . .'

Certainly the great back of the animal I saw in 1960 in direct early morning sunlight, and crystal visibility was a distinct reddish-brown – but it is of interest to note that in Lowrie/ *Finola* yacht sighting, at just a few yards range the animal is described as showing 'a large area of green and brown'.

Again, in the case of the Swedish Monster in Lake Storsjon, 'The colour is stated to be greyish; grey with black spots; in front dark-brown or reddish-brown, possibly greenish, and behind it is grey or light-brown.'

Thus the characteristics of colour and blotching appearing in my analysis are borne out, with a cross-reference to the greenish hue noted by Mr. Lowrie.

272

C

Lake Okanagan, British Columbia, Canada, is approximately 75–80 miles in length, and uniformly narrow, varying only from $1\frac{1}{2}$–3 miles in width. The observed maximum depth is 760 feet and mean 228 feet. The deepest region is north from the centre of the lake, with a 10-mile stretch at over 655 feet. The shores shelve rapidly in centre regions, into deep water. Only 15 per cent of area is less than 10 feet in depth, mostly at the two ends where shelving occurs gradually due to glacial deposits. A Morphometry index of 6·7 classifies the lake as 'Alpine'.

Topographical History: For history of 'Late Glacial and Surficial Deposits' refer to British Columbia Dept. of Mines and Petroleum Resources Bulletin, No. 46, (my copy of which is available for loan). This is an official detailed report, with maps: and under the section 'Physiography of the Okanagan Valley' it is stated that: 'The elevation of the underlying bedrock trench is unknown . . . and beneath the lake bottom lies an unknown thickness of unconsolidated sediment. A test well drilled in the Okanagan Valley north of Armstrong, starting at an elevation of 1,220, passed through slightly more than 1,300 feet of unconsolidated and unweathered sediments, apparently Pleistocene deposits, before bedrock was reached.'

This statement is not really as contradictory as it sounds, because on the strength of one bore hole results are purely of local significance. But, if bedrock is below current sea-level at this place it is possible the Okanagan Valley may once have been a long arm of the sea (at present some 600 miles distant via the Columbia River route) because with the melting of vast quantities of ice at the end of the last Ice Age, the oceans rose to some 200 feet above their present level, and there have also been gradual changes in the level of the earth's crust in different places during this relatively short period in Geological history.

Fish Population: Game fish are not overly abundant and consist mostly of Kamloop trout (a 10 pounder is considered large today) and the smaller Kokanee. Coarse fish include carp, squaw-fish and suckers – and sturgeon are suspected. Along the shore-line, crayfish, leaches, bullheads and minnows are found. Plankton is probably minimal. The water is clear, potable, and moderately hard (about 80 p.p.m.) the bulk being calcium carbonate. The bottom is silty with little visible weed.

The lake has frozen over only six times since 1928, despite extremes of climate – up to 110° F. and down to 20° below zero F. But more typical temperatures summer and winter are 90° and zero F. Surface water can reach 75° F. in summer.

Surface Observation: The lake runs roughly north and south with a bend to left and right about a third of the way up it. Population centres are at Penticton; southern extremity – Kelowna; middle of east bank – and Vernon at north-eastern extremity; each with about 10,000 people. Other much smaller communities are spaced along the shore. The southern half of the lake surface is well observed from west-shore houses and the main highway, which crosses over the new bridge at Kelowna leading away from the water to the north. There is a heavily settled lake-shore area below Kelowna, but northwards the water is observed intermittently from scattered houses and the eastern shore road. The extreme north-eastern shore being rocky and uninhabited. Generally the view of the surface is good, but the lake width of two or three miles calls for the use of good binoculars.

D

'On Fresh Theropod-like Tracks: Results of investigations carried out in Florida on giant three-toed tracks that appeared on the banks of the lower Suwannee River in October 1948.'

This is the heading to the report by Ivan Sanderson, the layout of which provides an indication of its thoroughness – covering origins, locale, procedure, background (similar tracks in other parts of Florida, Natal in South Africa, etc.), inferences, and then a most detailed analytical study of the Suwannee River tracks, and deliberate attempts to repeat them; resulting in the withdrawal of the first published conclusion suggesting the tracks were man-made.

Altogether difficult to summarize – and thoroughly mysterious – but if due regard is given to the mile or so of similar tracks reported from Clearwater Beach and other deserted stretches of coast near by during the previous few months, always emanating from the sea and re-entering it – and the depth and size of these indentations – and the local reports at Suwannee Gables of a large unknown 'something' splashing about and making 'gurgling growls' *before the tracks appeared,* it would seem to put the hoaxers into a most enterprising category: equipped with footprint making equipment weighing several tons and fired with the desire to use it on remote sections of the shore, and unhealthy swampland.

E

The model skeleton of a Basking shark hanging up in the British Museum (Natural History) has 103 vertebrae, which suggests that either the Hunda carcase had lost some of its spinal column or that it wasn't that of a Basking shark. If the former it must have been a fish of near-record size, because with only 65 vertebrae it measured almost 30 feet.

There is one other possibility. Could the number of vertebrae vary to any extent between different populations of this type of shark, even accepting there is only one species recognized at present? The answer seems to be that this is possible, because it does happen in the case of some other fishes of the same species, though the variation in number is liable to be small – much less than the difference between 103 and 65, which is more than a third. No one has found this characteristic in Basking sharks, which come from different areas – but again, information is lacking.

F

On Plate No. 12 it may be seen that the skull of a Basking shark possesses two curious rib-like appendages, which branch back from the snout, rather like the legs of a wish-bone.

These are known as the 'dorso-rostral' cartilages and are characteristic of the *Elasmobranchi* (sharks, skates and rays), but their precise purpose is hard to define. Unless I am mistaken there is a similar structure visible on the original Girvan Monster photograph, indicated by an arrow on the tracing (Sketch No. 14), and it also seems possible that if fractured, these cartilages might stick up through the rotting flesh of a skull, and look something like Mr. Graeme's 'antennae'. They would be of a flexible gristly substance.

G

Returning from my sixth abortive expedition to Loch Ness in late September of 1962, I called in at the Royal Scottish Museum at Edinburgh, with the object of trying to find the skull of the Deepdale animal. On a previous trip I had spoken to Dr. A. C. Stephen (now retired) on the phone about it, and he had said he thought it might still be in existence; although it might have been disposed of during the war when the museum was closed for a while, and some of its contents moved. It seemed to me that if the skull could be found it would remove any last vestige of doubt I had about it, because the skull of a Basking shark is unmistakable.

But, I had underestimated the task: in every museum for each exhibit on display there must be a dozen specimens or bottled parts of animals residing in the vaults – which together run into thousands. We searched methodically through tabulated files, boxes and cabinets and finally in the vaults below the building, through all the bony bric-à-brac, but to no avail – the Deepdale skull was not to be found.

It was a disappointment – but in compensation I did find something unexpectedly of great interest. When poking about amongst the bottles I espied one large flask containing a number of huge, flat, bioconcave vertebra. These great discs had bleached in the preserving fluid and were rather beautiful, with a fine tracery of cartilaginous bone radiating out from the centre, like the veins on an autumn leaf – but it was the label which attracted my attention. It read 'Spinal vertebra of a "Sea Serpent" washed ashore at Stronsa in 1808' – or words to that effect.

H

An excellent list of sightings for 1964 was drawn up by David James, and published by the *Observer* newspaper, 27th December, 1964. Summarized below, those reports with an asterisk have been the subject of interview, or correspondence, to establish *bona fides*.

January 11th.* Alex Campbell, water bailiff: Cherry Island: large hump 15 feet × 5 feet high: Speed 8–10 knots: Range ¾ mile: Visible 2½ minutes.

March 25th. A. Russell, J. MacKenzie, D. Gow all of forestry commission. Off Invermoriston: Hump some 25 feet long, cruising several minutes.

May 6th.* Five employees, Clansman Hotel: Object at speed creating big disturbance: Range 1 mile.

May 17th.* R. Eames, schoolmaster, wife and children: off Achnahannet: 15-foot long dark hump: range 400 yards.

May 18th.* F. Pullen (expedition member) sees similar object, same place: Submerges quickly: range 2 miles.

May 19th.* Peter and Pauline Hodge (expedition members): off Achnahannet: Pole-like object. Reacts to slamming car door and makes off: range 400 yards: filmed on 8 m.m. movie.

May 19th.* The Hodges, Ivor Newbury (expedition member): same place: large object: late evening.

June 9th.* Doctor and wife, submit formal report on five separate neck-like objects, at first close together, but changing relative positions. Range ½ mile: optimum conditions.

July 17th.*   Alex Campbell: Cherry Island: another hump.

August 9th.   J. Dawson: minor: off shore Fort Augustus: double hump: sinking after 5 minutes.

August 19th.   J. Thompson and three companions: Sandy Point: stationary hump 4 feet × 4 feet high: made off at great speed.

August 30th – September 5th.   Urquhart Bay: two large hump sightings: Clansman Hotel: one large hump. Local witnesses.

September 6th.*   Commander Quintin Riley (who will direct field operations for 1965 expedition) and his wife: dome-shaped object: Achnahannet: 400 yards.

September 8th.*   Mrs. H. MacNaughton: off Inverfarigaig pier: 6 foot head and neck, moving, distinct small head with protuberances: range 230 yards.

Early October.*   Mrs. Dallas: off Dores: head and neck.

Mid October.   'Lady of unimpeachable integrity': off Dores: head and neck.

The first published account for 1965 reads: *Aberdeen Press and Journal*, 3rd April, 1965: 'Nessie pops up to frolic in the sun – Mr. James T. Ballantyne (49) of 51 Fairfield Road, Inverness, was walking beside the loch with Miss Elizabeth Keith, a teacher from Rothienorman, Aberdeenshire. Mr. Ballantyne said there was a sudden commotion in the water . . . "We only saw the neck and head. I would say the neck was roughly six feet long. As we watched him paddle about he twice disappeared under the surface. It was fascinating," he said.

'Said Miss Keith: "Some may not believe our story, but it was the Monster all right. It was jet black, and obviously quite large. I lived beside the loch for seven years, but I never believed the stories about Nessie. As far as I was concerned it didn't exist," added Mr. Ballantyne who, (in his subsequent report to the L.N. Investigation Bureau) described the foreparts of the Beast in the following terms . . . 'The head was completely similar to that of a python, or indeed a large conger eel and was held at right angles to the neck. The neck was very elongated

278

and slim, thickening at a point some 1 foot or thereby above the water. The neck and head stood some 4–6 feet above water, something like a cobra standing up when charmed by an Indian piper. I saw no body or humps but the speed at which it went through the water with its head held high, and the distance travelled could only make one surmise that it had a huge body and a very strong method of propulsion. When I say speed I do not mean terrific speed. What happened was that the beast cruised leaving ripples but no great wash, yet travelled approx. 1 mile or more in the 5–7 minutes while watched. The loch at this point is about 1½ miles wide . . ." '

The Loch Ness Phenomena Investigation Bureau Ltd., 25 Ashley Place, London S.W.1. has been instrumental in collecting recent evidence through the media of standard sighting report forms, personal contact, tape-recordings, etc., and has done a vast amount of work in connection with the main expedition effort. Its Directors are Mr. Norman Collins (also director at ATV who has worked with Hans and Lotte Hass), Mr. Richard Fitter (also Director of the British Council for Nature), Mr. David James (Founder Member), Commander Peter Scott (Hon. Director of the Wildfowl Trust in Gt. Britain, and a Trustee for the World Wildlife Fund), and Mrs. Constance Whyte, M.B., B.S., whose book *More Than a Legend* in 1957 established the first post-war rallying point. Secretary is Mr. D. W. Suckling (the indefatigable Doug). None of these people receive any form of payment, and when the affairs of the Company are in due course wound up, the profits, if any, are to be divided equally between the World Wildlife Fund, and the Council for Nature.

I

During the course of the last week in July 1965 when acting as site-commander for the main expedition effort at Loch Ness, coinciding with the torrential rain and high water-level an extraordinary report appeared in the *Aberdeen Press and Journal*, 30th July edition and other local papers. Two businessmen, Mr. Hamish Ferguson, of Gullane, East Lothian and his assistant Mr. George McGill of Lambhill, Glasgow, were standing on the step of the Y.M.C.A. hall in Bank Street, Inverness, when they saw a large animal swimming down the river Ness towards the sea. (At this point the river is some 80 yards wide and perhaps 8–10 feet deep). About 15 feet of it was visible. It appeared black, with deep ridges across its girth, four triangular spikes along its back, and with humps at front and rear. Visible for about six minutes.

Mr. Ferguson told the *Press and Journal*: 'This has absolutely amazed me. It was very much alive and for all the world like one of those prehistoric animals you see in picture books . . . we first saw three humps in the water at about the centre of the river. . . . The skin on it appeared to be deeply ridged, and at one point I saw what I took to be a neck like a big half-submerged tractor tyre . . .'

It swam at quite a leisurely pace, and rippled the water in passing.

This report is very interesting, for several reasons. Firstly, with regard to the 'triangular spikes' along its back – in Mr. James Gavin's report of the Soay beast (refer back to page 65) he says: 'The line of its back was formed by a series of triangular-shaped spines, the largest at the apex and reducing in size to the waterline . . .'

Also, this is the second report I now have of a humped animal in the river Ness, which is some 7 miles in length, leading from Telfords Weir at the extreme north-east end of Loch Ness, to the sea. The first was from a Mr. and Mrs. Y. H. Hallam, of 11 Carlton Road, Filey, East Yorkshire, who were travelling in a pleasure boat in June of 1936. They saw a twenty-footer, with head and two humps, going 'very fast' towards the sea.

I had previously put this report to one side, having written off the river as a means of access to the sea, due to the barrier formed by the salmon weir – but in view of this new report, and the high lake water-level at the time one can no longer be so sure about it. Furthermore as female long-necked Plesiosaurs were known to lay their eggs in estuaries,[1] the whole question of access to the sea, and Loch Ness as a breeding ground becomes much more entertaining.

J

Excerpt from *Lone Voyager* – Joseph E. Garland, Hutchinson, London (1964). Being an account of the voyages of Howard Blackburn of Gloucester, Mass., U.S.A. The experience below being recorded on 1st July, 1902, during a west to east trans-atlantic crossing . . .

'1st July, 4 p.m. while sitting on the wheelbox steering . . . I saw something just abaft the starboard beam lashing the water into foam. I stood up and saw what looked like a coil of very large rope. I hove the wheel down and trimmed the sheets in sharp by the wind. The boat would not fetch it on that tack, but passed within 35 to 40 feet to leeward of it.

'As I drew near I could see that it looked like a large snake, but had a tail more like an eel. It was fully 12 to 15 feet in length. It was holding in its mouth either a small turtle or a good-sized fish, with which it was lashing the water into foam. Its head moved so rapidly from side to side that I could not tell its shape, but am inclined to think it resembled that of a serpent. The tail and parts of the body that I could see plainly appeared to be smooth and of a light lead colour.

'I put a running bowline into the end of the mainsheet, and when the boat got far enough by to fetch it on the next tack I hove the wheel hard down, and with every hair on my head like so many belaying pins, filled away on the other tack, taking the mainsheet in my hand, and as the boat passed within 8 or 10

[1] Dr. W. E. Swinton in *Fossils Amphibians and Reptiles* says, on page 59: 'Although the female Plesiosaurs laid eggs upon the shore and were thus in some measure tied to the land, the group was successfully adapted to a marine life and its members were distributed throughout the world during the later Mesozoic.'

feet of it I tried to lassoo it. But the rope must have struck its head, for without a bit of fuss it sank from sight. . . . It was no shark, for a shark of that length would be at least as big round as a five-gallon keg, whilst this was no stouter than my mast, which is 5 inches in diameter. It must have been a baby sea serpent.'

ACKNOWLEDGEMENTS

I would like to thank the following for permission to reproduce photographs: Mr. R. H. Lowrie, Plate No. 3; Pathé News, Plates 4 & 5; Mrs. Elizabeth MacLeod, Plate No. 8; *Pentiction Herald,* Plate No. 9; Scottish *Daily Express,* Plate No. 11; British Museum (Natural History), Plate No. 12; Edward Brian Mc-Cleary, Plate No. 13; Robert le Serrec, Plate No. 14; The American Museum of Natural History, Plate No. 16; David James (1964) expedition, Plates 17 & 19; Martyn Simmons, Plate No. 20; Mr. P. A. MacNab, Plate No. 28; Associated Newspapers Ltd., Plate No. 29.

I am indebted to Publishers and Authors for permission to quote excerpts from the following books: *Amazon Fortune Hunter* by Paul Gregor; *The Lost World of the East* by Stuart Wavell, as published by Souvenir Press Ltd.; *Sea Enchantress* by Gwen Benwell and Arthur Waugh; Hutchinson Publishing Group Ltd.; *Black Jack's Spurs* by C. W. Thurlow Craig, and Curtis Brown Ltd.; *On the Track of Unknown Animals,* by Dr. Bernard Heuvelmans, published in English by Rupert Hart Davis, and the original French by Librairie Plon.

I am indeed grateful to all the many friends and acquaintances who have contributed to this book, or helped with their advice and encouragement; particularly, David James, Gordon Creighton and Nikolai Vassilicv, Michael Painter, Elizabeth MacLeod, Ivan T. Sanderson, Dr. Bernard Heuvelmans, F. W. (Ted) Holiday, Gordon To, Mrs, Sybil Armstrong and Mrs. Mary Hamilton, Revs. Mathew Burke, Daniel Murray and Richard Quigley, Patrick J. N. Bury, James McM. Ure, James Gavin, R. H. Lowrie, Ken Anderson, Lt. Col. J. D. Blyth, Dr. S. K. Klumov, G. A. Smith, Karl Karlson and Knut Svedjeland, L. L. Björkquist and Björn Rosén, Major H. C. Butler, John S. Coleman, Mrs. Cicily M. Botley, Edward P. Smith, D. J. A. Briggs, Eric Robinson, Alec Patmore, Miss Helen Stitt, Miss Janc Best, Anthony Oliver, W. J. Williamson, C. F. Rae-Griffin, Robert le Serrec, Robin Brampton, O. D. Rasmussen, Peter J. Whitehead, Charles G. Lewin, Mrs. Hildegarde Forbes, Morton Marrian, Mrs. Mildred Nye, Peter Costello, Mr. and Mrs. Y. H. Hallam, Larry Foley, Miss J. Robb, Mrs. Hope Smeeton, Mrs Trude Bryant, Peter Hodges, Jock Gemmel, David Hanson, Dr. and Richard Kenchington and Dr. Eric Blank.

ACKNOWLEDGEMENTS

In the Expedition field I need to thank those who have given me their help and hospitality over the years, and some fifteen thousand miles of motoring. Especially, Alex. Campbell, the Water Bailiff at Loch Ness, the Brothers Carruth at St. Benedict's Abbey, Fort Augustus; Basil and Freddie Cary at Castle Urquhart; Hugh and Jane Rowand of Wester Farigaig; Mr. and Mrs. Halliday at Foyers Hotel. Also Ro-Camilla-Alex-McPherson, Janet Kronstadt, Alan Dance, Robin and Edwina Weston, Dick Hobbs, Martyn Simmons, Jim Ewing, John Addey – Peter and Margaret Dinsdale, whose 'half-way' farmhouse has saved the day on more than one occasion. But, to Wendy my wife, who has put up with me during the course of this marathon pursuit, I owe the most of all.

ILLUSTRATIONS

SKETCHES

MAPS

ILLUSTRATIONS

PHOTOGRAPHS

286

INDEX

Kinlochleven, 61
Kirkwall, 176
Klumov, Dr. S. K., 33, 35, 78, 160
Kokanee trout, 202
Komandorskie Islands, 160
Komsomol'skya Pravda, 36
Konecki, Mrs. Blanche, 27
Konefall, John, 29
'Kraken', 68
Kronosaurus, 167

Labynkyr, Lake, 35–36, 38
Land and Water, 154
Lane, Lt. Col. W. H., 17, 54
Lathangue, Mr., 26
Laughton, Andrew, 175
Lee, Boyd, 83
Lee, Henry, 133–4
Le Serrec, Robert, 80, 84–85
Leviathans, 58
Linnhe, Loch, 59, 63
Little, Mrs. E., 23
'Little Siberia', 7
Lochalsh, Kyle of, 59, 64
Loch Ness Monster, 3, 6, 17, 42, 48, 51, 74, 91, 156, 164
Loch Ness Phenomena Investigation Bureau, 5, 207
Lochy, Loch, 59, 61
Locke, Tom, 28
Lomond, Loch, 63
London, 7
Lone Voyager, 209
Long necked seal, 18
Lords Commissioners of the Admiralty, 130, 133
Lovell, Miss S., 90, 154, 155, 156
Lower Bray, 52
Lower Cretaceous, 167
Lowrie, R. H., 7, 9, 200
Lucas, Mrs. D. S., 196
'Lucio', 188
Lyle Stewart, 165
Lyme Regis, 18

McBeath, John, 176

McCleary, Edward Brian, 91, 93–94
MacDonald, Commander, 135
MacDonald, James, 175
MacDonald, Sir Murdoch, 57
McKay, John, 61
McKay, Valentine, 27
McKay, William, 54
MacKenzie, J., 205
McLeans Magazine, 29
McLean, R. P., 23
McLeod, Capt. Jack, 24
McLeod, Dr. James A., 26, 29
MacLeod, Elizabeth, 6
MacLeod, Torquil, 6, 9
McNaughton, Mrs. H., 206
Macrae, John, 70
Magnus, Olaus, 67, 142
Major, Lough, 151–2
Malayan Peninsular, 101
Malmesbury, Earl of, 61
Mammals of the World, 140
Manaos, 124, 126
Manatee, 140–1
Manchester Guardian, Weekly, 188
'Manipogo', 21, 26–27
Manipogo Beach, 28
Manitoba, Lake, 27–30
Manson, William, 138
Marine Iguana, 169
Marrian, Moreton, 108
Marwick, Provost J. G., 171, 173–4, 176
Mask, Lough, 49, 51
Maureen, 11
Maxwell, Gavin, 64
Meade-Waldo, E. G. B., 76
Memoirs of an Ex-Minister, 61
Memoirs of the Wernerian Society, 185
Mermen, 143
Mesozoic, 209
'Mighty Chasm of Glenmore', 53
Millar, Sqdn. Ldr. Bruce, 24
Miller, Robert F., 171
Mills, J. P., 105
Mirrimac Plains, 156